ALSO BY DAVID CRANE

Lord Byron's Jackal: A Life of Edward John Trelawny

THE KINDNESS OF SISTERS

THE KINDNESS
OF SISTERS

*Annabella Milbanke
and the Destruction
of the Byrons*

DAVID CRANE

ALFRED A. KNOPF

NEW YORK

2002

THIS IS A BORZOI BOOK
PUBLISHED BY ALFRED A. KNOPF

Originally published in Great Britain by HarperCollins Publishers, London

Knopf, Borzoi Books and the colophon are registered
trademarks of Random House, Inc.

Library of Congress Cataloging-in-Publication Data
Crane, David.
The kindness of sisters : Annabella Milbanke and the destruction
of the Byrons / by David Crane. — 1st American ed.
    p.   cm.
Originally published: London : HarperCollins, 2002.
Includes bibliographical references and index.
ISBN 0-375-40648-4
1. Byron, George Gordon Byron, Baron, 1788–1824—Family.
2. Byron, Anne Isabella Milbanke Byron, Baroness, 1792–1860.
3. Byron, George Gordon Byron, Baron, 1788–1824—Marriage.
4. Poets, English—19th century—Family relationships.
5. Poets, English—19th century—Biography.   6. Leigh, Augusta,
1784–1851.   I. Title.
PR4382 .C73 2002
821'.7—dc21
[B]   2002022815

Manufactured in the United States of America
First American Edition

Contents

Illustrations

Medora Leigh. *Reproduced from Moore, Doris Langley: Ada: Countess of Lovelace, John Murray, London, 1997.*

Lapeyre, Medora's final home.

Lapeyre from above.

Lapeyre centre.

Reverend Fredrick William Robertson. *Courtesy of the National Portrait Gallery, London.*

Coffin of Augusta, next to that of George Leigh, in the catacomb.

Grave of Annabella.

Byron and Ada's tomb. *Reproduced from Barber, Thomas Gerard, Byron and Where he is Buried, Henry Morley and Sons, Hucknall 1991.*

All photographs without credits are from the author's own collection.

THE KINDNESS OF SISTERS

PROLOGUE

The glory of mankind has been to produce lives,
to provide vivid, independent, individual men, not
buildings or engineering works or art, not even the
public good.

D. H. Lawrence[1]

You should not have warred with the World—it will
not do—it is too strong always for any individual.

Madame de Stael to Byron[2]

In the late afternoon of 15 June 1938, a small group of men stood
at a gaping hole at the south-west corner of the chancel of St.
Mary Magdalen, Hucknall. Beneath their feet a short flight of
steps led down to a low, cramped vault, and by the glare of a photographer's lamp they could make out a pile of coffins heaped on top of
each other in a mouldering jumble of wood and bone and twisted
lead that had lain undisturbed for over fifty years.

They had converged on the church in some secrecy. Earlier in the
day a lorry had brought builders' tools and planks to the north door,
and one by one through the afternoon a surveyor, antiquarian and
doctor had appeared. Finally a mason and three labourers arrived
and began lifting the massive, cracked slab of York stone that now
lay beside the open crypt.

It took them two hours to raise the stone, but by six o'clock in the
evening it was done. During the course of the work there were other
visitors in the church, but once the vault was open most of these, and
all the women, were asked to leave.

Even by English standards, those who remained were a curiously
prosaic lot to be indulging a taste in literary necrophilia. There was
clearly a generous streak of romance in the character of Canon Barber, the Vicar of Hucknall, but if a brace of churchwardens and half
the professional classes of the county were not ballast enough to
steady the most extravagant imagination, he had also co-opted the
Diocesan Surveyor and local MP in a bid for respectability.

A miner's lamp was swung into the vault to test the air, a ladder lowered to avoid the shallow, awkward steps, and Canon Barber climbed down, followed in turn by the surveyor, photographer and antiquarian. The purpose of the meeting, if the Canon is to be believed, was to establish the existence of a lost medieval crypt, and although it was soon plain that any such hopes were misplaced, measurements were duly taken and recorded, leaving the way clear for the real, if unacknowledged, business of the day.

The labourers were dismissed until the next morning, and the party adjourned to the church hall, only returning at the dead of night. Again, Canon Barber was the first down. Alone in the vault, lit now only by the photographer's lamps, he had time for a more careful inspection. It was a cramped, rectangular chamber six feet wide, just over seven feet long, and no more than eight feet beneath the floor of the nave. Its walls were of plastered brick, with two sloping slabs of stone making the vaulted roof. In three piles, running north to south rested the more or less intact shells of about half a dozen coffins, with the crushed debris of others beneath them. Round his feet lay the dust and bones of three centuries.

There seemed to be no order to anything. At the foot of the stairs, though, he identified the seventeenth century coffin of a baby, its lead lining buckled and twisted under the weight of a double-cube funerary chest, to which scraps of faded purple velvet still clung. On the lid was a brass plate with the following inscription:

Within the Urn
are deposited
the heart and the brain
of the deceased
Lord Noel Byron

The lid was loose, and inside was a sealed lead case, with a second inscription adding an oddly casual "etc" to the contents of the urn. Beyond the chest, Barber could now distinguish more easily the coffin for which he was searching. It was made of well-preserved oak and ornately decorated. Further shreds of purple material—faded since to crimson—clung to the brass headed coffin nails. On the lid rested the remains of a Baron's coronet. The velvet and ermine had rotted away, and the pearls had been wrenched from their finials.

Only the simple rim survived to identify the rank and probable identity of the dead.

There was no coffin plate to confirm Barber's guess, but the lid was loose and he could see that the lead casing had already been cut open. "Somebody," he recalled with an endearing disingenuousness,

> had deliberately opened the coffin. A horrible thought came over me that souvenirs might have been taken from the coffin. The idea was revolting, but I could not dismiss it. Had the body itself been removed? Terrible thought! From time to time visitors to the church had asserted in my hearing that the body of the Poet was not in the Vault. I wondered now on what ground this assertion could have been made. Had they known of the opening of the coffin, and received some secret information that the body had been removed? The more I thought about it, the more fearful I became of the possibility of the coffin being empty. There was the coffin before me—the lid was loose and easily raised—the leaden case within torn open. Within the case was another coffin of wood—the lid had never been fastened. What was beneath it? If I raised it, what should I discover? Dare I look within? Yes, the world should know the truth—that the body of the great poet was there—or that the coffin was empty. Reverently, very reverently, I raised the lid, and before my eyes there lay the embalmed body of Byron in as perfect a condition as when it was placed in the coffin one hundred and fourteen years ago. His features and hair were easily recognisable from the portraits with which I was so familiar. The serene, almost happy expression on his face made a profound impression upon me. The feet and ankles were uncovered, and I was able to establish the fact that his lameness had been that of the right foot. But enough—I gently lowered the lid of the coffin and as I did so, breathed a prayer for the peace of his soul.3

"Close thy Byron and open thy Goethe," that renegade Byronist Thomas Carlyle demanded in *Sartor Resartus*, but Barber's vandalism is only the most literal example of England's refusal to bend to the Sage of Ecclefechan. From the moment in July 1824 when Byron's black servant struggled for one last view of his master's coffin as it was lowered into the Hucknall vault, a defiant nation has shared his reluctance to let its most notorious poet go, a complex mix of curiosity and guilt driving it to re-stake its claim in the man it had once forced into exile.

It is as hard to exaggerate the impact of Byron's death on England as it is that of his life. In the orthodox histories of the nineteenth century the two seminal figures of his age are Coleridge and Bentham, but both men were pre-eminently "sires of sires," their influence disseminated through disciples until it was simply part of the zeitgeist—lived and breathed by men and women who would have been hard pressed to identify the source of their beliefs.

With Byron it is the opposite, and there is in this sense no English writer like him, no one who has stamped his image so firmly on the phenomenon that bears his name, no one who has so completely made his life the measure of his art. It is difficult to imagine that anybody in their right mind has ever allowed a dislike of Wordsworth to stand in the way of his *Prelude* for instance, but from the first triumph of *Childe Harold*, Byron and his art have been inseparable, his personality and life validating or threatening the poetry in ways that have no obvious parallel. "We shall, like all others who say anything about Lord Byron," *Blackwood's* declared,

> begin, *sans apologie*, with his personal character. This is the great object of attack, the constant theme of open vituperation to one set, and the established mark for all the petty but deadly sneers, shrugs, groans to another. . . . Is there a noble sentiment, a lofty thought, a sublime conception in the book? "Ah yes!" is the answer. "But what of that? It is only the roué Byron that speaks!" Is a kind, a generous action of the man mentioned? "Yes, yes!" comments the sage; "but only remember the atrocities of 'Don Juan.' Salvation is thus shut out at either entrance: the poet damns the man, and the man the poet.[4]

With the solitary exception of Milton, no English writer has so polarised opinion or posthumously stirred such visceral responses as Byron. In the wake of Shelley's death off the coast at Lerici the Tory press might lash him with a cruel and casual contempt that still has the power to shock, but the entrenched battle lines that formed around Byron's memory are of another order altogether, scars that define not just a world of coterie politics but the permanent cultural life of a whole nation.

It is notable, in fact, that it is not with other literary reputations that the posthumous cult of Byron can be compared, but with those deaths that seem to reveal some crisis of confidence or national identity. In more recent times the great state funeral of Sir Winston Churchill patently belonged to an order of its own, but if the sombre mood of that week was of an empire mourning its own passing, one only needs to think of other such funerals—Wellington's, Nelson's, the torch-lit procession of the old, mad George III—to recognise the context in which Byron's needs to be seen. "We have been stunned from another quarter," Sir Walter Scott wrote,

> by one of those deaths . . . as from an archangel's trumpet to awaken the soul of a whole people at once.[5]

"Hark! forth from the abyss a voice proceeds," Byron himself wrote of Princess Caroline—lines doubly prophetic of the mood that would greet his own death and that of another thirty-six year old aristocratic exile whose funeral cortege followed the almost identical journey northwards through the streets of London,

> *A long low distant murmur of dread sound,*
> *Such as arises when a nation bleeds*
> *With some deep and immedicable wound . . .*
>
> *Scion of chiefs and monarchs, where art thou?*
> *Fond hope of many nations art thou dead?*
> *Could not the grave forget thee, and lay low*
> *Some less majestic and less beloved head?*[6]

There was something else about Byron's death, however, something alien and atavistic, that not even the politicised guilt and pseudo-Catholic trappings of Princess Diana's funeral can quite match. Some years ago there was a documentary film of a Bengali village terrorised by a man-eating tiger, and in the ritual celebrations that greeted its killing, the frenzy of hands that stretched up in a bizarre mixture of fear and reverence to touch the garlanded corpse, we probably come as close as we can to the mood in which England awaited the return of Byron's body.

For Byron *was* that tiger (an image he used of himself—for that matter an image his mother-in-law used of him)—Blake's tiger, a thing of "fearful symmetry," an elemental force, beyond comprehension—too dangerous to be allowed to live and too vital to live without. "Alas poor Byron," Carlyle wrote in the flush of pentecostal panic that greeted the news from Greece,

> The news of his death came down on my heart like a mass of lead; and yet, the thought of it sends a painful twinge thr' all my being, as if I had lost a brother! O God! That so many souls of mud and clay should fill up their base existence to the utmost bound, and this, the noblest spirit in Europe, should sink before half his course was run! . . . We shall hear his voice no more: I dreamed of seeing him and knowing him; but the curtain of everlasting night has hid him from our eyes. We shall go to him, he shall not return to us. Adieu my dear Jane. There is a blank in your heart, and a blank in mine, since this man passed away.[7]

With his looks and glamour, his aristocratic pedigree, and the scandals that clung to his name, it is no surprise that Byron excited this attention in life, but the oddity is that death only intensified the cult of personality that surrounded him. For Jane Welsh the blank in creation his death left could have been no greater if the sun or moon had fallen from the skies, and it was as if no one could quite believe the enormity of their loss without the evidence of the body. "Don't look at him, he is dangerous,"[8] a horror-struck Lady Liddell had warned her daughter, covering her eyes when she saw the exiled Byron in Rome, but in death that was just what everyone wanted to do. In Missolonghi the wretched Julius Millingen and the rest of Byron's doctors had hacked at his corpse in a brutal parody of an autopsy, measuring his skull and weighing his brain, slapping vital organs on their scales as if the mystery of genius and personality was there to be found in his remains. In the same room, only days later, his companion and biographer, Edward Trelawny, pulled back the burial sheet to stare down on Byron's body with a similar confidence—"the great mystery was solved," he later wrote with a ruthless disregard for truth; "Both his feet were clubbed, and his legs withered to the knee—the form and features of an Apollo, with the feet and legs of a sylvan satyr."9

Back in England, it was little different when after almost six weeks at sea the *Florida* docked with his coffin just below London Bridge. While Byron's old friend Hobhouse waited on deck for the undertakers to drain the preserving spirit off the corpse, crowds lined the banks and watched from the flotilla of small boats that bobbed around the ship, as eager to glimpse his return as they had been to watch his departure from Dover eight years earlier.

A French officer from Le Havre delivered Hobhouse a request from General Lafayette asking to see the body. Down in the hold, a boy was caught cutting a relic from Byron's shroud. Over the next days, as the sense of loss sank in, the crowds only grew, men and women queuing in their thousands to pass the coffin as it lay in state in Great George Street, cramming the pavements and windows along the route of the funeral cortege and packing the church at Hucknall so full that there was scarcely room for the coffin.

Nor was this just the morbid excitement of a season, as the Parish Clerk's Album at Hucknall, placed there by John Bowring more than a year after the funeral, underlines. The church was then a more modest structure than the building which Victorian improvers bequeathed to Canon Barber, but for the mass of visitors who made the pilgrimage, the intimacy of the old St. Mary's ministered to their grief in ways that Westminster Abbey or St. Paul's could never have done. "So should it be," Bowring had written in the front of the album,

> *let o'er this grave*
> *No monumental banners wave;*
> *Let no word speak—no trophy tell*
> *Aught that may break the charming spell*
> *By which, as on the sacred ground*
> *He kneels, the pilgrim's heart is bound.*
> *A still, resistless influence,*
> *Unseen, but felt, binds up the sense;*
> *While every whisper seems to breathe*
> *Of the mighty dead who rests beneath.*10

The extravagant grief of the young Tennyson, the maudlin reflections of Mary Shelley as she watched the funeral cortege from her Kentish Town window, the lecture extemporised by Coleridge as it passed up Highgate Hill—all these quite properly belong to literary history, but skimming down the lists of names below Bowring's poem the most striking thing as ever with Byron is the sheer breadth and cosmopolitanism of his appeal. The two names that head the album, for instance, are those of the royal Duke of Sussex and of Pietro Gamba, brother of Byron's last Italian mistress, who visited Hucknall before sailing for Greece to die in the cause that Byron had made Europe's. There are visitors here, too, from New Orleans and Baltimore, representatives from the Spanish Cortes and the American Congress, comedians and Grenadier guardsmen, writers, theatre managers and clergymen, school parties, ships' crews, and—in 1832—a John de Bracken, home from Calcutta, where eight years earlier prayers for the repose of Byron's soul rose from a Greek chapel on the banks of the Hoogly.

After the seismic convulsion of grief that greeted Byron's death, these quieter after-shocks recorded in the Hucknall Album might come as no surprise, but they still raise teasing questions about his place in English cultural life. Among those hundreds of visitors many might have been hard pressed to say what had brought them, and yet in a curious sense it is the presence of the "common man"—the great battle cry of Diana's funeral—rather than of Washington Irving or the Duke of Sussex that is the most intriguing aspect of the Byron cult.

For a man of Sussex's liberal pretensions, the pilgrimage carried clear and deliberate political overtones, but precisely what kind of "fane" did those hundreds of obscure admirers imagine they were visiting at Hucknall? What were parents doing, signing the visitors' book with their daughters, paying homage at the shrine of a man who had publicly ridiculed every tie of family life? Why were army or naval officers at the tomb of a poet who took such pride in sharing Napoleon Bonaparte's initials? What did good protestant Englishmen think they were up to, leaving messages that would not look out of place at the foot of the Bambino in Rome's Aracoeli? What was it that brought so many clergymen to the grave of a writer the Bishop of Calcutta had labelled the "systematic poet of seduction, adultery and incest; the contemner of patriotism, the insulter of piety, the raker into every sink of vice and wretchedness to disgust and degrade and harden the hearts of his fellow-creatures"?[11] What was nineteenth century England doing longing after "a perfected idol . . . as the Israelites longed for the calf in Horeb"?[12]

The most exciting answer to these questions is that Byron had come to represent a subversive element in the national character for which the encroaching morality of the nineteenth century allowed less and less expression. In his wonderfully contrary study of the Byrons, A. L. Rowse once went so far as to claim that Byron was scarcely English at all, and if this is a characteristic overstatement, Rowse is right that the values Byron embodied have always prospered on the margins of English life rather than at its centre, a source of equal fascination and fear to a country reluctant to recognise its own complex identity.

"Into what dangers would you lead me, Cassius," a nervous Brutus asks in *Julius Caesar*,

> *That you would have me seek into myself*
> *For that which is not in me?*

and the fear that accompanied Byron to the grave was the fear of what he had shown them in themselves.* "Every high thought that was ever kindled in our breast by the muse of Byron," *Blackwood's* protested, expressing the sense of outrage and almost self-disgust that his readers came to feel as the full implications of their "idolatry" were brought home to them,

> every pure and lofty feeling . . . is up in arms against him.
> We look back with a mixture of wrath and scorn to the
> delight with which we suffered ourselves to be filled.[13]

It is this that gives the history—and the posthumous history—of Byron its continuing importance because he raised demons that no

---

*This was illustrated vividly by figures such as W.G. Whitcombe, who followed Byron to Greece. In 1825 the nineteen year old Whitcombe arrived in the town of Nauplia, assumed the name, identity and morals of the Byronic hero of a popular novel, *Anastasius*, attempted to assassinate Byron's friend Trelawny in an incident that might have come straight out of one of Byron's Eastern tales, and promptly went mad with fear and guilt when he realised what he had done.

community could afford to acknowledge or allow to live. In a wonderful sequence near the beginning of Stanley Donen's *Charade* George Kennedy opens the west door of a church, strides down the aisle to where an open coffin rests between banks of candles on its bier, stares for a moment at the body, takes a pin out of his raincoat lapel, jabs it into the corpse to make sure it is dead, turns on his heel and strides out again.

There was something of *that* about Byron's funeral—the mood along the Tottenham Road seemed to George Borrow like that of an execution—because for all its beauty and fascination the tiger was safer dead. There was nothing feigned in the grief and loss of the young Tennyson or Carlyle, and yet from the notorious day that his closest friends burned his memoirs in John Murray's offices to the letters George Eliot sent Harriet Beecher Stowe, even Byron's most passionate admirers needed to deny or suppress the truths that his life embodied. John Cam Hobhouse, that loyal "bulldog," told Tom Moore in a conversation about the memoirs, that he knew more of Byron than anyone else, and much more than he should wish anyone else to know.

"Yet each man kills the thing he loves"[14] wrote a later exile from these shores, and along with the adulation, Byron has always inspired an anxiety that ranges from comic wariness to suspicion, fear and open hatred. Through the novels of the nineteenth century Byronic imitators would continue to stalk the Caucasus or the moors with all the misanthropic glamour of their original, but from *Persuasion* to *Jane Eyre*, from *Glenarvon* to *Dracula*, from Mary Shelley's Raymond to Polidori's Ruthven—the first vampire in English fiction—"Byronism" is a physical threat to be feared, shunned, exiled, immolated, staked through the heart or—that most English of solutions,—blinded, crippled and then, "Dear Reader," married.

It is only too appropriate that Mary Shelley's name should feature on this list, because no one has so painfully united what D. H. Lawrence called the *"prédilection d'artiste"*[15] for the aristocrat with a bourgeois fear of everything he stands for. "For there does exist, after all," Lawrence wrote in his great essay on Thomas Hardy—an essay characteristically less about Hardy than Lawrence himself—

> . . . the great self-preservation scheme, and in it we must all
> live . . . But there is the greater idea of self-preservation,

which is formulated in the state, in the whole modelling of the community . . . In the long run, the State, the Community, the established form of life remained, remained intact and impregnable, the individual, trying to break forth from it, died of fear, or of exhaustion, or of exposure to attacks from all sides, like men who have left the walled city to live outside in the precarious open. This is the tragedy of Hardy, always the same: the tragedy of those who, more or less pioneers, have died in the wilderness, whither they have escaped for free action, after having left the walled security, and the comparative imprisonment, of the established convention. This is the theme of novel after novel: remain quiet within the convention, and you are good, safe and happy in the long run, though you never have the vivid pang of sympathy on your side; or, on the other hand, be passionate, individual, wilful, you will find the security of the convention a walled prison, you will escape, and you will die, either of your own lack of strength to bear the isolation and the exposure, or from direct revenge from the community, or from both. This is the tragedy, and only this.[16]

This book is the story of that tragedy, because supreme among the Lawrentian outsiders is Byron, an aristocrat in the conventional sense by a convoluted accident of inheritance, an aristocrat in the Lawrentian sense to the core. It has been plausibly argued that Byron was never in fact at ease with the chance that brought an impoverished Aberdeen schoolboy a title, but from that day in 1812 when, as the author of *Childe Harold*, he "woke to find himself famous" his life became a paradigm of Lawrence's struggle between the individual and the community—the archetype of all those artists forced into exile, compromise or silence by the hostility of the crowd, of the men and women who have had to pay with their freedom or security for their integrity, the living victims of that same communal, English instinct for self-preservation that pushed Hardy to sacrifice his heroes and heroines on the altar of social convention.

Crippled with a deformity of his right foot, abandoned by his rake of a father, brought up in poverty by his violently possessive mother, alternately abused and terrified by his Calvinist nurse, Byron might have had little choice in the matter, but no psychological pleading can disguise the gusto with which he embraced his fate. In recent years it has become the fashion among biographers to present him as some kind of "monster-victim" of this childhood, but the exhilarating truth about Byron is that he was an outsider by intelligence and will, an enemy by instinct, sensibility, temperament and politics of all that this "tight little island"* stands for.

No major English poet—except perhaps his hero, Alexander Pope—has made such creative capital out of a sense of alienation and grievance. It would take most of his life before the combination of exile and technical mastery matured these feelings into the great verse of *Don Juan,* but from his first callow satire the poet fed ruthlessly off his sense of difference, transmuting all the social and physical insecurities of childhood into the antinomian hauteur of the Byronic hero.

And the key word there is "Byronic," because it was the glee with which Byron seized on the idea of hereditary doom that has made his name synonymous with the rebel outsider. The more unstable elements of his character probably owed as much to his mother's Gordon blood as the paternal line, but it was exclusively through the history of crime and excess that was "Mad Jack" Byron's bequest to his son that a perverted Calvinism and the curse of deformity coalesced into a single, liberating myth of predestined damnation and revolt.

From the moment when, as a nine year old child, after the successive deaths of father, cousin, uncle and the "Wicked Lord," he came into the title and first saw the ruins of his ancestral home near Nottingham, the shape of this rebellion was set. Newstead had originally been founded as an Augustinian priory in the reign of Henry II, and for all the changes it was still the great west front of the former church that gave the house its special character, a soaring, pinnacled and traceried façade behind which nothing stood, a piece of history preserved as theatre as wonderfully and spuriously evocative as everything else about the child's bankrupt inheritance.

If it is impossible to imagine any nine-year old would be impervious to the romance of Newstead, no one but a Byron could have glo-

---

*Oh! what a snug little Island,
A right little, tight little Island!

Thomas John Dibdin, "The Snug Little Island," in *The British Raft,* 1797 ried so in its evidence of ancestral ruin. The priory had first come into the family in 1537 at the Dissolution of the Monasteries, but the ruthless transforming energies of Henrician England had long disappeared there, leaving house and lands mouldering in the same irreversible decay, the Byron name stained by murder, its deer slaughtered, woods felled, mining rights leased, rooms bare, its ruined east wing open to the skies.

Among the great English Romantics, Byron is unique in an almost complete absence of feel for his native landscape, and the cloistered world of Newstead quite literally set in stone a sense of physical alienation that had begun in his infancy. In his earliest verse there was a certain amount of Ossian-like posturing over the mountains of his childhood, but it was significantly the ruined priory that became what Pope's Twickenham grotto and garden had been to another crippled outsider—the emotional and physical context of his creative life, the "other place" of the imagination where he could reinvent himself in the successive alter-egos with which he would take on the world. "Newstead, fast falling, once resplendent dome," Byron saluted it in one of his juvenile poems,

> *Religion's shrine! Repentant* HENRY*'s pride!*
> *Of warriors, monks, and dames the cloister'd tomb,*
> *Whose pensive shades around thy ruins glide,*
> *Hail to the pile! More honour'd in the fall*
> *Than modern mansions in their pillar'd state;*
> *Proudly majestic frowns thy vaulted hall,*
> *Scowling defiance on the blasts of fate*[17]

In his adult life Newstead would be more a financial burden than a retreat, but its blend of history and loss retained a central place in his imagination. As a boy at Harrow and then Cambridge his sense of identity was wrapped up with the Byronic inheritance it embodied, but even after he had been compelled to sell it, the lessons of pride and vulnerability he had learned under its roof always remained with him.

It influenced everything in his life, his strengths and weaknesses, his politics and social manner—the awkward mix of arrogance and uncertainty—and above all the poetry that can often seem an emanation of childhood alienation. In the last great poem of his life he returned to Newstead with a freshness that underlines its importance to him, but if it is impossible to imagine the satirist of *Don Juan* without acknowledging the role Newstead played in his development it is as hard not to see its influence in the lack of "place" that is such a glaring weakness of his descriptive verse.

Nothing is ever as simple as that with Byron, of course, but his deliberate, "aristocratic" obtuseness about the *business* of poetry that clouds the issue here was ultimately no more than a manifestation of the same insecurity. One only has to think of the ease with which Keats can move through an English landscape in darkness and identify every scent and sound to see what is missing from Byron's verse, but in some adolescent way it would have seemed *beneath* him to look with that kind of particularity. "Where is the green your friend the Laker talks such fustian about," Trelawny recalled in an anecdote which—true or not—neatly brings Byron's hostility to a world with which he was at odds and poetic sensibility into a single focus,

> "Who ever," asked Byron, "saw a green sky?"
>
> Shelley was silent, knowing that if he replied, Byron would give vent to his spleen. So I said, "The sky in England is oftener green than blue."
>
> "Black, you mean," rejoined Byron; and this discussion brought us to his door.[18]

This insensitivity to his surroundings might seem an odd criticism of a poet whose evocation of the Greek landscape inspired a generation to fight and die for its freedom, but even then it was an *idea* of landscape rather than landscape itself that quickened his creativity, a sense of decline and loss that was as much imaginative projection as classical association.

It is no coincidence, either, that the one place that could genuinely vie with Greece in Byron's mind was Venice, and again it was the palpable air of decay that clung to the Serenissima in her dotage that gripped his imagination. There are times in fact when this almost reflex melancholy can strike an oddly adolescent note in a writer of his wit and sophistication, and yet it is precisely this quality of arrested growth that links boy and man, and—critically—man and *poet* in a sense of alienation that found its first and deepest expression in Newstead.

The greatness of D. H. Lawrence's novels, as F. R. Leavis remarked, was the proof they give that he *lived*, and the same could be said with even more validity of Byron's poetry. In the wonderful satires of his last years he produced some of the finest comic poetry in the English language, and yet for all its brilliance and fun the ultimate fascination of his verse lies in the testament it offers to the courage and defiance with which Byron lived his life.

It was a defiance that darkened everything, from the wounded bitterness with which he responded to rejection, to the reckless and self-destructive exhibitionism with which he greeted success. There are other outsiders for whom success comes as a kind of belated membership card, but it was perhaps the defining hallmark of Byronic rebellion that triumph only propelled him from the defence onto the attack, driving him in an ascending trajectory from Newstead on an inevitable collision course with the community he despised.

This is not another biography of Byron—nor even of the notorious marriage that led to his final rupture with England—but an exploration of this timeless battle between the values he stood for and those of the community. There are any number of English authors around whose lives a similar argument might be built, but the unity of his life and art and the fame which surrounded Byron make him the one writer whose history defines in some permanent way what it means to be English.

At the height of the marriage crisis, it was claimed with a breathtaking simplicity that men and women's attitudes to him demonstrated whether they were "good" or "bad," and nearly fifty years after his death Harriet Beecher Stowe berated the English nation for any softening in its attitude to him. It seemed to the American novelist that the moral sinews of the nation had been radically weakened by his verse and life, and while she was in some ways a case apart, there was too much agreement on all sides of the political spectrum to dismiss hers as the naïve voice of New England puritanism.

"England, England!"[19] she lamented, and if she was wrong in her diagnosis, she was right that the threat Byron offered had not died with him. For the dozen years which followed the triumph of *Childe Harold*, his poetry and personality had sent his contemporaries scuttling for cover behind the city walls, and yet it was only in death that his rebellion was revealed in its full destructiveness, consuming and maiming lives with all the inexorable power of Greek tragedy until it reached its final, savage climax in the "High Noon" of Byronic Romanticism that forms the core of this book.

This was the first and last confrontation in twenty years between the two women who had been brought together by his marriage and fought over his corpse, the sister he had loved and the wife who had brought about his exile. It took place at the White Hart at Reigate, a small town some twenty miles south of London, on 8 April 1851, the year of the Great Exhibition, the year Victorian England gloried in its prosperity and moral superiority with a complacency Byron would have loathed.

Byron, though, had been dead for almost twenty-seven years. Of his great contemporaries, Shelley had been gone for twenty-nine, Keats thirty, Coleridge seventeen, even Wordsworth—the "Words-words" of *Don Juan* as he had long since become—one.

And thirteen years into Victoria's reign, it was a different world. Tennyson, who as a schoolboy had carved Byron's name into a rock on hearing the news from Missolonghi, had just been presented to the Queen as the new Poet Laureate, his tortured frame tightly trussed in the same court dress that Samuel Rogers had once lent his predecessor. Matthew Arnold—that other representative voice of the mid-century—had just become engaged. Trollope was wondering if he would ever make a novelist. Dickens, never one to be seduced by national prosperity, was beginning *Bleak House,* Mayhew publishing his *London Poor.* George Eliot was editing at the *Westminster Review,* Charlotte Brontë squabbling with Thackeray, her sisters Emily and Anne, already dead. Byron's half-sister, Augusta Leigh, was sixty seven; his widow, Annabella Byron, fifty-eight.

Byron had been dead for almost as long as he had lived, but for the two women who met at the White Hart his memory had all the sharpness of recent bereavement. For the best part of forty years his presence or legacy had alternately enriched and shattered their lives, and this Reigate meeting was the final testament to his dominance, one last dramatic demonstration of the fear and adulation that had convulsed a generation and for which in their polar antagonisms Annabella Byron and Augusta Leigh stand the perfect surrogates.

It is this that gives both the fascination and significance to this meeting, because the battle that climaxed at Reigate is also in minia-ture the archetypal struggle of the outsider and the community that had raged around Byron ever since the first publication of *Childe*

Harold. The secret histories of these two women have a misery that no repetition can dim, and yet for all the melodrama of the story this book tells, it is the *representative* quality that gives a kind of Aeschylian grandeur to the history of incest, bastardy, betrayal, love and hate that in Byron's name and memory bound them together.

If this focus on the Reigate meeting needs no justifying, the form that has been adopted here requires some explanation. In the first and last parts of this book the methods are those of any conventional biography, but if there is a single episode in the whole Byron saga that *demands* a freer, more speculative approach, it is this last confrontation between Annabella and Augusta at the White Hart.

With that in mind, the form is that of an "imaginary dialogue," and if this is in part because we do not *know* what was said, it is not necessity that has determined this option. There can be few lives or deaths that have ever been subjected to the same scrutiny as that of Byron's, and yet as so often with him the most compelling truths of this narrative lie in regions for which the traditional tools of history or biography are simply not enough.

It is not only that scholarship can never deliver the certainties to which it aspires, but that this meeting has less to do with "objective truth" or ascertainable fact than with the kinds of subjective experience that gradually take on an independent and destructive life of their own. Within the restrictions of orthodox biography it would have been possible to chart the chronological path that took Annabella and Augusta from their first meeting to this last, but what biography could never do is dissolve the barriers between past and present or capture the distorting operations of memory, the co-existence of contradictory but equally valid "truths"; could never re-open those avenues that, one by one, are closed by life but remain in the mind; could never, most important of all, do full justice to that sense of waste, that consciousness of other possibilities—other "selves," resolutions, aspirations, untapped or thwarted potentialities of human growth—that was Byron's terrible gift, not just to these two women, but to his whole generation.

There is, too, another—entirely fortuitous—advantage to a dialogue of this kind, in that the inevitable whiff of Victorian melodrama about it, the sense of characters speaking out of "role," of addressing not each other but the audience beyond, perfectly captures the way in which they spoke. In a letter written just before the meeting at Reigate, Annabella accused Augusta of never saying or writing anything without a third person in mind, and whether or not that is fair to her it certainly is to Annabella herself whose natural mode of address was the statement or deposition made and obsessively recorded with the judgement of posterity in her sights.

And if this reconstructed dialogue is essentially a fiction, it is a fiction that is strictly circumscribed by historical evidence. The old White Hart in Reigate had passed its Regency peak by the time that Annabella chose it and is now long since gone, and the setting here is essentially a theatrical rather than an historical space, its symbolism and props those of a Pre-Raphaelite painting—this after all is the year Ruskin championed the Brotherhood—rather than a Victorian coaching inn doomed by the advent of the train.

There has, too, been a compression of time to contain within the classical unities the final unfolding of these lives, but those are the only liberties taken. There is nothing here, otherwise, that does not have its source in the thousands of letters, statements, depositions, reminiscences and journals that document the relationship of the two women. Much of it, too, is in their own words, spoken, written or reported over a period of more than thirty years. We have the letters that they exchanged before Reigate, and the minutes taken after. We have the notes, written on a slip of paper in a nervous, almost indecipherable hand, that Byron's widow took with her to the meeting. We have the correspondence that followed. We know their state of health, how they looked, how they dressed, how they sounded, how they stood and walked, their physical responses to pain. Above all, though, in the mere presence of two elderly women—the one frail from chronic ill-health, the other dying—we have the ultimate proof of that obsession with the memory and influence of Byron that makes their story the story of the age itself.

I

A MEETING OF OPPOSITES

On a chill and blustery Tuesday in April 1851, an elderly woman, accompanied by a man in his early thirties, emerged from the entrance at the top of Trafalgar Street in Brighton to take the north-bound railway for Reigate. If anyone in the crowded terminus had noticed either of them it would almost certainly have been the man, a tall and striking figure, whose charismatic preaching at the Holy Trinity had made the names of "Brighton" and "Robertson" synonymous across the English-speaking protestant world.

With her air of genteel invalidism, and discreet, unassuming appearance, it is unlikely that the woman beside him would have attracted a second glance. She had never been more than five foot three in height and in her late fifties seemed scarcely that, a fragile, neat creature with a slight, "almost infantine"[1] figure, fine delicate hands, deep and striking blue eyes, silver hair, high forehead, and the preternatural pallor of the permanent invalid.

To the circle of her friends, in fact, who watched over her prolonged decline with a complete and willing devotion, it seemed that Annabella Byron hardly belonged to this world at all. There was a calm certainty about her that struck a note of unearthly detachment, an ethereal refinement that seemed to the chosen "soul-mates" of these last years to be that of "one of the spirits of the just made perfect . . . hovering on the brink of the eternal world."[2]

If anyone had taken a closer look at this pair, however, as they made their way under the soaring gothic of Brighton's new terminus to the first-class carriages of the London train, there would have been little doubt where the balance of power lay. Thirty-five years earlier the young Annabella Byron had appeared to her sister-in-law less as a visiting angel than an avenging spectre, and in the remote and concentrated self-possession of her bearing, it was as if all the frailties or pleasures of life had been purged away to leave behind only a pure, indomitable will.

And yet behind this "miracle of mingled weakness and strength,"[3] as Harriet Beecher Stowe called her, there was a nervousness, an emotional and physical excitability, that raged all the fiercer for its ruthless suppression. In a self-portrait she wrote in the last year of her life she spoke of the "burning world within"[4] that so few ever saw, and as she took her place beside Robertson, and sat compulsively folding and refolding her scrap of paper with its illegible instructions to herself on it, she knew only too bitterly the cost at which any outward calm had been won.

If she had caught her reflection in the glass before it was swallowed up in the blackness of the Clayton tunnel, she would have been forced to recognise there the evidence of the same grim truth. Forty years earlier, in her second London season, Hayter had painted her with the louche abandon of some Regency Magdalene, but if she had looked now for the face of the young Annabella Milbanke in the reflection that stared back, searching for some trace of all those potentialities and hopes that were frozen when pain and humiliation petrified her strength into the obduracy of a long widowhood, she would have looked in vain.

There would have been something in its unyielding expression, however, in the set of the mouth, in the air of conviction, the concentration, that anyone who had seen her as a child would have had no difficulty recognising. Some years after her death Robertson's biographer, Frederick Arnold, remarked on the doctrine of "personal infallibility" to which Annabella Byron subscribed in these late years, and if a lifetime of alternating sycophancy and hostility had done their worst to make her what she was, the foundations at least of her old age were laid in the cosseted, self-absorbed childhood of Annabella Milbanke.

· · ·

To have any real sense of the woman in the train bound for Reigate, or the forces that had shaped her life, it is necessary to go back even further than that, to another generation and world that is best glimpsed in a family portrait by Stubbs that now hangs in the National Gallery in London. On the left of Stubbs's grouping a young woman of seventeen sits high in the seat of a light carriage, reins and whip competently and prophetically in hand, her face, simultaneously "unfinished" and determined, framed by a white bonnet, her eyes boldly, almost immodestly, engaging with a future that seems in her control.

The girl, Elizabeth Lamb, is pregnant, although it is impossible to tell from the painting. At her side, her father, Sir Ralph Milbanke, his expression serious, leans against the carriage; in the centre, holding the reins of a dappled grey that matches her carriage pony, stands her brother, John; on the right, slightly apart, elegant in profile on a superb bay, is her husband of a year, Peniston Lamb, the future first Lord Melbourne.

There is a sense of calm to the piece, a reserve and unforced serenity that can only come of an unconscious collaboration of artist and sitters. In the distance a rocky outcrop looms over a stretch of water with some vague suggestion of domesticated wildness, but Stubbs's figures need no background, confidently filling their social and pictorial space, sufficient to themselves under the enveloping protection of a darkly spreading oak.

The oak and the girl, the past and the future, both linked in an unbroken chain to which the figures bear silent, unruffled witness. There is no conversation in this "conversation piece," no interaction almost, just a shared strength that needs no articulating. From the side Peniston Lamb looks across—as well he might—to his formidable young wife, but the gaze is unreturned. Even the horses seem entirely self-contained, blinkered or cropping the grass, indifferent to each other, their owners, or the two dogs that, like a pair of attendant saints, stare up, in that eternal gesture of English portraiture, with unnoticed devotion at their masters.

There is none of the golden glow of other Stubbs paintings here, none of the bucolic ease of his *Haymakers*, but a cool silvery light warmed only by the pink of Elizabeth's dress and the answering tinge of the clouds. On a nearby wall an elderly couple also painted by Stubbs aboard their phaeton might be Jane Austen's Admiral and

Mrs. Croft, but this group is not about affection or fulfilment but hierarchy and power, about dynastic and cultural certainties, and about what David Piper memorably called that "obscure but potent directive of fate" that gives Stubbs sitters their air of unchallenged and unchallengeable authority.

According to tradition, the Milbanke family traces itself back to a cup-bearer at the court of Mary Queen of Scots, who fled the country after a duel, settling in the north of England. Whatever the maverick promise of these origins, however, the next two hundred years saw a blameless decline into respectability, all taint of romance erased, in a family progress that took the Milbankes from Scottish exile by way of aldermanic and mayoral office in Newcastle to a baronetcy and a safe seat in Parliament.

It was Charles II who granted the title to the first Sir Mark Milbanke in 1661, and over the next century the Milbankes' influence was consolidated in the network of alliances and marriages that inevitably underpinned eighteenth-century political life. In generation after generation of Sir Marks or Sir Ralphs the same pattern emerged, as the Milbankes of Halnaby Hall married into other northern families, extending their land and connections across the north-east of England, augmenting agricultural interests in one marriage or mineral interests in another before, in the middle of the eighteenth century, forging the key alliance with the powerful Holderness family that gave Stubbs's 5th Baronet a place in the Commons.

There is something so reassuringly dull about the Milbankes' political careers, so entirely lacking in individuality, that one feels instinctively with them that one is in touch with the solid bedrock of Sir Lewis Namier's England. Sir Ralph had first entered parliament as one of two unopposed members for Scarborough in 1754, and at the first election of the new reign stood in the Holderness interest for Richmond, loyally and uncritically supporting successive administrations, before retiring in 1768 without having spoken a single word in fourteen years an MP.

Over twenty years were to pass before another Milbanke sat in Parliament, but through the 1770s and 80s Sir Ralph's son, another Ralph, continued the same process of family consolidation, hitching his political fortunes first to Lord Rockingham and then, on his death, to Charles James Fox. In 1790 after a ruinous campaign that is reckoned to have cost the family £15,000, he was finally returned in second place for Durham Co, and for the next twenty-two years remained its MP, a genial and ineffectual "Uncle Toby" whose fidelity to the Whig cause, in his daughter's succinct phrase, was "as little valued as doubted."[5]

It was into this family and this world, on 17 May 1792, that Anne Isabella Milbanke was born. The future Lady Byron has always seemed to belong so completely to the nineteenth century that it is easy to forget that this is where her roots lie, that her moral and social being was shaped by the inherited virtues and limitations implicit in Stubbs's painting or her family's dilettante public service.

But if the young Annabella was brought up in a political milieu, behind the web of alliances and obligations that supported two generations in parliament lay realities of landed life that had a far more profound effect on her vision. From the middle of the seventeenth century the principal seat of the Milbankes had been Halnaby Hall, a red-bricked Jacobean manor house, now gone, that lay just off the Great North Road outside the village of Croft in Yorkshire. In the village church of St. Peter's a wonderfully grandiose tomb and pew still evoke the dynastic ambitions of the early Milbankes, but Annabella's affections remained all her life with the modest estate at Seaham on the north-east coast where she grew up. "If in a small village," she recalled many years later, in a passage that might have come from George Eliot,

> you cannot go out of the gates without seeing the children of a few Families playing on the Green, till they become "familiar faces," you need not be *taught* to care for their well-being. A heart must be hard indeed that could be indifferent to little Jenny's having the Scarlet Fever, or to Johnny's having lost his mother. . . . I did not think property could be possessed by any other tenure than that of being at the service of those in need.[6]

The Milbankes and Seaham may have given Annabella a sense of the rooted interdependency of country life, but through her mother she could lay claim to a more exotic strain of English history. Judith Noel was born in 1751, the eldest daughter of Sir Edward Noel of

Kirkby Mallory, first Viscount Wentworth and heir through the contorted female line to the sixteenth century Wentworth barony. It
would be dangerous to describe any title that has survived with the
tenacity of the Wentworths as "doomed," but when a family branch
can provide a Lancastrian standard-bearer at St. Albans, a Governor
of Calais under Mary Tudor, and the devoted mistress to the Duke of
Monmouth, it is at least guilty of the kind of ill-luck that might pave
the way to a marriage with Byron.

For someone so outwardly prosaic as Annabella, there was, too, a
curiously vivid streak of romanticism that fed directly off her sense
of history. In a self-portrait written as a woman of thirty-nine, she
looked back on her childhood self, on a miniature Dorothea Brooke
pulled backwards and forwards between the claims of the imagination and the stern imperatives of a protestant conscience.
"Impressed from earliest childhood with a sense of duty, and sympa-
thising with the great and noble in human character," she wrote,

> my aspirations went beyond the ordinary occasions of life—I
> wasted virtuous energy on a visionary scene, and conscience
> was in danger of becoming detached from that before me.
> Few of my pleasures were connected with realities—riding
> was the only one I can remember. When I climbed the rocks,
> or bounded over the sands with apparent delight, I was *not
> myself*. Perhaps I was shipwrecked or was trying to rescue
> other sufferers—some of my hours were spent in the Pass
> of Thermopylae, others with the Bishop of Marseilles in
> the midst of Pestilence, or with Howard in the cheerless
> dungeon . . .

> About the age of 13 . . . I began to throw my imagination
> into a home-sphere of action—to constrain myself, from reli-
> gious principle, to attend to what was irksome, and to submit
> to what was irritating. I had great difficulties to surmount
> from the impetuosity and sensitiveness of my character . . .
> It was this stage of my character which prepared me to sym-
> pathise unboundedly with the morbidly susceptible—with
> those who felt themselves unknown . . .7

It would clearly be absurd to try to define her exclusively in terms of
ancestry, but there is a sense in which the solidity of the Milbankes

and the romanticism of the Wentworth inheritance combined to produce in Annabella something distinctly new, a kind of fierce ordinariness, a strident centrality that raised the commonplace to the realms of genius, orthodoxy to the stuff of crusade.

Along with this dual inheritance, the circumstances of her own contented upbringing can only have sharpened the feeling of singularity with which she coloured the most ordinary imaginative experiences of childhood. In the same *Auto-Description* she lamented a "want of comparison" in her Seaham life that blinded her to the advantages of birth, and yet of greater importance than the inevitable isolation of a small Durham village was the simple fact that she was the only child of parents who had waited fifteen years for an heir.

Ralph Milbanke and Judith Noel had married in 1777, and although they had brought up a niece as if she was their own child, there is no mistaking the ferocious joy that greeted Annabella's birth. It is often admiringly noted that she was encouraged in her opinions from her earliest days, but if her childhood self can be back derived from her adult character, hers was the kind of independence that might have flourished more safely in the face of opposition than indulgence, her character one that would have fared better outside the warmth and admiration of a family that placed her firmly and uncritically at its centre. "It was indeed Calantha's misfortune to meet with too much kindness," her cousin Caroline Lamb wrote of herself in a passage in *Glenarvon* that throws an unexpected light on this—a passage that sufficiently stung Annabella when she read the novel to have her mark and angrily refute its psychology in a criticism that survives still among her papers,

> or rather too much indulgence from all who surrounded her. The Duke, attentive solely to her health, watched her with the fondest solicitude, and the wildest wishes her fancy could invent, were heard with the most scrupulous attention, and gratified with the most unbounded compliance.[8]

This regime of indulgence was made more dangerous in Annabella's case by an intelligence that in and outside the home had little to challenge it. Even as a child she was conscious of being cleverer than most of those around her, but it was a cleverness dangerously at the service of unchallengeable moral certitudes, an intelligence that

seems never to have broadened with reading or turned on itself in
any genuine spirit of criticism. From the evidence of her letters and
journals there was certainly a kind of scrupulousness about her, and
yet even here her scruples and self-doubts were, like her shyness, the
self-referential workings of an imagination that ultimately appealed
to no other judgement but its own.

If Annabella Milbanke had simply married as Milbankes had traditionally married, none of this might have much mattered, and it is
likely that she would have done no more than add one more name to
history's forgotten roll of mute, inglorious husbands. From the earliest family descriptions one can glimpse the formidable chatelaine she
should have been, but substitute the name Byron for that of George
Eden or any of her earlier suitors, see that ten-year-old girl with the
determined pout Hoppner painted as the future Lady Byron, and
the warmth, the love, the privilege and security of her sheltered
upbringing suddenly seem the laboratory conditions for breeding the
disaster of the most notorious marriage in literary history.

It is the inevitable condition of biography to shape a life with the
benefits of hindsight in this way, and yet it is only hindsight that casts
a shadow over the prelapsarian happiness of Annabella's childhood.
In her own eyes the memories of Seaham would always have the
poignancy of blighted innocence, but the horror is that it could have
ever equipped anyone so essentially limited in experience or culture
to imagine that she could understand or tame a Byron.

It is often forgotten, in the feeding frenzy that invariably accompa-
nies her name, how vulnerably young she was when she first met him
in 1812, and yet nothing suggests that another summer or two would
have made the difference. She had come up to London for her first
season in the previous year, and although there were suitors enough
to satisfy anyone's vanity, not even a future governor-general of India
or Wellington's adjutant general in the Peninsula had been sufficient
to jolt her out of the complacent certainties of her Seaham world. "I
met with one or two who, like myself, did not appear absorbed in the
present scene," she later wrote of this period,

> and who interested me in a degree. I had a wish to find
> among men the character I had often imagined—but I
> found only parts of it. One gave proofs of worth, but had no
> sympathy for high aspirations—another seemed full of affec-

tion towards his family, and yet he valued the world. I was clear sighted in these cases—but I was to become blind.⁹

It was a misfortune, too, for a woman who could think like this to see her future husband for the first time in his *annus mirabilis*, because if there were far more interesting "Byrons" than the triumphant author of *Childe Harold*, there was none more likely to appeal to a romantic moralist of Annabella's stamp. "Lavater's [the phrenologist] system never asserted its truth more forcibly than in Byron's countenance," the portrait painter Sir Thomas Lawrence wrote at the height of Byron's fame, wonderfully capturing the mix of glamour and threat in the figure that seduced London's "golden parallelogram" in the spring and summer of 1812,

> in which you see all the character: its ken and rapid genius, its pale intelligence, its profligacy, and its bitterness; its original symmetry distorted by the passions, his laugh of mingled merriment and scorn; the forehead clear and open, the brow boldly prominent, the eyes bright and dissimilar, the nose finely cut, and the nostril acutely formed; the mouth well made but wide and contemptuous even in its smile, falling singularly at the corners, and its vindictive and disdainful expression heightened by the massive firmness of the chin, which springs at once from the centre of the full under-lip; the hair dark and curling but irregular in its growth; all this presents to you the poet and the man; and the general effect is heightened by a thin spare form, and, as you may have heard, by a deformity of limb.¹⁰

Byron was just twenty-four when, after more than two years' travel across Europe and the east, the sudden and unprecedented success of *Childe Harold* changed his life and the course of Romantic literature. He had already produced some feeble juvenilia and a long and scabrous satire he had since come to regret, but nothing in his literary or private life, nothing in the intense and homo-erotic friendships of his Harrow and Cambridge days or the bisexual philandering in the Levant had prepared him emotionally for the loneliness of fame that swamped him on his return, a poet without conviction, an aristocrat without a sense of belonging, a liberal without the stamina or will for political life, an icon with a morbid sensitivity to his lameness.

It would have been odd in fact if Annabella alone had not felt drawn to Byron that summer, and yet even in the privacy of her diary and letters she felt she owed her intelligence some more refined expression of her feelings than the general excitement that gripped Regency society. She had first seen him at a morning waltzing party given by Caroline Lamb on 25 March, and after filling her journal that night with her impressions, the next day reported back to her mother in Seaham. "My curiosity was much gratified by seeing Lord Byron, the object at present of universal attention," she wrote,

> Lady Caroline has of course seized on him, notwithstanding the reluctance he manifests to be shackled by her . . . It is said that he is an infidel, and I think it probable from the general character of his mind. His poem sufficiently proves that he *can* feel nobly, but he has discouraged his own goodness. His features are well formed—his upper lip is drawn towards the nose with an expression of impatient disgust. His eye is restlessly thoughtful. He talks much, and I heard some of his conversation, which is very able, and sounds like the *true* sentiments of the Speaker.
>
> I did not seek an introduction myself, for all the women were absurdly courting him, and trying to *deserve* the lash of his satire. I thought that *inoffensiveness* was the most secure conduct, as I am not desirous of a place in his lays. Besides, I cannot worship talents that are unconnected with the love of man, nor be captivated by that Genius which is barren in blessings—so I made no offering at the shrine of *Childe Harold*, though I shall not refuse the acquaintance if it comes.[11]

The acquaintance finally came the next month at a party of Lady Cowper's, and with it the note of ironic detachment became increasingly hard to sustain. In her letters home to her mother she continued to insist that "calm benevolence"[12] alone could touch her heart, but no amount of dissembling to her parents or herself could disguise the fact that curiosity was rapidly turning into the crusade that would shape her whole life. "Do you think there is one person here who dares to look into himself?," she later recalled the question that had inspired her first mute "offering" at the shrine of *Childe Harold,*

> . . . I felt that he was the most attractive person; but I was not *bound* to him by any strong feeling of sympathy till he uttered these words, not to me, but in my hearing—"I have not a friend in the world!" It is said that there is an instinct in the human heart which attaches us to the friendless. I did not pause—there was my error to enquire why he was friendless; but I vowed in secret to be a devoted friend to this lone being.[13]

There is something unsettling in the reveries of the young Annabella, or at least in her incapacity to see them for what they were. The descriptions of Byron that litter her diary and letters are as banal as those of anyone else that season, but running through them is that old and dangerous sense of election, the conviction of some private and silent understanding that set her apart in a city swept along on the rhythms of the waltz and the voyeuristic thrill of Caroline Lamb's pursuit of Byron.

If there was nobody to blame for these delusions but Annabella, however, it is clear that she had not just imagined Byron's interest in her. In the wreck of their marriage she once accused him of only ever wanting what he could not have, but if there is something in that, the more brutal truth is that he simply could not see her for what she was—could not see the provinciality that passed for independence, the rigidity latent in her strength, the narrowness which, with the nostalgia of the jaded sophisticate, he wistfully put down to moral superiority. "I set you down as the most puzzling person there," he later told her of the first time he had seen her, across a room full of morning-visitors at Melbourne House,

> For there was a quiet contempt of all around you & the nothings they were saying & doing in your manner that was so much after my own heart. There was a simplicity—an innocence—a beauty in your deportment & appearance which although you hardly spoke—told me I was in company with no common being.[14]

As the spring of 1812 wore on, and Byron's life drifted dangerously and publicly into the chaos of his notorious affair with Caroline Lamb, it was not so much what Annabella was as what she was *not* that attracted Byron. The kinds of virtues and solidity with which he invested her would always hold a theoretical attraction for him, but it is hardly an exaggeration to say that if there had been no Caroline Lamb to escape then there would have been no marriage to her cousin, Annabella.

Byron had first come across Caro Lamb, the twenty-seven-year-old, fragile, androgynous-looking child wife of William Lamb, when she had written to him under a thin veil of anonymity after the triumph of *Childe Harold* in February 1812. Even before she had set eyes on him she had declared that she would know its author if he was "as ugly as Aesop,"[15] and within weeks of meeting she had made sure their affair was public property, played out with a kind of arriviste relish on his part and on hers with a reckless exhibitionism hovering on the edge of insanity.

There is not a moment of an affair that defined and caricatured the Romantic passion in all its delinquent intensity that has not been raked over a hundred times, but in the context of his relationship with Annabella it still has its place here. In later years Byron came to hate Caroline with a passion that only Claire Clairmont could otherwise inspire, but in its first weeks at least what attracted him to the maddest of all the Spencers was precisely the wayward and uncontrollable element in her that he eventually came to loathe.

There was a wonderfully sane and balanced side to Byron that would always in the end tire of romantic excess, and yet after the initial excitement had passed something more than boredom turned him against Caroline Lamb. An illicit element to some of his earlier, male relationships had sometimes unnerved him, but as he tried to distance himself from Caroline he found himself contending with a woman ready to call the Childe's bluff, to live out the implications of his Romanticism with a patrician contempt for convention that in his first year of success he had neither the courage nor the confidence of "belonging" to match.

Even with the contrast of Caroline Lamb to concentrate his mind, it is unlikely that his interest in Annabella would ever have quickened into anything more important had it not been for the intervention of her aunt (Caroline Lamb's mother-in-law), Lady Melbourne. By the time that Annabella made her London debut, the girl in Stubbs's portrait had reigned as the "spider queen" of Whig society for over a generation, "a sort of modern Aspasia" with the brain and morals to match, tolerant, attractive, intelligent, cynical, corrupt and—to Byron at least—"the best, the kindest, and ablest female I have ever known, old or young." "She was a charming person," he later told Lady Blessington,

> uniting the energy of a man's mind with the delicacy and tenderness of a woman's. She had all of philosophy, save its moroseness, and all of nature, save its defects and general *faiblesse* . . . I have often thought, that, with a little more youth Lady M. might have turned my head, at all events she often turned my heart, by bringing me back to mild feelings, when the demon passion was strong within me. Her mind and heart were as fresh as if only sixteen summers had flown over her, instead of four times that number—and the mind and heart always leave external marks of their state of health. Goodness is the best cosmetic that has yet been dis-covered . . . She was a captivating creature, *malgré* her eleven or twelve lustres, and I shall always love her.[16]

Even in her early sixties, the "spider" or the "thorn" still retained the power, desire and intelligence that had once made her the mistress of Lord Egremont and the Prince of Wales. As a young bride she had been forced to stand and watch her husband's ludicrous pursuit of the actress Sophia Baddeley, but with the ambition and purpose Stubbs caught so well, disappointment had simply deflected her energies into the ruthless pursuit of family influence that was to con-sume the rest of her life. "The charms of her person and the endow-ments of her mind were worthy of a better fate than that she was preparing for herself," Caroline Lamb wrote savagely of her in *Glenarvon*, the *roman à clef* with which she took her revenge not just on Byron but on the Whig world that had turned its back on her,

> But, under the semblance of youthful gaiety, she concealed a dark intriguing spirit, which could neither remain at rest, nor satisfy itself in the pursuit of great and noble objects. She had been hurried on by the evil activity of her own mind,

until the habit of crime had overcome every scruple, and rendered her insensible to repentance, and almost to remorse. In this career she had improved to such a degree her natural talent of dissimulation, that, under its impenetrable veil, she was able to carry on securely her darkest machinations; and her understanding had so adapted itself to her passion, that it was in her power to give, in her own eyes, a character of grandeur, to the vice and malignity, which afforded an inexplicable delight to her depraved imagination.[17]

With daughter and mother-in-law both living in Melbourne House, a delicate balancing act was required, but from the moment Byron tried to extricate himself from the affair with Caroline, he found Lady Melbourne a subtle and determined ally. To a woman who had charmed and slept her way to the top of Whig society, her daughter-in-law's morals were of no great concern, but the one crime the lax Regency world would not forgive was indiscretion and as Caroline's antics began to threaten the dynastic ambitions "the spider" held for her family, Lady Melbourne moved to neutralise her.

In spite of all her cynicism, though, it can no more have occurred to Lady Melbourne than it had to Byron that the solution to their mutual problem lay in her cool, self-contained country niece. For their different reasons both Caroline Lamb and her sister-in-law "Caro George" had done their best to convince him that Annabella was already engaged, but he had hardly needed their warnings to keep a wary distance from a woman he instinctively recognised as his opposite. "My dear Lady Caroline," he had written as early as 1 May, after reading some verses of Annabella's,

> I have read over the few poems of Miss Milbank with attention.—They display fancy, feeling, & a little practice would very soon induce facility of expression . . . She certainly is a very extraordinary girl, who would imagine so much strength & variety of thought under that placid countenance? You will say as much of this to Miss M. as you think proper.—I say all this very sincerely, I have no desire to be better acquainted with Miss Milbank, she is too good for a fallen spirit to know or wish to know, & I should like her more if she were less perfect.[18]

There is no reason to doubt Byron—Annabella is not mentioned in his letters for more than four months—but the *idea* of her had taken a dogged hold of his imagination. There was no pretence on his part that he was in love with her, or anyone else, but as over July and August the pressure from both the Lambs and Caroline's mother to end the affair grew, he was faced with the fundamental need of the outsider to assimilate or face destruction. "I see nothing but marriage & a *speedy* one can save me," he wrote to Lady Melbourne on 28 September,

> if your niece is attainable I should prefer her—if not—the very first woman who does not look as if she would spit in my face.[19]

"You ask 'if I am sure of myself,' " he had already written to Lady Melbourne ten days earlier, after first hesitantly broaching the idea of Annabella to her in a letter from Cheltenham on the 13th,

> I answer—no—but *you* are, which I take to be a much better thing. Miss M. I admire because she is a clever woman, an amiable woman & of high blood, for I still have a few Norman & Scotch inherited prejudices on the last score, were I to marry. As to *Love*, that is done in a week (provided the Lady has a reasonable share) besides marriage goes on better with esteem & confidence than romance, & she is quite pretty enough to be loved by her husband, without being so glaringly beautiful as to attract too many rivals.[20]

At the beginning of October Lady Melbourne approached her niece on his behalf, and on the 12th received Annabella's refusal from Richmond, complete with a "Character" of Byron explaining her decision. "The passions have been his guide from childhood," she wrote, up on her "high stilts" as her aunt described her,

> and have exercised a tyrannical power over his very superior intellect. Yet among his dispositions are many which deserve to be associated with Christian principles—his love of goodness in its chastest form, and his abhorrence of all that degrades human nature, prove the uncorrupted purity of his moral sense.

There is a chivalrous generosity in his ideas of love and friendship, and selfishness is totally absent from his character. In secret he is the zealous friend of all human feelings; but from the strangest perversion that pride ever created, he endeavours to disguise the best points of his character. When indignation takes possession of his mind—and it is easily excited—his disposition becomes malevolent. He hates with the bitterest contempt; but as soon as he has indulged those feelings, he regains the humanity which he had lost—from the immediate impulse of provocation—and repents deeply.[21]

It is difficult to be sure of Byron's real feelings at this rejection, or even whether he knew himself, but whatever they were he would never have dropped the tone of cool worldliness with Lady Melbourne that had become their common language. "*Cut* her! My dear Ly. M. marry—Mahomet forbid!"—he wrote to her on receiving the news, anxious to allay any suspicion of resentment,

I am sure we will be better friends than before & if I am not embarrassed by all this I cannot see for the soul of me why *she* should—assure *her* con tutto rispetto that The subject shall never be renewed in any shape whatever, & assure yourself my carissima (not Zia what then shall it be? Chuse your *own* name) that were it not for this embarras with C I would much rather remain as I am.—I have had so very little intercourse with the fair Philosopher that if when we meet I should endeavour to improve our acquaintance she must not *mistake* me, & assure her I never shall mistake her . . . She is perfectly right in every point of view, & during the slight suspense I felt something very like remorse for sundry reasons not at all connected with C nor with any occurrence since I knew you or her or hers; finding I must marry however on *that* score, I should have preferred a woman of birth & talents, but such a woman was not at all to blame for not preferring me; my *heart* never had an opportunity of being much interested in the business, further than that I should have very much liked to be *your relation*.—And now to conclude like Ld. Foppington, "I have lost a thousand women in my time but never had the ill manners to quarrel with them for such a trifle."[22]

The address on this letter—Cheltenham again—suggests, though, that Byron's good humour was not simply feigned for Lady Melbourne's benefit. He had gone to the fashionable spa town for the waters earlier in the summer, but long after it had been abandoned by most of London society he was still there, held by a growing fascination with that other "Aspasia" of Regency England that he would have been reluctant to admit to Lady Melbourne, the beautiful, serially faithless forty-year-old Countess of Oxford, Jane Harley.

There is as much pseudo-psychological nonsense talked of Byron's predilection for older women—as if everyone over the age of thirty were somehow identical—as there is over his fastidious distaste at the sight of a woman eating.* In the wake of *Childe Harold* it was inevitable that he should gravitate towards the great hostesses who dominated Whig society, but among even that disparate group it would be hard to imagine two women with less in common than Lady Melbourne and Lady Oxford, the one all caution, cynicism, and dynastic ambition, the other generous, impulsive, radical and careless of the proprieties she had so successfully defied from the first loveless years of marriage.

The daughter of a clergyman, Jane Scott had been born in Inchin, and at the age of twenty-two "sacrificed," as Byron later told Medwin, "to one whose mind and body were equally contemptible in the scale of creation."[24] If Lord Oxford had never been much of a match for his dazzling and ambitious wife, however, he was no gaoler either, and by the time that she began her affair with Byron the "grande horizontale" of Whig political radicalism was already the mother of five children by as many fathers, "a tarnished siren of uncertain age," as Lord David Cecil described her with patrician distaste,

---

*Captain Gronow, who fought at Waterloo, recalled a dinner with Byron that the Psychoanalysts have carefully ignored. "I recollect his saying," Gronow wrote, "that he disliked seeing women eat, or to have their company at dinner, from a wish to believe, if possible, in their more ethereal nature; but he was rallied into avowing that his chief dislike to their presence at the festive board arose from the fact of their being helped first, and consequently getting all the wings of the chickens, whilst men had to be content with the legs or other parts."[23]

who pursued a life of promiscuous amours on the fringe of
society, in an atmosphere of tawdry eroticism and tawdrier
culture. Reclining on a sofa, with ringlets disposed about her
neck in seductive disarray, she would rhapsodise to her lovers
on the beauties of Pindar and the hypocrisy of the world.[25]

Byron had first met her during the London season, but it was at
Cheltenham and then at Eywood, the Oxfords' country house in
Herefordshire, that their friendship developed into the infatuation
that absorbed him for the next six months. "She resembled a landscape by Claude Lorraine," Lady Blessington—no ingenue herself—
recalled him saying,

> with a setting sun, her beauties enhanced by the knowledge
> that they were shedding their last dying beams, which threw
> a radiance around. A woman (continued Byron) is only
> grateful for her *first* and *last* conquest. The first of poor dear
> Lady [Oxford's] was achieved before I entered on this world
> of care, but the *last* I do flatter myself was reserved for me,
> and a *bonne bouche* it was.[26]

It is impossible to imagine Byron speaking of Lady Melbourne in this
tone, but if Lady Oxford never exerted the same dominance over
him as the "spider" had done, in the sensual and intellectual licence
of the "bowers of Armida,"[27] as he labelled Eywood, he found a
retreat from any fleeting disappointment at Annabella's rejection
and the continuing assaults of Caroline Lamb. "I mean (entre nous
my dear Machiavel)," he had written to Lady Melbourne,

> to play off Ly. O against her, who would have no objection
> *perchance* but she dreads her scenes and has asked me not to
> mention that we have met to C or that I am going to E.[28]

"I am no longer your lover," he wrote to Caroline herself, as good as
his word, if the letter she reproduced in *Glenarvon* is the faithful copy
of Byron's that she claimed it to be,

> and since you oblige me to confess it, by this truly unfemi-
> nine persecution,—learn, that I am attached to another;

whose name it would of course be dishonorable to mention. I shall ever remember with gratitude the predilection you have shewn in my favor. I shall ever continue as your friend, if your ladyship will permit me so to style myself; and as a first proof of my regard, I offer you this advice, correct your vanity, which is ridiculous; exert your absurd caprices upon others; and leave me in peace.[29]

In spite of the callousness of this letter—a cruelty that forms the counterpart to Byron's generosity—his relationship with Caroline had stirred him in ways that Lady Oxford never did. There is no disguising the sense of almost bloated content that runs through many of Byron's letters from Eywood, and yet at some level both he and Lady Oxford knew that the demons that drove him were not ones that could be contained within Armida's bowers or the boundaries of Whig politics she had marked out for him.

For all the sexual and intellectual freedom Byron enjoyed at Eywood, the affair with Lady Oxford was too tame ever fully to satisfy him. In all his most important relationships there had been an element of risk and social danger, but there was something almost institutional in the sexual abandon of Lady Oxford, a kind of *licenced* immorality that paradoxically took Byron closer to one branch of the Whig political establishment than he had ever been before.

And there was never a time, either, when Byron was more dangerous than when made aware of how little he wanted what English society had to offer him. "I am going abroad again," he announced in March 1813, in the middle of his affair with Lady Oxford,

> . . . my parliamentary schemes are not much to my taste—I spoke twice last Session—& was told it was well enough—but I hate the thing altogether—& have no intention to "strut another hour" on that stage.[30]

Byron was being partly disingenuous—for all the kind words that greeted his debut speech it had only had a limited impact—but his suppressed unease of this period was more than a defensive reflex to disappointment. It is clear from his own comments that he knew that he would never make a parliamentary orator, and yet it is hard to believe that success could any more have reconciled the creator of

Childe Harold—still less the "Titan battling with religion and virtue"[31] that Nietzsche admired in Byron—to the limitations of English public life and a career in politics.

If it seems inevitable that the young Nietzsche should be drawn to Byron—and in particular to the creator of the defiant Manfred—the quality that he most admired in him was the courage to follow his instincts that Lawrence also saw as the defining characteristic of the "aristocrat." In his Hardy essay Lawrence wrote that "the final aim of every living thing . . . is the full achievement of itself,"[32] but as Byron's affair with Lady Oxford guttered towards its untidy end, it was precisely that goal of self-realisation—the supreme ambition of the Romantic imagination—that he recognised with an ever increasing clarity he could never achieve in England.

In an age that is as ready to recognise the tyranny of sex as ours is, it is possibly enough to point out that for a man of Byron's sexual ambivalence a country that still sent homosexuals to the gallows was no place to be. From the publication of the spurious "Don Leon" poems in the mid-nineteenth century, Byron has always been an icon and spokesman for homosexual freedom, and yet the vital thing in this context is not so much the question of his sexual identity *per se*— who now cares?—but the wider issues of creative fulfilment or frustration with which it was inevitably and intimately bound.

For Byron, as for Lawrence, the test of "*being*" was "*doing*," and as the year dragged on he was conscious of how little he had achieved as a poet. For all his aristocratic disdain for the business of versifying he was keenly aware that he had "something within that 'passeth show,' "[33] and yet for a man whose lameness, childhood and sexual ambiguities all supremely equipped him to challenge political, moral, or physical injustice in every form he found it, he had precious little to show. The adolescent anger of *English Bards and Scotch Reviewers*, which he had long since repudiated? The stagey and harmless posturing of *Childe Harold*? A clutch of cautiously disguised tributes to the dead Cambridge chorister, Edleston? "At five-and-twenty, when the better part of life is over," he wrote in his journal,

> one should be *something*;—and what am I? nothing but five-and-twenty—and the odd months.[34]

But if, in these early months of 1813, Byron still lacked what Lawrence called the "courage to let go the security, and to *be*,"[35] this

sense of self-dissatisfaction and estrangement was gradually pushing
him towards a crisis. As early as May he was writing to Lady Melbourne of the need to escape a world that was stifling him, and at the
end of June he returned with increased irritation to the same theme.
"I am doing all I can to be ready to go with your Russian" [Prince
Koslovsky, a visiting Russian diplomat], he told her,

> depend upon it I shall be *either* out of the country or
> nothing—very soon—all I like is now gone—& all I abhor
> (with some few exceptions) remains—viz—the R[egent]—
> his government—& most of his subjects—what a fool I was
> to come back—I shall be wiser next time.[36]

It is a curious, if somehow irrelevant, thought that Byron might have
gone abroad in the summer of 1813, either with the Oxfords to Sicily
as was planned at one time, or farther east to the Levant. Byron himself had such a strong sense of his own destiny that even with the
benefit of hindsight it is hard to see his life in any other shape than
that which it finally took, and if this ignores those elements of
chance and sloth that right up to his death might have disposed of
him in a dozen different ways, one only has to picture him for a
moment harmlessly cruising the Mediterranean to recognise the
inherent implausibility of the vision.

Because if Byron was to grow as a man or a poet, he did not need
simply to *escape* England, but to smash with a complete and final violence everything that held him to it. In his relationship with Caroline
Lamb during the previous year he had come dangerously close to
doing this, and while he had pulled back from the edge then it was
only a matter of time before he recognised that the conformist elements in his nature could never be squared with the vocation for
opposition he claimed as the Byron birthright.

"I have no choice"—Byron put the words in Manfred's mouth—
and it is this sense of necessity that attracted both Lawrence and
Nietzsche to the dramatic parabola of Byron's life and career. There
is of course a world of difference between the Lawrentian "aristocrat" and the *übermensch* that Nietzsche hailed in the figure of Manfred. Yet if Lawrence's ultimate concern was with *fulfilment* in the
deepest and most human sense of the word, he never shirked the fact
that for an outsider of Byron's stamp that inevitably meant war.
"This is the tragedy," Lawrence wrote,

... that the convention of the community is a prison to his natural, individual desire, a desire that compels him, whether he feels justified or not, to break the bounds of the community, lands him outside the pale, there to stand alone, and say: "I was right, my desire was real and inevitable; if I was to be myself I must fulfil it, convention or no convention ..."[37]

It is this sense of inevitability that gives the air of a "phoney war" to the period of Byron's affair with Lady Oxford. When at the end of June she left England with her husband he confessed that he felt more "Carolinish"[38] about it than he had expected, despite the fact that for all her attractions she could no more satisfy him than Caroline Lamb herself had done before her.

Still less could one of the great *regnantes* of Whig society answer his need for a rupture with everything that held him to England. It did not, though, matter. By the time that Lady Oxford finally sailed, on 28 June, the one woman had re-appeared in his life who could fill both roles: a woman who by her birth and temperament was not only uniquely placed to define the full nature of Byronic rebellion but also to meet with a peculiar psychological and emotional fitness what Lawrence called "the deepest desire" of life,

a desire for consummation ... a desire for completeness, that completeness of being which will give completeness of satisfaction and completeness of utterance.[39]

The woman in question was the Hon. Mrs. Augusta Leigh, the twenty-nine-year-old daughter of Byron's father by his first, scandalous, marriage to Amelia Darcy, Baroness Conyers in her own right and the wife of the heir to the Duke of Leeds, the Marquess of Carmarthen.

The son of that famous sailor and womaniser, "Foulweather Jack," "Mad Jack" Byron seemed "born for his own ruin, and that of the other sex."[40] Six years before Augusta's birth, the dazzling and wealthy Marchioness had met and fallen for him, picnicked with him one day and abandoned her husband for him the next, living defiantly with him in a "vortex of dissipation"[41] until a well-publicised divorce left her free to marry him and move to France.

Whatever fondness his son might retain for his memory, "Mad Jack" was as callous a rake as eighteenth-century gossip portrayed him, with all the Byron charm and none of its generosity. For five years he lived off his wife's fortune in either Chantilly or Paris, but when shortly after Augusta's birth he lost wife and income together, Jack Byron abandoned the child to the first in a long succession of guardians and relatives, and set off on the predatory hunt for another heiress that finally led to Bath and Catherine Gordon.

For a few months, as a four-year-old, Augusta lived with her father and his pregnant new wife at Chantilly, but from the moment she was handed over to her grandmother, Lady Holderness, she left behind the depravation and uncertainty that was Jack Byron's only obvious legacy to his children. During the crucial years when Catherine Gordon and her son were struggling under the indignities of poverty and isolation, the orphaned Augusta was growing up among a clutch of aristocratic relations into a tall and graceful girl, "light as a feather," with a long, slender neck and heavy mass of light brown hair, a fine complexion, large mouth, *retroussé* nose, beautiful eyes, gentle manner, and a pathological shyness that eclipsed even that of her unknown Byron half-brother.[42]

If these formative years among her Howard cousins and the half-brothers and sisters of her mother's first marriage gave Augusta an uncritical, aristocratic ease that Byron never matched, as a grounding in emotional subservience they had more corrosive consequences. There was a fundamental docility to her character that probably ran deeper than any social conditioning, but for a girl of such natural reticence and limited prospects, a childhood of gilded dependence in the great houses of her relations can only have compounded the instinct for self-surrender that was to mark her adult life.

It was an instinct confirmed, too, when after a six-year courtship she finally married her feckless cousin, George Leigh, and sank into a life of straitened domesticity from which she never escaped. Colonel George Leigh has always had one of those roles in the Byron story that never quite swells even to a walk-on part, but for his wife at least he was real enough, an irascible and incapable husband and father in equal measure, a cavalry officer whose career ended in financial scandal and a gambler whose sharpness, even in the world of Newmarket and the circles of the Prince of Wales, placed him on the wrong side of social acceptability.

It can seem at times as though Augusta only existed in and through other people, so it is little wonder that a woman with such a genius for self-effacement has always proved hard to pin down. From the first day that her character was dragged into the public domain it has been open season on her, but after a hundred and fifty years of legal and biographical prodding she remains as elusive and unknowable as ever, leaving behind only a kind of erotic charge that is as close as we can get to her, an impression of femininity so endlessly and placidly accommodating as to obliterate all individuality.

A "fieldsman," Thomas Hardy wrote in *Tess*, is never anything more than a man in a field but a woman is continuous with the natural world, and something of that universality clings to the finest surviving image we have of Augusta Leigh. There is little contemporary evidence to suggest she ever looked like Hayter's lovely drawing of her, but in the languor and passivity of that face, the tilt of the head and the long curve of the neck, he has surely left us the essential Augusta—the "sleepy Venus" of Byron's *Don Juan*, the Zuleika of *The Bride of Abydos*, the mother of seven children by a husband she hardly ever saw—the woman whose idle and easy sexuality could disturb and attract both men and women every bit as much as her half-brother's flagrant aggression.

Augusta had first met Byron when she was a girl of seventeen and he an awkward and overweight schoolboy of thirteen. From their first exchanges of letters the two were natural allies in his endless battles with his mother, but in spite of a protective—and on his side almost seigneurial—affection they saw very little of each other as children. At the age of seventeen Augusta was already infatuated with her Leigh cousin, and as Byron himself moved from Harrow to Cambridge and then on to his travels in the east she inevitably became more of an idea than a reality to him.

In the long run there could have been nothing more dangerous than this legacy of intimacy and distance, and no more vulnerable time for Augusta to re-enter his life than the summer of 1813, when his affair with Lady Oxford was petering out and Caroline Lamb was taking her last melodramatic revenge. The correspondence between Byron and Augusta for the preceding months is missing, but it seems almost certainly his idea that she should come up to London. She had written to him the previous January in need of money to meet her husband's gambling debts, and although financial troubles over Newstead left Byron in no position to help, his answer emphasises the sad hollowness she alone would fill. The "estate is still on my hands," he began a long list of complaints, "& your brother not less embarrassed . . . "

> I have but one *relative* & her I never see—I have no connections to domesticate with & for marriage I have neither the talent nor the inclination—I cannot fortune-hunt nor afford to marry without a fortune. . . . I am thus wasting the best part of my life daily repenting and never amending. . . . I am very well in health—but not happy nor even comfortable—but I will not bore you with complaints—I am a fool & deserve all the ills I have met or may meet with.[43]

There was something prophetic in that last line, because almost from the moment she arrived in London, Byron seems to have been bent on disaster. If "form" is anything to go by, he would inevitably have turned to someone on the rebound from Caroline and Lady Oxford, but if anyone might have done, Augusta seemed to offer everything, the excitement of novelty and the comfort of familiarity, the danger of the forbidden with the guarantee of safety implicit in her name.

Because above all she was a *Byron,* and for someone so self-absorbed and yet utterly lacking in self-love as her brother that was an irresistible attraction. In the years since their childhoods he had formed some of the most intense friendships of his life, but it was only with a more attractive version of himself, as he now saw Augusta, a woman with so many of the same mannerisms and the same shyness, that he found his deepest, almost platonic desire for completion realised. "For thee, my own sweet sister," he addressed her,

> *in thy heart*
> *I know myself secure, as thou in mine;*
> *We were and are—I am, even as thou art—*
> *Beings who ne'er each other can resign;*
> *It is the same, together or apart,*
> *From life's commencement to its slow decline*
> *We are entwined—let death come slow or fast,*
> *The tie which bound the first endures the last!*[44]

With her endless good-humour and sense of fun, her charm and talent for nonsense—her "damn'd crinkum-crankum"[45] as he called it—Augusta also represented a simple release from the tensions of London life. Almost immediately she became an integral part of his routines, included in his invitations and plans, the novel half of a double-act that was part spontaneous and part calculation. "If you like to go with me to ye. Lady Davy's tonight," he wrote in a note that nicely captures the blend of pride and vanity with which he looked on her,

> I *have* an invitation for you—There will be the Stael—some people whom you know—& *me* whom you do *not* know & you can talk to which you please—& I will watch over you as if you were unmarried & in danger of always being so . . . I think our being together before 3d. people will be a new *sensation* to *both*.[46]

With anyone except Augusta this might have led nowhere, but with her chronic habit of subservience, it was only a matter of time before affection and familiarity slid into something more perilous. It is impossible to know with any absolute certainty when brother and sister became lovers, but if the malicious gossip of Caroline Lamb—or Byron's own boast to Tom Moore that her seduction had cost him little trouble—has any substance it was probably only a matter of weeks or even days.

The mere use of the word "seduction" in this context however—Byron at his coarsest—wilfully trivialises and misrepresents a relationship that he would always more honestly recognise as the most important of his life. If these things can ever be judged from the outside, it would seem that sex was always of secondary significance in their affair, on Augusta's side to a limitless capacity for self-surrender, and on Byron's to the expression of a kindness and generosity that was at the core of his personality.

And yet when that is said, his letters and verse make it clear that he inspired in the twenty-nine-year-old mother of three a passion that surprised them both with its violence and abandon. In the best known celebrations of their love it is always a platonic ideal of union that Byron is anxious to stress, but in Zuleika's language in *The Bride of Abydos* we are almost certainly taken closer to the earthier reality of

its early days. "To see thee, hear thee, near thee stay," Zuleika tells
the man she believes to be her brother, in a passage which uncon-
sciously echoes the startled self-discovery of Shakespeare's Perdita in
the great fourth act of *A Winter's Tale*

> *And hate the night I know not why,*
> *Save that we meet not but by day,*
> *With thee to live, with thee to die,*
> *I dare not my hope deny:*
> *Thy cheek, thine eyes, thy lips to kiss,*
> *Like this—and this—no more than this;*
> *For, Allah! Sure thy lips are flame:*
> *What fever in thy veins is flushing?*
> *My own have nearly caught the same,*
> *At least I feel my cheek, too, blushing.*[47]

Even when this is recognised, however, the seamless, almost
inevitable transition from sister to lover was for Augusta only one
stage in a more complete annihilation of self. "Partager tous vos sen-
timents," she wrote to him in November 1813, enclosing with the
note a lock of her hair: "Ne voir que par vos yeux"—"to share in
your feelings, to see only with your eyes, to act only on your advice, to
live only for you, that is my only desire, my plan, the only destiny that
could make me happy."[48] "To soothe thy sickness," Zuleika continues
in the same vein in *The Bride,*

> *watch thy health,*
> *Partake, but never waste thy wealth,*
> *Or stand with smiles unmurmuring by,*
> *And lighten half thy poverty;*
> *Do all but close thy dying eye,*
> *For that I could not live to try;*
> *For these alone my thoughts aspire:*
> *More can I do, or thou require?*[49]

The tragedy for Augusta, however, was that Byron *did* require more,
because for him the affair was more complex and guilt-ridden than
her simple devotion could comprehend. In reckless moments he
might publicly ridicule the moral parochialism of an incest taboo,

but at other times it could disturb him with a fear that stopped him naming Augusta even in the privacy of his journal. "Dear sacred name, rest ever unreveal'd," he quoted from Pope's *Eloisa* in his November 1813 journal, adding his own gloss: "At least even here, my hand would tremble to write it."[50]

Somewhere behind this fear lies the legacy of his Calvinist childhood, and yet as his deathbed shows, Byron was too intellectually and morally courageous to be cowed by the demons of the "Scotch School." Throughout his life he habitually dramatised himself in terms of Miltonic defiance, but for all the swagger of Cain or Heaven and Earth, Byron's sense of sin and exclusion was ultimately bound by this world rather than the next, his instinct for rebellion against man and not against God.

And this is perhaps the key to his behaviour with Augusta, because the fear he had of what they had done was less to do with a theological sense of sin than the growing recognition that he was prepared to push his defiance of convention to any limits. In his affair with Caroline Lamb the previous year, the courage or recklessness had seemed almost exclusively hers, but as he paraded Augusta in London and followed her to Newmarket and talked of exile together, as he trailed the affair in his letters and flaunted their incest in his poetry—as he pitted the Byrons against the world in the most public and symbolic way he could find—he discovered in Augusta not just his ideal refuge but his perfect weapon.

It would take the imaginative sympathy of a novelist to do justice to the complex and contradictory rhythms of Byron's life as it slid towards open rupture with the society that had embraced him only eighteen months earlier. If one simply believed the evidence of his journal for the winter of 1813–14, the frustrations of the previous year were as acute as ever, but as one turns from that to his verse, the contrasting boldness of the poetry suggests rather an artist and man growing into a defiant sense of his own power and vocation.

In the space of a few days in November 1813 he wrote *The Bride of Abydos*, and the following month, in another spasm of creative energy, threw off the third of his Eastern tales, *The Corsair*. In his letters and journals he was as dismissive as one would expect of these achievements, and yet no amount of Byronic self-mockery or defensive irony could deflect the central importance these poems had for him.

The Bride of Abydos, written with Augusta and the theme of incest constantly in mind, had been, in his own words, his first "complete" poem but in its own harsher way *The Corsair* was every bit as subversive. He had written the *Bride* in the first place to keep himself sane, but with its violent and antisocial rage *The Corsair* was in itself a kind of deliberate public madness, brilliantly conceived simultaneously to alienate and seduce his public. "Fear'd, shunn'd, belied, ere youth had lost her force," Byron described his hero whom he must have known by now his readers would associate with himself.

> *He hated man too much to feel remorse,*
> *And thought the voice of wrath a sacred call,*
> *To pay the injuries of some on all.*
> *He knew himself a villain—but he deem'd*
> *The rest no better than the thing he seem'd;*
> *And scorn'd the best as hypocrites who hid*
> *Those deeds the bolder spirits plainly did.*
> *He knew himself detested, but he knew*
> *The hearts that loath'd him, crouch'd and dreaded too.*
> *Lone, wild, and strange, he stood alike exempt*
> *From all affection and from all contempt:*
> *His name could sadden, and his acts surprise;*
> *But they that fear'd him dared not to despise:*
> *Man spurns the worm, but pauses ere he wake*
> *The slumbering venom of the folded snake:*
> *The first may turn, but not avenge the blow;*
> *The last expires, but leaves no living foe;*
> *Fast to the doom'd offender's form it clings,*
> *And he may crush—not conquer—still it stings!*[51]

"I have just finished the Corsair—am in the greatest admiration," Annabella Milbanke, wilting forgotten in the wings since her rejection of Byron's proposal, wrote to Lady Melbourne,

> In knowledge of the human heart & its most secret workings surely he may without exaggeration be compared to Shakespeare. He gives such wonderful life & individuality to character that from *that* cause, as well as from unjust prepossessions of his *own* disposition, the idea that he represents

himself in his heroes may be partly accounted for. It is difficult to believe that he could have known these beings so
thoroughly but from *introspection* . . . I am afraid the compli-
ment to his poetry will not repay him for the injury to his
character.[52]

For a brief period in the autumn of 1813—probably to placate Lady
Melbourne—Byron did his best to draw back from the edge with his
pursuit of the young, newly married Lady Frances Webster, but by
the end of the year Augusta was pregnant with a child which the
dates suggested might well be his. In the middle of the following January, with a crisis mounting, brother and sister drove north to Newstead, "through more snows than ever opposed the Emperor's
retreat." Once arrived, there was no possibility of leaving. The roads
beyond the Abbey were impassable, but their coals were excellent, he
told his publisher, John Murray, the fireplaces large, the cellar full, his
head empty, his only desire "to shut my doors & let my beard
grow."[53]

For the moment, defiance and refuge were in perfect equilibrium.
"Never was such weather," Byron wrote contentedly after ten days,
"one would imagine Heaven wanted to raise a Powder-tax & had
sent the snow to lay it on."[54] Never had his ancestral home seemed so
all-sufficient as with Augusta. "And what unto them is the world
beside," Byron later demanded in *Parisina*, his drama of incest and
family doom that echoes the mood of these weeks,

> *With all its change of time and tide*
> *Its living things, its earth and sky,*
> *Are nothing to their mind and eye.*
> *And heedless as the dead are they*
> *Of aught around, above, beneath;*
> *As if all else had pass'd away*
> *They only for each other breathe . . .*
> *Of guilt, of peril, do they deem*
> *In that tumultuous dream?*[55]

There is something, in fact, of the magic of Pasternak's *Dr. Zhivago*
about Byron's and Augusta's illicit exile at Newstead, isolated from
criticism and responsibilities by the impenetrable winter landscape,

as safe among the ruins of the abbey as Yuri and Lara in the frozen wastes of Varykino. At the edge of Newstead's cloistered world lurked the wolves, but like Zhivago watching their shadows in the half-light of dusk, Byron could pretend for the moment that they were merely dogs. To be alive, and to live in the present, was enough. All his restless search after sensation was sunk in "sluggish" content. Even the desire or need to write—for Byron the "lava of the imagination"[56]—was gone. Happy, he had neither need nor urge to create. He felt, he told Murray in a revealing metaphor for his poetic life, as he did when recovering from fever in Patras—"weak but in health and only afraid of a relapse." "I shall keep this resolution," he wrote of his determination to give up scribbling, "for since I left London—though shut up—*snow*bound—*thaw*bound—& tempted with all kinds of paper—the dirtiest of ink—and the bluntest of pens—I have not even been haunted by a wish to put them to their combined uses."[57]

The wolves, though, were not dogs, and with the Tory press in full voice following the publication of his poetic squib against the Prince of Wales, Caroline Lamb still primed for trouble and his friends increasingly nervous, Byron was never going to be allowed to forget it. Characteristically, just as the previous year Caroline's antics had frightened him back from the abyss, his moods now swung between defiance and compromise, between talk of the exile he had been threatening for almost a year and a marriage—any marriage—that might yet be his "salvation" from the feelings that he confessed to Lady Melbourne "are a mixture of good and diabolical."[58]

After his first impetuous talk of exile, Augusta too was beginning to look on the idea as the only way of averting catastrophe. There is little doubt that she would have gone abroad with him the previous summer if he had pressed her, but in the nature of things she had more to lose than he did and for a mother as indulgently devoted as Augusta, the thought of abandoning any of her children—Georgiana, her eldest, had been born in the first week of November 1808, Augusta Charlotte, a little over two years later and a son, George, in June the next year—could never have been a bearable option.

George was still only a baby when Byron first proposed exile to Augusta, however, and it was probably her two daughters who most exercised her concern. From an early age Augusta Charlotte had begun to exhibit the symptoms of autism that would eventually lead her to an asylum in Kensal Green, and yet in her different way the oldest, "Georgey"—traditionally Byron's favourite—was as much of a worry as her sister, constantly ill and as cripplingly and elusively shy as Augusta herself had been as a child.

And even with Augusta's easy belief in the workings of a benevolent providence—virtually the only legacy from her pious Holderness grandmother—she must have felt that she had used up not just her small stock of courage but her luck when the birth of a third daughter in April passed without any gossip. It is impossible to tell from the few elliptical comments in Byron's letters how anxious they had been in advance, but whatever his thoughts on the child he was certainly concerned enough for Augusta to journey up from London to the Leighs' home outside Newmarket in the days before her confinement.

For all the space and time that has been expended on the subject, the only thing that can be said with any certainty of the paternity of Elizabeth Medora Leigh, is that it cannot be known. It would seem likely that Byron and Augusta both initially believed that she was his child, and yet there is not a single scrap of evidence—not a remark or silence—that cannot be equally well interpreted to support either side of the argument. "Oh! but it is worth while," Byron reported to Lady Melbourne—in the one notorious, throw-off paragraph on which a whole speculative industry has been raised,

> I can't tell you why—and it is *not* an "*Ape*" [an apparent reference to medieval incest superstitions] and if it is—that must be my fault—however I will positively reform—you must however allow—that it is utterly impossible I can ever be half as well liked elsewhere—and I have been all my life trying to make someone love me—& never got the sort I preferred before. But positively she and I will grow good—and all that—& so we are *now* and shall be these three weeks & more too.59

For all Byron's resolutions, however, the choice of the name Medora—the heroine of his *Corsair*—smacks of the kind of brinkmanship that threatened disaster at any moment. It has been argued, with some plausibility, that she was in fact called after the Oaks winning filly of 1813, but even if that is true Augusta—for all her "goosiness"—was astute enough to know that in anything to do with Byron it was the perception rather than the reality of things that mattered.

She had, in fact, her own idea for Byron's wife, Lady Charlotte Leveson-Gower, but since the previous autumn an alarmed Lady Melbourne had been keeping a far more serious candidate waiting in the wings. For a time during his Eywood idyll there had been a slight froideur between her and Byron, but one of the great secrets of Lady Melbourne's influence was a talent for absorbing slights and from the first threatening appearance of Augusta in Byron's life she had been as ready to sacrifice her niece for his safety as she had been a year earlier for her own dynastic needs.

There are moments in the relationship of Byron and Annabella Milbanke that tilt the sympathies violently in one direction or another and the intervention of Lady Melbourne is one of these. There is no need to sentimentalise the broadly "Austenish" attitudes to marriage of Annabella herself, but the machinations of her aunt over the next fifteen months belong to another league altogether, raising the cynicism of the Regency marriage market to levels for which *Glenarvon* or *Les Liaisons Dangereuses*—the constant point of reference among her family for Lady Melbourne—provide no real preparation.

Lady Melbourne's letters to Byron were always cooler, more discreetly circumspect, than his to her, and so it is difficult to be sure of her motives in this matter. It is clear that she was both genuinely fond of Byron and alarmed for him, but for a woman who only had to see a happy marriage, it was said, to want to destroy it, the appeal of the match must have been as much aesthetic as practical—the pure unalloyed pleasure of uniting two people so symmetrically ill-suited as Annabella and Byron, "the spoilt child of seclusion, restraint and parental idolatry" and "the spoilt child of genius, passion, and the world,"[60] as Mrs. Stowe later described them.

Lady Melbourne's performance was one of dazzling cynicism as she brought them together again, interpreting one to the other, revealing or concealing as needed, playing equally on the weaknesses of Byron and Annabella until each imagined the initiative their own. There was a streak of passivity in Byron's nature that had always made him putty in Lady Melbourne's hands, but with her romantic high-mindedness and naivety her niece proved no less easy to manage.

After almost a year in which she had time to reflect on the loneliness of moral superiority and the dullness of domestic life without the *frisson* of Byron's attentions, Annabella was ripe for persuasion. "I have received from Lady Melbourne an assurance of the satisfaction you feel in being remembered with interest by me," her first direct letter to him had begun on cue on 22 August 1813—midway between the beginning of his affair with Augusta and his half-hearted pursuit of Lady Frances Webster,

> Let me fully explain this interest, with the hope that the consciousness of possessing a friend whom neither Time nor Absence can estrange may impart some soothing feeling to your retrospective views.[61]

One of the supreme temptations of the novel, E.M. Forster once confessed, is the desire to give characters the happiness that "real life" denies them, and this first letter of Annabella's can stir the same kind of emotions. She was so much in the habit of regarding herself in fictional terms that it would be hard not to follow suit anyway, but the cruelty of her fate now was to find herself less the heroine of her own shaping than the dupe of a Leclos plot over which she had no control. "You have remarked the serenity of my countenance," she went on,

> but mine is not the serenity of one who is a stranger to care, nor are the prospects of my future untroubled. It is my nature to feel long, deeply, and secretly, and the strongest affections of my heart are without hope. I disclose to you what I conceal even from those who have most claim to my confidence, because it will be the surest basis of that unreserved friendship which I wish to establish between us . . . Early in our acquaintance, when I was far from supposing myself preferred by you, I studied your character. I felt for you, and I often felt with you. You were, as I conceived, in a desolate position, surrounded by admirers who could not value you, and by friends to whom you were not dear. You were either flattered or persecuted. How often have I wished that the State of Society would have allowed me to offer you my sentiments without restraint.[62]

With its oblique and frustrated demand to be heard this might antic-
ipate the great climax of *Persuasion,* but Annabella was no more an
Anne Elliot than Byron was Captain Wentworth. From her earliest
youth she had dramatised herself as the self-sacrificing heroine of
her historical daydreams, and the girl who had stood by Howard in
her fantasies now abandoned herself to the role of Byron's redeemer,
uniting herself with him in an imaginary communion of souls that
transcended time, place or vulgar self-interest. "Surely the Heaven-
born genius without Heavenly grace must make a Christian clasp the
blessing with greater reverence & love, mingled with a sorrow as a
Christian that it is not shared," she wrote to her old confidante Lady
Gosford in her most ecstatic vein,

> Should it ever happen that he & I ever offer up a heartfelt
> worship together—I mean in a sacred spot—*my* worship will
> then be most worthy of the spirit to whom it ascends. It will
> glow with all the devout and grateful joy which mortal breast
> can contain. It is a thought too dear to be indulged—not
> dear for *his* sake, but for the sake of *man,* my brother man,
> whomever he be—& for any poor, unknown tenant of this
> earth I believe I should feel the same. It is not the poet—it is
> the immortal soul lost or saved.[63]

In one of her "Auto-descriptions," Annabella confessed this inability
to distinguish fiction from fact, but what had been harmless enough
in the child was profoundly dangerous in the adult. In the early days
of their acquaintance she had self-consciously distanced herself
from the "Byromania" of London, but as she realised with something like panic how much she had lost in turning him down, she set
about desperately trying to re-create Byron in an image she could
square with her conscience, blindly moving with every exchange of
letters towards marriage with a man she scarcely knew. "I entreat
you then to observe the more consistent principles of unwearied
benevolence," she wrote to Byron in the language of a tabloid
astrologer,

> No longer suffer yourself to be the slave of the moment, nor
> trust your noble impulses to the chances of Life. Have an
> object that will permanently occupy your feelings & exercise

your reason. Do good. Your powers peculiarly qualify you for performing those duties with success, and may you experience the sacred pleasure of having them dwell in your heart![64]

It is clear from Byron's reply that Annabella's tone had startled him, but if he had to sacrifice Augusta, it hardly seemed to matter whom he married. "To the part of your letter regarding myself," he wrote back, having first assured her that she was the only person with whom he had ever contemplated marriage,

> I could say much—but I must be brief—if you hear ill of me it is probably not untrue though perhaps exaggerated—on any point in which you may honour me with an interest I shall be glad to satisfy you—to confess the truth or refute the calumny.—I must be candid with you on the score of Friendship—it is a feeling towards you with which I cannot trust myself—I doubt whether I could help loving you—[65]

There was not a scrap of hypocrisy about Byron, but what was almost as hazardous as he renewed his interest in Lady Melbourne's niece, was the artist's ability to conjure imagined feeling out of the depths of genuine experience. He would have found it impossible to preserve his illusions about a future with Annabella had he seen anything of her, but in the safety of letters he could indulge in an emotional transfer that enabled him to create an idea of her and himself that could sustain him through the travesty of an epistolary courtship.

If it was a serious error of judgement on Annabella's part to imagine she could reform Byron, it was a more culpable misjudgement on his to think that he would ever allow it. It is unlikely that with Augusta so compulsively in his mind anyone could have filled her place, but as he edged inexorably towards a second proposal, it was Annabella's fate to be almost diagrammatically the wrong person at the wrong time—a poor woman's Dorothea Brooke, capable of change but not growth, of ardour but not compassion, sensibility but no real sympathy.

It is possible still that Byron could have forgiven Annabella for what she *was*, and yet he must have known, as he finally steeled himself to propose, that he could never forgive her for *not* being Augusta. In the early days of their courtship her virtues had been thrown into relief by the extravagances of Caroline Lamb, but seen now through the distorting prism of his "perverse passion"[66] everything about her would inevitably come to seem different, her goodness primness, her certainties dogmatism, and her learning pedantry—the five foot three incarnation of all the cultural and moral littleness he despised.

Byron's courtship of Annabella through the late summer of 1814 seems so reckless, so wantonly obtuse in the refusal to recognise the warning signals, that no conventional explanation of his actions seems quite sufficient. In his journals and letters he might describe her as his last hope of salvation, and yet if at some superficial level he managed to convince himself of that, his choice betrays a deeper compulsion to make her the *causa bella* of a rift with the world she embodied that had been threatening since the first success of *Childe Harold*.

It is this secret, unconscious, destructive agenda that gives such an air of inescapable misery to the story that unfolds with his second proposal to Annabella. On 9 September, having prevaricated as long as he could, he wrote to her from Newstead, sealing and despatching the letter "with the greatest haste," according to Tom Moore, before he could have second thoughts.[67] On the same day that she received it at Seaham, Annabella wrote back, a letter of touching and honest simplicity. "I have your second letter," she told him,

> and am almost too agitated to write—but you will under-
> stand. It would be absurd to suppress anything—I am and
> have long been pledged to myself to make your happiness
> my first object in life. If I *can* make you happy, I have no
> other consideration. I will *trust* to you for all I should look up
> to—all I can love. The fear of not realizing your expectations
> is the only one I now feel. Convince me—it is all I wish—that
> my affection may supply what is wanting in my character to
> form your happiness.[68]

As Byron opened the letter, Augusta at his side, he turned so pale that she thought he might faint. It never rains but it pours, was his only comment. Even so, he probably did not understand the forces he had set in motion. Nor did a fraught, uncomfortable week at Seaham at the beginning of November, that left him and Annabella as ignorant as ever of each other's character, open his eyes.

On 24 December 1814, after further delays over the marriage settlement, he once more set off for the north, accompanied by his old travelling companion, Hobhouse, and stopped near Newmarket to spend a last Christmas with Augusta. On the 26th the two men continued their reluctant journey towards Seaham. "Never was lover less in haste,"[69] recorded Hobhouse in his journal, and he was right. As the wedding day approached, the air of foreboding spread. In later life Annabella would speak of the sense of inexplicable dread that seized her. At the Leighs' house at Six Mile Bottom, near Newmarket, on the morning of 2 January, at the exact time she knew that the marriage service had begun, Augusta later said that she felt as the sea must do when an earthquake moves it. The panic, the fear, the emotional turmoil were justified. She knew, as Byron had told Lady Melbourne, that her own security and reputation were wrapped up with the success or failure of the marriage. It was, though, already too late.

Almost forty years after that journey north, on the same morning that Annabella Byron and Frederick Robertson boarded the Reigate train at Brighton station, a woman in her late sixties, dressed in mourning and walking with a slow, shuffling step, made her painful way up the first-class staircase of London Bridge's new terminus, and onto the narrow platform of the Brighton line.

It is unlikely that anyone who had ever known Augusta as a young girl, or seen the drawing that Sir George Hayter had done of her in her late twenties, would have recognised her. She might never have been in any conventional sense a beauty, but there had been a charm and elasticity about her that had long since gone, the woman Hayter so wonderfully captured worn away to the faded creature for whom every anxious step seemed an act of atonement to the world around her.

There was even something in the way she carried herself, her long, black shawl pulled tight around her as though she might disappear into it, that suggested the same air of surrender. For most of her lifetime she had struggled with whatever resources she could muster to keep a hostile world at bay, but just two months past her sixty-eighth birthday, and with "death in her face,"[70] the Hon. Mrs. Augusta Leigh had at last nothing more to give or ask than to die in peace.

She had only travelled once before on the railway, but even for someone less nervous and sick, the prospect from her window would have been a bewildering one. As the train swung southwards and left the Greenwich line and the teeming slums of Bermondsey behind, the soaring glass house of the Great Exhibition visible in the distance, it began to cross a city that was changing by the week and almost by the day, spreading and growing with the railways that were transforming it, sprouting new villas and settlements, degrading suburbs into slums and villages into suburbs in a thrusting dialectic of population, railway and building that had left any world Augusta had known far behind.

It was a new age that Augusta instinctively and rightly feared, but as the train gathered speed and finally escaped the tentacular spread of London, moving through a landscape still relatively unchanged from her youth, it was this older world that threatened most danger. For more than twenty years she had looked forward to this journey with all the optimism and placatory desire to accommodate that had characterised her youth, but as the train slowed across the common land and farms near Reigate, coming to a standstill at the heart of what one contemporary guide called England's "forgotten Eden," this older, less resilient Augusta must have known that for the last representative of a "serpent race"[71] there was little mercy to be expected.

If there had been any doubts about that, the letter she had received, sent from Brighton on 11 February, would have ended them. "Since the cessation of our personal intercourse," she had read in a neat, firm hand she had not seen in two decades,

> you have more than once asked me to see you. If you still feel that wish, I will comply with it. We may not long have it in our power, Augusta, to meet again in this life, and to do so might be the means of leaving to both of us a remembrance of deep though sad thankfulness. But this could not be the effect unless every worldly interest were absolutely excluded from our conversation, and there were the most entire and mutual truthfulness. *No other expectations* must be entertained by you for a moment. On any other terms I cannot see you again, unless summoned to your Death-bed.[72]

She had, too, her instructions. A fly would be waiting at the station to take her to the White Hart. When the train stopped she remained sitting where she was, a dowdily dressed figure from a previous age, waiting like some sacrificial victim at the altar of Victorian self-justification and moral rectitude to which she had been brought. After a short while a servant in drab livery carrying a visiting card appeared at her window. On the card was a name: Lady Byron.

II

THE MEETING

Tuesday, 8 April, 1851. The White Hart, Reigate. A large room decorated in an oppressive clutter of different periods and styles, an amalgam of the Georgian coaching age and Victorian, the walls sombre maroon relieved only by the glint of frames, the woodwork dark, the scattered chairs covered in chintzes. A door, ajar, opens into the left wall, against which is a long, black, horse-hair sofa. On the opposite side of the room a wood fire burns low in an open grate. Under a glass dome on the mantel is an elaborate ivory-faced clock, its pendulum swinging with an insistent, audible ticking. Above, a mirror; on either side, open bookcases. In the left foreground a heavy square legged mahogany serving table, with a cut glass vase of dried flowers, papers scattered across it, a small travelling case with its lid open, outdoor bonnet, gloves etc. Back right, a window opens onto the garden beyond, which drops away and rises again to a skyline of still bare beech trees, and a cold, grey sky. Back left a large corner cupboard, and between them a regency pier table, with a gilded, finialled bird cage. Above it, incongruously flanked on either side by sporting prints, hangs a large framed print of Manfred on the Jungfrau, the face of Manfred contorted by suffering, his fist raised in one last gesture of defiance.

In front of the picture, a woman in her late fifties, in a lavender coloured dress stands staring silently up, her arms folded across her chest, the fists clenching and unclenching in a compulsive gesture. She can be no more than a little over five feet in height, with an unusually high forehead, the habitual pallor of her face slightly flushed with agitation, hard blue eyes, sharp features, pursed mouth, silver hair under a widow's cap of transparent material.

At the table, papers in his hand, a man stands looking anxiously at her. He is a tall and impressive figure in his early thirties, brown hair just receding at the temples, a broad forehead, deep set eyes, a strong, straight nose, wide, thin mouth, cleft chin, and side whiskers, his whole manner an uneasy mix of deference and authority.

I

ROBERTSON   (*Hesitantly*)
               If you would prefer another room, I'm sure—

LADY BYRON   (*Without answering, slowly turns from the picture, and walks to the window. She stands there, looking out to the bare trees, her back to Robertson*)
               Was that the fly?

ROBERTSON   (*He takes a watch from his waist-coat pocket, and glances up at the clock*)
               She should have been here by now—

LADY BYRON   (*Almost to herself*)
               Oh, she will be here soon enough, she'll be here.

ROBERTSON   If she has never taken the railways—
               (*He breaks off as a sudden spasm of pain seems to run through the slight figure standing with her back to him*)
               Lady Byron?

LADY BYRON   (*Her body relaxes, she waves away his concern with a slight gesture, turns slowly away from the window, and returns to the picture*)
               She will be here.

ROBERTSON   I do wish you would let me bring you something—

LADY BYRON   And the papers? Is everything there?

ROBERTSON Yes, yes I think you have everything that we went through, though I really can't see that you will need them—

LADY BYRON (*Interrupting, her voice quiet, her eyes still on the picture*)
But then you have not met Mrs. Leigh.
(*She makes a slow circuit of the room, pausing again momentarily in front of the same picture. Her voice is measured*)
I have long since had to learn, that with a certain—
(*She pauses, letting the words hang between*)
with a certain kind of forgetfulness, it is as well to be prepared.
(*She moves on, the subject dismissed*)
And the child's letters, are they with the others?

ROBERTSON (*Watching her, his voice registering a note of defeat*)
Yes,—yes, I think they are all here.

LADY BYRON Then if you won't stay, I'll only trouble you for some water—

ROBERTSON Yes, of course—
(*Takes a jug up from the table, begins to pour a glass, and pauses hesitantly*)
And you know that in any other circumstances I would gladly, but the poor creature is surely going to be more at ease—

LADY BYRON (*Dryly*)
I thought it was Mrs. Leigh's soul that we were concerned with, Mr. Robertson, and not her ease.

ROBERTSON (*Defensively*)
Yes indeed, but in common charity—

LADY BYRON (*Her tone as measured as ever*)
I would not have imagined that I had given you much cause to doubt my charity.

ROBERTSON   *(He takes up his hat from the table, and stands with it in hand, looking down, his voice almost inaudible)*
No, no. Certainly. But—but when Mrs. Leigh has made her wishes so plain, I can't in all conscience see how I can simply ignore them—
(His voice peters away, as he looks at the figure at the table, seemingly absorbed in pushing papers about as if he was not there)
But we have been over all this, so if you will excuse me—
(He places the glass of water down on the table, moves towards the door, and opens it)
And I will be in the next room if you need me.

LADY BYRON   *(She pauses beside the table, adjusting the papers on it without any obvious purpose, her voice ironic)*
Ah. Need.
(She moves away from the table, and towards the fire, her back to Robertson)
Why are people so keen to bring up my needs when they are most bent on thwarting them?

ROBERTSON   *(Pauses at the door)*
That hardly seems fair—

LADY BYRON   *(Underneath the control, her voice has a nervous edge to it)*
I sometimes think, too, that you imagine that I enjoy this. There is nothing I could wish more than to take your view of things, but there are duties—a duty to truth—
(Her voice becomes more composed, as if the phrase has a soothing, almost mantric familiarity)
a duty to Mrs. Leigh herself, Mr. Robertson,
(She turns and looks fixedly at him)
that as she and I stand on the brink of eternity I will not shirk.

ROBERTSON   *(Inaudible almost)*
No, indeed.

LADY BYRON   (*Turning away from him, and moving to the window*)
You will tell a servant, that if Mrs. Leigh has
arrived she is to be shown in.

ROBERTSON   Of course.

LADY BYRON   And say that we are not to be disturbed.

ROBERTSON   No, indeed.
(*With a final defeated stare at the woman standing with her
back to him, Robertson leaves, shutting the door behind him.
As she resumes her pacing, she takes out a folded slip of
paper tucked into her cuff, begins to unfold it and tucks it
back unread into her sleeve. She stops again under the
Manfred. As she stands in silence looking up at it, her fists
clench and unclench in another spasm of pain. Behind her,
unnoticed, the door opens, and a woman in her late sixties,
slightly taller and fuller in figure, dressed in heavy but shabby
mourning, the black crepe bodice mottled with damp stains,
the hem of her dress spattered with mud, her movements
slow, her air uncertain, appears. She stands by the door a
moment looking across at Lady Byron*)

AUGUSTA   (*Her voice softly attractive, affectionate*)
Annabella.
(*Without waiting for a reply, she moves tentatively forward,
her two hands stretched out in greeting*)
Dearest Annabella!
(*Half way across the room she stops as the figure of Lady
Byron remains with her back to her, the only recognition a
tensing of her whole body. Slowly Augusta's hands drop
back to her side*)

LADY BYRON   (*Quietly. Without turning*)
Augusta.
(*Without looking at her she moves away from the picture to
the window, only her hands betraying her agitation. When
she speaks again there is a note of strained control in her
voice*)
You found Bridges, then?

AUGUSTA   Yes, yes, or at least he found me.

LADY BYRON   And your journey? Easy I trust?

AUGUSTA   (*Uncertain at her reception*)
             Thank you, yes

LADY BYRON   (*Staring out of the window, her tone wandering and incon-
             sequential*)
             I find the railways so much better—the roads can
             be so disagreeable at this time of the year. Did you
             come alone?

AUGUSTA   Yes. Yes, I had thought to ask Emily, but—

LADY BYRON   (*Her voice remote*)
             Ah, of course, Emily. The child, is she well?

AUGUSTA   Thank you, yes. It has been hard on her since her
             father's death, but—

LADY BYRON   And yourself?

AUGUSTA   (*Her tone almost apologetic*)
             Perhaps now with the warmer days—

LADY BYRON   (*Breaking in, dryly impatient of weakness*)
             I find with age I have less and less time for illness,
             what with my schools—and—
             (*She seems to lose the thread of what she is saying*)
             And other duties . . .
             (*There is a slight pause as she looks out of the window, her
             thoughts elsewhere*)
             I ought in fact to be in Ealing now, but this was the
             only day that Mr. Robertson could join me.

AUGUSTA   Yes, you wrote.

LADY BYRON   Perhaps you noticed him as you came in? He has
             been very useful to me over these last years, and he
             would have wished to have stayed—

(*She turns away from the window, her manner and voice firm again*)
But as you made it clear that you would rather we were alone, I have asked him to wait for us—

AUGUSTA (*Quietly*)
Thank you.

LADY BYRON You ought to know, too, that he was against this meeting at all, but though he has only my welfare at heart—
(*Each phrase is carefully weighed*)
I find—I find that I have been thinking of you more and more since Colonel Leigh's death, and while I can accuse myself of no injustice, I have not been easy at the thought that we might never meet again—uneasy—
(*She pauses for a moment in front of the bird in the cage, looking at it with a remote detachment*)
that certain things should remain unsaid between us.

AUGUSTA (*Softly*)
I am glad.

LADY BYRON (*She resumes her circuit, with an almost imperceptible movement motioning Augusta to sit down in a chair at the centre of the room*)
Is there anything I can have them bring you?

AUGUSTA (*Dropping into the chair, removing her black gloves, and placing them on a small table beside her*)
Thank you, no.

LADY BYRON Some wine after your journey?

AUGUSTA No, nothing.

LADY BYRON (*Indifferent*)
Probably wise.

(*She pauses at the side table, and runs a finger along a surface, examining it for dust, before casting a slow, look around the cluttered room*)

Though I begin to find myself oddly at ease in places of this sort—something to do with the restlessness of age I dare say—or merely the price perhaps of having nowhere that one is tempted to think of as home.

(*She stops again in front of the picture, studying it with distaste. Still looking at it, she continues*)

Do you know that when I was a child, I thought Seaham would be my home forever. I used to visit our cottagers with my father, and I would have my own purse to give out pennies and I believed— believed that so long as I could be there nothing could ever harm me, that I would always be happy—

(*There is a slight break*)

and now—

(*With a weary sigh*)

But I have not asked you here to speak of Seaham.

AUGUSTA   (*Almost to herself, as if in a private reverie*)

Seaham. I don't know when I last heard that name.

(*There is a slight pause*)

It seems a world away—a lifetime ago—

LADY BYRON   (*Slowly and without even seeming to hear*)

Thirty-six years.

(*There is a pause*)

Thirty-six years years, three months—

(*Another pause*)

and seven days. The second of January eighteen hundred and fifteen. I often think how blindly we live our lives, of all those childhood years before that date—all those Januaries that I watched that day glide past unnoticed, unconscious of what that anniversary would come to mean to me—the beginning—

(*Her voice has an ominous and measured flatness to it*)
and the end of my life crushed into a single
moment. From Spring to Winter
(*She moves out of the window, the panes spattered now with
rain, to the bare trees*)
and nothing in between.

AUGUSTA   (*Softly*)
Please.

LADY BYRON   (*With a forced lightness*)
Oh I know how he used to like to mock me, think
me dull—and what was his name for me among
you all,
(*She glances round momentarily*)
with Moore and Hobhouse and the rest of you?—
the Princess of the Parallelograms was it? But there
is a kind of poetry in figures too. Each year as that
anniversary approaches, I can say to myself, "On
this day
(*She resumes her pacing*)
"On this day one year ago—on this day ten years
ago—on this day—

AUGUSTA   (*She is looking at the ground, her voice low and pained*)
Annabella.

LADY BYRON   "On this day twenty years ago my life ended."
And I can still recall that day that finished it as if it
were yesterday, still see the room—the two kneel-
ers side by side on the carpet—and the cushions—
(*She glances at Augusta for corroboration*)
—and how like him, don't you think, even on his
wedding day to make a fuss over a cushion!—and
Mama at the window—Mrs. Clermont—

AUGUSTA   (*Quietly*)
Annabella.

LADY BYRON   (*Entirely caught up in her memory*)
I never looked at him, you know, the whole time. I remember as I walked in on Papa's arm I saw Hobhouse, and I can see his face still, long and severe, those staring eyes of his on me as if he was watching me walk to my execution—
(*There is a slight mirthless laugh*)
And perhaps it had been better that it was, rather than live to—

AUGUSTA   (*Gently*)
Please.

LADY BYRON   (*She collects herself with a weary sigh*)
Did I tell you I was at Leamington last year? There was a man at the table behind me, and I could hear him talking, telling whoever it was he was with that he had seen the hotel register, and that Lady Byron was staying, and that you only had to look at her— oh, and he was very humorous about it, had passed my carriage in Piccadilly years ago, he claimed— that you only needed to see her once to understand why Byron fled the country.
(*There is a pause*)
Something about the primness of the mouth, it seems. And the eyes.
The eyes. As if they had not once been different. As if they had always been an old woman's eyes, as if—
(*She breaks off and turns suddenly to face Augusta, looking at her intently, as if seeing her for the first time. When she continues, there is a reluctant fascination in her voice*)
As if they had not once been as young as yours. And yours! How right the child was—the same still as ever—the same look to them—the same— soft—

AUGUSTA   (*So quiet as to be almost inaudible*)
You're very kind.

| LADY BYRON | (*With a slight laugh, as she turns away*) |

(With a slight laugh, as she turns away)
Ah, kind!
(She walks towards the window, and stands at it, looking out, brooding)
Kind. "Be kind to Augusta"—
(She turns again, her voice less controlled)
Do you know that's the only thing your brother ever left me, the only message?—"Be kind," he wrote from Italy, "Be kind to Augusta, and her children."

AUGUSTA   *(Warily, uncertain)*
And you were.

LADY BYRON   *(Dismissively)*
Oh I know you don't think so, but I have always done what was right.

AUGUSTA   And do you think I have ever forgotten it?

LADY BYRON   *(Slightly querulous)*
And as if he had ever needed to ask! Do you know from the first time I met you—no even before that, when I had no more than heard of you from him—I used to pray that if I could get close to you—if I could only get you to love me as I was ready to love you—
(She clasps and unclasps her hands)
then perhaps I could make him love me too. Augusta will know, I used to tell myself—
(Her tone becomes more agitated)
Augusta can teach me. Augusta will know how to humour him, Augusta can quieten him, Augusta understands him—and that's what he used to say, you know—"Augusta would understand," he'd say, only Augusta—why couldn't I understand him in the way Augusta did? Why could I not be more like Augusta? How did I think that he could ever have loved someone like me when—

AUGUSTA   (*Pleading*)
                 Annabella!

LADY BYRON   (*More collected again*)
                 I was so young too when we married. You can't
                 think what it is to have spent your life loved and
                 cosseted on all sides, to be the centre of your own
                 universe—and oh I was spoiled enough, I know!—
                 knew it then I suppose—and then—suddenly—to
                 find yourself hated in the way that he hated me. To
                 wake at night and discover your husband standing
                 over your bed, knife in hand—
                 (*She turns*)
                 Do you know the first words he spoke, as we drove
                 away from Seaham after the wedding? Before we
                 had even left the park? The first words of our
                 married life?
                 (*She gives a short laugh*)
                 "It must come to a separation," he said. He
                 couldn't even look at me as he spoke—couldn't
                 bear even the sight of me. It must come to a
                 separation. "It is enough"—he said—"it is enough
                 that you are my wife for me to hate you"—
                 (*She turns back to the window, and stands there seeming to*
                 see nothing, her voice without emotion)
                 I thought that journey would never end. Hobhouse
                 had given me a set of Byron's poems as a wedding
                 present, and there they lay—between us—
                 (*She glances round at Augusta, an ironic smile*)
                 the man I had loved bound in his yellow morocco,
                 the man I had married as far from me as he could
                 get.
                 (*She turns back to the bare landscape*)
                 It was so cold too. My pelisse so thin. I remember
                 huddling in the corner of the carriage, staring out
                 of the window, desperate for something I could
                 recognise—anything—and finding nothing—
                 nothing I knew—only snow—an endless white
                 waste, stretching ahead as far as I could see—

(*She moves from the window and walks over to the fire*)
Did he ever tell you that they rang the bells for us
as we drove though Durham? "Ringing for our
happiness, I suppose," he said. And then began to
sing. I wondered if he had gone mad—he told me
all the Gordons were mad—half hoped even that
he was, but it wasn't madness—
(*She picks up the poker and jabs at the fire*)
Not madness. Hate. I could hear it in his voice, in
the dark of the carriage. "I'll be even with you," he
kept murmuring. "I'll be even with you—I'll be
even—"

AUGUSTA (*Breaking in agitated*)
And do you think I hadn't tried to stop him, hadn't
tried to keep him—

LADY BYRON (*Softly*)
I'll be even with you.

AUGUSTA I tried all I could to save you—

LADY BYRON (*With a slow heavy irony, staring at Augusta*)
Oh yes, you tried, I can still see how you tried to
save me. Have you forgotten the first time we met,
your brother with his new bride? And how I was
sent packing as if I was a servant—how he stood at
the fire with you on the rug at his feet, and told me
that I was to take myself to bed, that he wanted to
talk to his sister—that there was no place for me
there. Now I have her, he said, you'll see I have no
use more for you. Oh yes, I know how you tried.
(*There is a silence. Lady Byron turns away and walks back
to the window. Augusta is motionless. After a pause, Lady
Byron goes on, her voice flat*)
It's raining.
(*There is another pause. When she resumes each sentence is
deliberate, unemotional*)
It was raining that first night at Newmarket. I don't

know how long I lay listening to it on the roof, waiting for the sound of his footsteps, my eyes straining the dark for a crack of light at the door. I don't know how long I lay there. Heaven knows when I fell asleep. Only that when I woke he was there,

(She moves across to the picture, and stands looking up at it)

standing at the bed, his face lit by the candle, with that look, muttering. "Why did you not say yes when I first asked, when we might have been happy, when there might still have been time!"

(She pauses, wrapped up in the scene. Augusta bends forward in her chair, her face buried in her hands)

He didn't even know I was awake. Why? he kept saying. Why? Why? When we might yet have been happy; why—

AUGUSTA   *(With sudden passion, rising from the seat, half-sob, half anger in her voice)*

And why couldn't you, when all London was throwing itself at his feet and only you—you

(Her outburst brings on a fit of coughing, and she steadies herself against the chair before dropping back into it. When she continues all the passion is gone)

Could you be so kind as to pour me some water?

(Without answering, Lady Byron goes over to a table, pours water into a glass from the jug, and carries it to Augusta. She takes it in silence, drinks from it, and hands back the glass)

Thank you.

LADY BYRON   I could never understand what he meant. I used to think at first that it was his pride I had hurt, and that only pique had driven him to persist—that he only ever wanted what he could not have—only married to revenge himself against me for having said no. But then—sometimes—just sometimes during those first weeks in Piccadilly before you came with Georgey—when for a moment we were happy together—he would look at me, and a pain would cross his face—

(*She turns to Augusta, as if for understanding, and then her eyes move back to the picture*)
a pain like I have never seen on any other face—
like a lost soul and—I would have died to spare
him that pain if I could. I didn't know it was
possible to feel so alone or helpless as in those
months. I don't know, either, which I feared more,
his pity or his anger. I used to hear him pacing his
study late at night, his voice raised as if he had
someone—or something—in there with him,—
struggling and arguing—but if I ever asked him—
Ever tried to get near to him—help him—all he
would say was "Ask Augusta." Ask Augusta.
(*She stops in front of Augusta, facing her, confronting their shared past. With a quiet hostility*)
Ask Augusta.

AUGUSTA (*There is a silence. When she speaks she does so without looking at her antagonist, her tone suddenly weary*)
What is there to say that was not said long ago?
(*She pulls herself heavily to her feet*)
Why now? What good can it do either of us?
(*She moves slowly towards the picture, her head shaking in a kind of wondering puzzlement. She glances around at Lady Byron before returning her attention to the picture*)
Or him. What more now can you want?

LADY BYRON Want? Do you imagine I am here for myself?

AUGUSTA Do you know I could have wept when I first saw
your letter, when I saw again after twenty years my
name written in your hand. You cannot think how
often in that time I have wanted to write, to beg
you that just once more before I die I could hear
your voice again, to hear you say as you once used
to "Dearest Augusta"—and now—
(*She breaks off and moves towards the bird, staring into its cage. When she speaks again it is with a quiet fatalism*)
But that is not what you want me for. In my heart,
too, I think I knew. Knew that you would not have

changed. Knew that I could never do penance
enough to satisfy you—

LADY BYRON   (*Coldly*)
Do you think it is to me that you'll have to answer?

AUGUSTA   (*She puts a finger through the cage bars, absorbed*)
Has there ever been anyone else? All these years?
(*She lets her hand drop from the cage*)
Poor thing.
(*She moves away from the bird cage, and walks slowly to the
other end of the room, the table between them, as far away
from Lady Byron as is possible. When she speaks it is with
the slightly detached voice of a deposition*)
I don't know either that I could ever make you
understand.
(*She takes a stem from the vase of dried flowers and stands
examining it as she speaks*)
What it was like for him. For me. What it is to be
born a Byron. Do you know that when my mother
died and my father married again, my
grandmother took me in—
(*She puts the stem back in to the vase, and moves slowly
towards the fire*)
and I don't know how it was, but I knew even then
that I should never mention the name—that I
should never ask after my father—never ask when I
might see him again. When he might come for me.
When he might take me home.

LADY BYRON   I don't see—

AUGUSTA   I remember once—I can't have been more than
six or seven—it was at her house in Hertford
Street—standing at an open door and hearing the
name "Byron," and shrinking back—
(*She pauses at the mirror, and looks at the faded figure
reflected back in its clouded surface*)
"There's nothing of the Byron in her," my

grandmother was saying—and I remember
running upstairs to look at myself in a glass—
trying to recall what he looked like —and sitting
there in front of it dreaming up schemes for us
both—romantic fantasies—not knowing what he
was really like—knowing nothing about him.
(*She turns from the mirror, and begins slowly to pace the
room*)
I am not even sure when I first knew that he had
given me a brother. I suppose it must have been
when my cousin was killed, and he became heir—
he can only have been six I suppose, but I
remember picturing him, wondering if he was like
our father—like I'd imagined him anyway—and,
ah!—
(*She breaks off with a slight laugh*)
You would never dream how little like it he was
when we met—a thirteen-year-old boy—fat—and
awkward—and almost as shy as I was—
(*Her voice is quieter, ruminative*)
I don't know why I had never been allowed to see
him before. I think there had been some ill-feeling
with my grandmother, but his mother wrote to me
when she died—and—
(*The pressure of memories momentarily banishes the reserve
between them*)
do you know for the first time in my life when I met
him I felt needed. Everyone had always been kind
but no one had ever needed me. I was not an
heiress. I was not clever. I was not even very pretty.
He used to write to me, though—dull, serious,
boy's letters to a sister four years older than
himself—letters full of his friends—of Clare and
Long—letters inviting me to Harrow—messages to
Colonel Leigh on my engagement—
(*She looks across at her*)
the letters of a child, Annabella, who had no one
else to love, no family but a wretched mother who
shamed him with every word she spoke—

(*There is a slight pause*)

Letters to an imagined sister he had hardly ever
seen. He would write to remind me of some purse
I had promised him, and then in the same breath
of what we would do when he came of age—how
his home—the Byron home—

(*Her face clouds over*)

how Newstead would always be my refuge so long
as ever it was his.

(*There is a silence until she seems to shrug off the memory,
and walks over to the window*)

A refuge! You can't think how remote a dream that
had become when we at last met again. I was
twenty-nine with three children and a husband
who—

(*There is a slight hesitation*)

But then I need hardly tell you of Colonel Leigh.

(*She allows her words to hang in the air for a moment, their
meaning unspoken. When she eventually goes on, her voice
gradually strengthens, and becomes more animated*)

It was at Lady Harrowby's that I saw him again,
the year after his return from the east. He was
talking at the far end of the room as I came in, and
as I stood in the doorway, he suddenly looked up,
and as he walked towards me with that quick
sliding gait of his, his arms outstretched—it was as
if for the first time I was—

(*The voice trails away, the words too elusive. After a pause,
musing*)

He always used to say himself that I was his other
half, that apart we were nothing. And he was
always such an egotist too, such a child when he
was in his "Wertherish" moods—

(*She smiles with a warmth that robs it of any malice*)

that I think that in loving me he found something
to love in himself—something to be kind to—that
he did not have to hate. It even pleased his vanity
that I looked like him—my form, my features—
lineaments—eyes—hair—

(*Her voice takes on a soft incantatory note*)
"— all to the very tone
Even of her voice, they said were like to mine—
(*There is a pause. Lady Byron stares at her. When Augusta speaks it is to herself*)
"But softened all and tempered into beauty."
And ah!
(*She seems suddenly aware of Lady Byron*)
If ever he needed a friend it was that season when he had the whole of London at his feet! He would always rage against the bitterness and humiliation he had known as a child, but success—success and fame!—I think he found them harder still—
(*She turns to Lady Byron*)
Did he ever tell you of the day that he learned our uncle had died? That the title was his?
(*Lady Byron says nothing*)
A lame boy, without a father, at his grammar school in Aberdeen. He burst into tears when he had to answer to his new name at roll call.
Dominus de Byron. He was sent for by the master later, and offered wine and cake—
(*She walks slowly away from the window*)
a lesson in deference he never forgot. Oh I know how conscious he was of rank and position, but it made him despise too what others valued—distrusted whatever it was in himself that the world wanted—despise the fame that was his.
(*There is a silence*)
I don't think any man was lonelier than he was that summer when he could call the world his own.

LADY BYRON   (*With a quiet resentment*)
And do you think you were the only one who could see that?

AUGUSTA   (*In a lighter tone suddenly, seeming not to hear the interruption*)
And I could make him laugh as well.

(*She turns with a bright look to Lady Byron, impervious to her cold stare*)

No one else could in the way I did. At my ignorance—my nonsense—my "damn'd crinkum-crankum." From the day that we met again it was as if we had known each other all our lives. We sometimes used to dream of an imaginary childhood we had shared—make up things that no one but us could know—memories of a father neither of us had known—signs when we wrote—

(*The voice trails away, and she turns away from Lady Byron, walks to the fire, staring absent-mindedly into it. When she speaks, her voice is again serious and low*)

I could comfort him too. When he was afraid—of himself—what he might do—who he was. He did really believe that we Byrons were all cursed. Wasn't he himself—wasn't his crooked foot proof of that, proof of his damnation, proof that we belonged to none but our own sort? He would see the whole line in his dreams, standing over him and beckoning, waiting to claim him for their own, their sins loaded on his head,—threatening him—

(*She stares into the fire as a log catches and bursts into life*)

challenging him. He used to say that he would never marry—that no Byron ever should—that the name should die with us—that only with me could he be safe.

(*A pause stretches out into a prolonged silence, each woman locked in her own thoughts. When Augusta finally speaks, almost inaudibly, she is still staring into the fire, her back to Lady Byron*)

But even there he knew he wasn't.

(*There is a pause. She goes on slowly, picking her way through each sentence*)

There above all.

(*She turns away, her eyes still averted*)

I remember the winter—the January of '14 it would have been—the year before you married—when we were snowed in at Newstead. I don't think

I have ever been more happy in my life. The lake
frozen. The roads blocked. The world shut out. No
one but the two of us.
(*She turns to look at Lady Byron*)
But even then, though, he lived with its ghosts—
there was no sin that the Byrons had not
committed, he'd say, no crime that hadn't taken
place inside those walls, nowhere on earth we
could go to escape our curse—
(*She turns again to look at the picture of Manfred*)
And the misery of it is that it was true too—true in
ways he never even dreamed—
(*She breaks off. When she resumes it seems as though it is on
a different tack*)
As a child I used to have a portrait of my mother in
my room. It was strange, but I don't think I ever
felt anything for her—had never known her—but I
used to love to look at it, and try to see her as my
father had seen her—dream that if I could grow
up to look like her I could somehow bring him
back. But I was wrong—because it was never her
he loved—not his wife—not my mother—not
anyone, I think, but his own sister—

LADY BYRON   Are you mad?

AUGUSTA   (*Ignoring the interruption*)
              Frances. My Aunt. My husband's mother.

LADY BYRON   Dear God, are you all insane?

AUGUSTA   I never knew at the time. Not till much later.
              Never knew how far he was from everything I had
              pictured—everything I had wanted.
              (*She walks slowly from the fire, her eyes turned away from
              Lady Byron*)
              We used to visit her sometimes in her old age, and
              in all those years that she never spoke of him,
              never mentioned his name even, she had his letters

by her—love letters—no, not love letters—fiercer,
harsher, more possessive than that—a packet of
them, tied in a ribbon, and just waiting for her
death for me to see them.
(*She pauses by the bird in the cage*)
And all those times I was with her, and she would
sit there, almost motionless, watching, she must
have known it. Known that I would see them.
Wanted me to have them. Not George. Me.
Wanted me to know. Wanted me to know what
they had done. That it was in my blood. That there
had never been a choice.

LADY BYRON   No choice?—

AUGUSTA   (*Her voice is low*)
And she was right too. Because that first time I saw
Byron again, walking across towards me—a
stranger and familiar all at once—the figure I had
cherished in my imagination all my life—I knew
from that moment that there was nothing I would
not have done for him.

LADY BYRON   (*Her voice harder than ever*)
Have you no shame?

AUGUSTA   (*She runs a finger across the wires of the cage*)
It seemed so inevitable, too. That first summer in
London he was never away from my side, at the
theatre—dance—felt the most natural thing in the
world too that a brother and sister should be
together, and by the time—
(*She pauses*)
By the time it became more it was too late. When I
tried to leave for Newmarket he followed me. We
were each others' fate, he would say, there was no
escape if we wanted, no way out but exposure and
disgrace. The idea of it tortured him too, filled
him—and
(*There is a baffled incomprehension in her voice*)

this is what I could never understand—
(*Quieter*)
what I still can't—filled him with a sort of reckless despair—made him loathe himself all the more, made him hate himself—me—for being what we were even as he plunged us towards ruin. He wanted us to leave England together. The East. Italy. There was nowhere we could have gone, though,
(*She looks up to the picture of Manfred*)
he could not flee himself. His horror at what he had done and would do again. I sometimes feared that winter before your marriage that it would destroy him, dreaded what he might do—what would happen if ever—
(*The voice trails away. When she speaks again it is without emotion, prosaic but firm*)
I would have sacrificed anything to save him.

LADY BYRON   (*With a quiet anger*)
Including me?

AUGUSTA   (*Without rancour*)
Including myself.
(*She moves over to the window*)
I don't think you have ever had any idea what I gave up for you. You said that all you could see that day was a white desert—
(*She glances around and then turns back to the cold, bleak view*)
How do you think I felt that morning of your marriage? Watching the hand of the clock move towards eleven. Imagining him. You. And poor Charlotte screaming—and screaming. And then suddenly I heard the clock strike and began to shake—tremble—until—
(*She breaks off*)
Do you think it was nothing to let him go? Do you think, too, I couldn't have held him,
(*She turns with the first resentment*)

if I hadn't wanted his safety—his happiness—
more than anything else on earth? I had to make
myself love you, make myself hope and pray that
you could be happy, that he could love you—make
myself smile and laugh with him when he said that
you would redeem him—that you had goodness
enough for the two of you.

LADY BYRON   (*Breaking in bitterly*)
Oh yes, I can hear the two of you—

AUGUSTA   And can you have forgotten so much—forgotten
those months in Piccadilly when there was nothing
I would not have done or undone to shield you
from him—forgotten how I would argue with
him—defy him—plead with him in his drink until
you and I became one in his eyes—a single enemy
who had trapped him into marriage—betrayed
him—

LADY BYRON   You can talk of betrayal? Do you know what he
told me when we were married, when I had been
prised away from everything I loved?—
(*She grips at the chair to steady herself*)
when he had me safely in his power? He told me
that he had wagered my own aunt that he could
win me over—that he would have my money and
my love—have me as mad for him as every other
fool-woman in town—
(*She moves swiftly to the window, close to Augusta, her voice
a harsh whisper*)
Oh yes, I can hear all of you. I can still hear, when
I shut my eyes, the sound of your steps on the stairs
with his, the sound of your voices, your laughter.
And what was I to you? Cover, was that it?—A
screen for the two of you? Never anything more?
Not even my money he wanted? Not even his pride
I'd hurt?

AUGUSTA   I tried to stop him hurting you.

LADY BYRON   (*Not hearing*)
And you won me over—made me silence every
jealousy—made me love you—made me trust you
and confide in you. I remember when we first
married, pressing him to invite you, even when he
insulted me in front of you, even when he gave me
every cause to be jealous, longing for you as I
would for my own sister if I had ever had one,
thinking—praying—that with you, with us it would
be all right—smothering my fears—my
jealousies—telling myself they were foolish—
punishing myself—
(*With a laugh she breaks away from the window, her step
and voice agitated, her fingers twisting compulsively on the
slip of paper tucked into her sleeve*)
And all those months of his hatred, of his insults
and drunkenness, you let me appeal to you, let me
write to you, let me ask what it was that I had done.
What it was that had come between us. I would
write, begging you to help me, begging—
begging!—you to intercede for me, and you would
smile and weep with me, console me—talk to him
for me—and all the time—
(*There is a break in her voice*)
And all the time, all those months I wondered what
I had done—
(*She looks at Augusta as though betrayed*)
My only crime was that I was not you.

AUGUSTA   (*Almost inaudibly*)
God knows, I never meant you harm.

LADY BYRON   (*With renewed energy*)
What a child I was! Right to the end! When I think
how you let me think him insane, made me think
his taunts and boasts the ravings of a madman!
(*She closes on Augusta*)

So scared were you of what he might say—
frightened that he would drag you down with
him—scared that duty and love—

AUGUSTA   (*Turning away from her, and looking round the room
slightly distractedly*)
Is that what it was?
(*She moves from the window across to a side table, and rings
a small hand bell. Muttering*)
Come on—
(*She rings the bell again*)
Is that what you gave him? God knows, you
wanted to own him,
(*She rings the bell*)
wanted to possess him—save him—
(*She stops, facing Lady Byron*)
But do you think you know what it is, to love him—
love anyone—
(*She rings again, more agitatedly*)

LADY BYRON   (*With a menacing control*)
I have told them that we are not to be disturbed—
(*She turns away from Augusta, as if the sight of her carries
some contagion*)
(*Sotto voce*)
And how dare you with your criminal passions,
your unnatural lusts,—
(*She rounds on her again with sudden venom*)
How could you know what I went through, those
nine long months that I carried his child, praying
and hoping against hope that it would win him
back to me—protecting him and lying for him—
writing to my parents of our happiness—of his
kindness—bearing up through his insults—
silencing my suspicions of you as unworthy of any
woman—
(*She breaks off, determined to control herself. When she
speaks again her tone is more prosaic, flat*)
I would have died if it could have made him love
me as I loved him. During those last days before

Ada was born, I would sometimes hear his step
pause outside the door and—God forgive me!—I
would pray that I could die there and then,
knowing that for the moment at least I was in his
thoughts.
(*She pauses, reviewing the memory in her own mind*)
And sometimes I thought if he would just let me
speak to him, or just see me, but he never would.
Not even at the end. Only a note, after Ada's birth.
"Madame," he wrote—I have the words by
heart—"as I am to leave the country and have no
plans to return pray make arrangements to return
with our child to your parents. My carriage is at
your disposal."
(*She gives a half-laugh*)
My carriage is at your disposal. Can you imagine
what it is to be sent back by your husband,
(*There is an odd detachment in her voice, as if she was
speaking of someone else*)
to be woken by servants in the freezing early hours,
and to crawl with your child out of your own
home, weak and sick in the dark, like a fugitive—
and still
(*Her voice breaks as the reality of it intrudes*)
Still love the man who has done it to you? Do you
know that I had to stop myself, as I passed his
room, from lying down on the mat for his dog at
his door? Had to stop myself.
(*There is a silence. She stares out of the window, her back to
Augusta*)
So do not say, madam, that I did not know what—

AUGUSTA   (*Passionately, ringing the bell again vigorously*)
Then why, why would you not take him back.
(*In her agitation she begins to pace the room again*)
Why when he wanted you—pleaded with you,
when he was half-mad with debts and brandy—
when he had hardly known what he was doing—
why in the name of all that's merciful, if you loved
him, would you not forgive him? Why if you loved

him did you set out to see him destroyed?
Destroyed by the lawyers you set on him.
Destroyed by your silence.

LADY BYRON   (*She speaks as if to herself, almost as though she was un-
              aware of Augusta's presence*)
              But wasn't that all he ever wanted? All that he was
              born for? To be destroyed? An outcast? He knew
              that I could bear with his actresses and his
              drunkenness, but that wasn't enough for him—
              (*She looks at Augusta*)
              wasn't enough for him even to have you but he had
              to fling you in my face until I could blind myself no
              longer—had to drag you out before his public—
              His Astarte!—Goddess of Love
              (*With a bitter emphasis*)
              "of all earthly things that lived, the only thing he
              seem'd to love"
              (*There is a pause while the words echo between them. When
              she resumes it is with a cold and inflexible sense of
              righteousness*)
              I have never, in all my life, done anything but my
              duty as I saw it. When I first accepted Byron I
              swore that I would do all I could to save him from
              himself, to rescue what was fine and noble in him
              and—and when I left him it was only for a higher
              duty—
              (*There is stiff primness to the formulation*)
              a duty to truth, to my child, to womanhood.

AUGUSTA   (*Quietly*)
              Ah, duty?
              (*She turns to Lady Byron, her tone wondering in its
              disbelief*)
              And has anyone ever enjoyed her duty as you
              enjoyed yours? I remember when Hobhouse
              brought the news—

LADY BYRON   How dare you throw that creature in my face—

AUGUSTA   Remember when it was you he blamed, telling him that you could never have sanctioned the whispers—that no wife could ever turn on her husband like that, but—ah
(She moves towards Lady Byron, who is still at the window looking out, and stands close behind her)
I should have known—should have known that first time I saw you again in London—
(Her voice registers her bewilderment at the intensity of the vision)
in Mivart's—after the separation—so thin and pale you seemed more a ghost than flesh and blood— with nothing left to hold you to anyone—nothing left of what you had been except the will to avenge yourself—

LADY BYRON   *(Almost inaudibly)*
And who made me that?

AUGUSTA   *(She turns away)*
I should have seen too just how well you played your part—the silent wife while your lawyers did your work for you. Duty?
(She moves round again to get a better view of Lady Byron's face as she talks)
How does it feel, Annabella, to enjoy all the pleasures of revenge and call it duty? To watch your husband pilloried and humiliated—severed from his child—branded with every nameless crime and yet remain blameless?

LADY BYRON   *(Without meeting Augusta's look, her voice hard and prim)*
I stood by you when a word could have destroyed you forever.

AUGUSTA   *(Turning away, and moving across the room, until she stands behind the chair. She rings the bell again, but when she speaks her tone is oddly mild)*

Oh yes, you stood by me! And what a price you exacted! I remember how you stood by me during those long months after he had gone abroad, how you bound me to you, held me fast by the fear of your displeasure—the fear of exposure. How you broke me. Made me betray myself. Made me betray him. Oh yes Annabella,

(*She moves away from the chair, pacing the room, her tone more agitated*)

I remember how you stood by me while everyone could say how kind you were to Mrs. Leigh, how you used the unspoken threat of the world's hatred—held it over me—wallowed in my penitence, how you enjoyed your duty. Let us save Augusta! Save her from her own weakness. Let us teach her to suffer—remind her every day of what she is. How could I forget how you stood by me or what you made me become? When Byron had no one to turn to, you kept me from him. When he wrote to me you would make me bring his letters to show you. When I answered them you would be there, standing over me, watching, silently guiding and—may God forgive me—

(*She covers her face with her hands*)

when you were sure enough of me—when I had become what you wanted—you would hand his letters to me without comment—"leave me to my own conscience"—leave me to betray him, certain that I was too much the coward to resist.

(*There is a pause. She is more collected when she continues*)

Too frightened of the world. And you were right. I never had his strength. You knew that, knew that even if he could escape your malice, so long as you still had me, so long—in the name of duty—that you could control the one person who wanted nothing from him—then you could enjoy all the satisfaction of virtuous revenge.

(*She looks round, all energy exhausted. Her tone is prosaic*)

I have put my gloves somewhere.

LADY BYRON (*Without looking round. Her voice equally flat*)
You have never understood me, have you?

AUGUSTA (*She moves over to a table, and picks up her gloves. There is a sense almost of release in her reply*)
Oh yes, I understand you, Annabella, understand you at last. I know now, too, why you wanted me here. You were afraid weren't you, afraid that after all these years that I was no longer yours—afraid that I might have slipped beyond the reach of your "kindness"—

LADY BYRON (*Her voice hard with resentment*)
Still the same!

AUGUSTA (*In control*)
No, not quite. I have never had the strength to resist you, but I see now that I have always had something you could never touch—that nothing you could do or make me do—could threaten—something through these weary years to place me beyond even your resentment—that love, Annabella, that you demanded of him and was always mine.

LADY BYRON (*Her voice frigid with anger*)
And you believe that, do you?
(*Moving swiftly to the table, and fumbling for a letter among her papers. With a bitter laugh*)
Believe you can defy every decency and imagine there is no reckoning?—Are you so bereft of sense or shame—so much the moral idiot to believe the world will just forget what you are? That your own family will forget?
(*Fumbles at the letter, she begins to read, rapidly, triumphantly*)
"My Dearest Pip"—And you know that's what he called me—I taught her to call me it too—Pip, her

dearest Pip—"I have this instant met my Mother.
She was crossing the square"—
(*She looks up*)
and did you know your child was watching you?
see—see—
(*She moves to Augusta, brandishing the letter in her face*)
do you recognise the hand, your daughter's—see
what she says of you, of her own mother

AUGUSTA   Stop it!

LADY BYRON   (*Reading on over her*)
"She was crossing the square coming from York
Street as the carriage drove up to the door. I
instantly recognised her—she is unchanged in
face . . . Her large eyes are ever & indeed
unchanged—she shuffles along as if she tried to
carry the ground she walks on with her & looks
WICKED."

AUGUSTA   Stop it!

LADY BYRON   (*Continues reading, inexorably*)
"Oh, were there a thing I had hoped to be spared it
was this . . . This has shocked me, pained me, but it
is over. I have drunk quantities of wine since, &
now there is nothing left for me to suffer that I
dread. Oh how dearly fondly I loved her, and had
she only stifled the existence her sin gave me—"

AUGUSTA   (*Her voice a cry of pain as she collapses back into the chair*)
Stop it, stop it!
(*Broken*)
Stop it—

LADY BYRON   (*Her voice hard with triumph as she reads on*)
"— but God is there & I will do my best to bear as
I have ever done—God forgive her. Oh how
horrible she looked—so wicked—so hyena-like.

That I could have loved her so! Bear in mind one
feeling the sight of her has given me yet more
strongly—for my good—intimidate her—she will
grovel on the ground, fawn, lick the dust—all—all
that is despicable and bad."

(*As she is reading, the door behind her opens, and Robertson
appears, stands there aghast as he hears these last words.
Without being aware of him, Lady Byron lowers the letter
and looks down in victory on the sobbing figure of Augusta.
She speaks with a slow emphasis*)

"All that is despicable and bad." Even my own
daughter was called after you, the child I bore
Byron in misery and hope, called after his sister—
Augusta Ada. Well.

(*It is pronounced like a sentence*)

A child for a child, Augusta, a daughter for a
daughter—

ROBERTSON   (*Moving quickly forward towards the weeping figure of Augusta, and speaking with scarcely restrained anger*)
Lady Byron, for pity's sake!

LADY BYRON   (*Turns and for a moment holds Robertson's gaze before she
continues, ignoring him*)
Did you think you could be allowed to keep the
child, Augusta—

ROBERTSON   (*Bending over Augusta, stretching for the water glass as he
props her up*)
For God's sake, Lady Byron, can't you see what you
are doing—can't you—
(*He looks around for the bell*)
And where in Heaven's name are the servants in
this place!—
(*He calls out loudly*)
Boy!

LADY BYRON   (*Turning away from them, and speaking with cold certainty*)
I don't think Mrs. Leigh would thank you for
bringing the servants here.

ROBERTSON   (*Continuing to fuss over Augusta*)
             Can't you see the poor creature is ill?

AUGUSTA   (*Trying to get up*)
             Please. You're very kind, but if you could just ask
             them to fetch a fly—

ROBERTSON   You are in no fit state to travel—

LADY BYRON   (*Remorseless*)
             No fit state to exist. Did you imagine, Augusta, she
             could be allowed to grow up ignorant of what you
             are? Not know what you had done to her? And
             who all these years did you think it was who told
             her, Augusta, saved her from you? Who told
             Medora who she was? What she was. The child of
             incest. Byron's ape.

             II

             (*Augusta stands at the window looking out, her back to the
             seated Lady Byron. When she speaks it is quietly, baffled*)

AUGUSTA   You cannot bear anyone to show me kindness, can
             you? No one—except you.

LADY BYRON   (*Grimly*)
             Why should I watch while another man falls for
             your wiles.

AUGUSTA   Nobody. Not even my daughter. Why did you have
             to tell her?
             (*There is no answer. Lady Byron watches her back with a
             cold and still concentration. After a moment Augusta turns,
             searching the other woman's face for an answer to her
             unanswered question*)
             Wasn't Byron enough? Wasn't it enough to take
             him from me, that you had to take Medora too,
             make her hate her own mother—

LADY BYRON   (*Bitterly breaking in*)
And she should love you, I suppose?

AUGUSTA   (*She seems scarcely aware to whom she is speaking, her eyes no longer on Lady Byron, her whole being caught up in the memories*)
All these years and I never dreamed that it could have been you—
(*Almost to herself*)
that any woman with a child of her own—anyone who had ever once loved Byron could do that—take from her—

LADY BYRON   (*Sullenly*)
Take what from her? A mother who abandoned her to sin—a father whose vices coursed through her veins?

AUGUSTA   Take from her the only thing the poor creature had left to her—the memory of her childhood happiness.
(*She turns from the window, walks slowly to the table, picks up the letter that lies on it*)
And turn her into that. She was so beautiful too. So alive. Do you remember her, then—remember how like him she was—not—
(*She breaks off with an involuntary smile*)
Not so much in her face, but the way she carried her head, the sudden petulance—the charm—
(*Her voice trails away as she is absorbed by one memory. When she speaks again it is slowly, abstracted*)
I don't think I ever knew how much it meant to have her with me until that week they brought his poor body home. Do you know sometimes at night I walk my rooms at Flag Court, and I can still see Hobhouse when he brought the news that the Florida had docked, standing there in the open door, the tears running down his face—and I remember—I could take in nothing that he was telling me—but I remember him saying that he'd

thought he had no more grief left in him until he
saw Byron's dogs playing on the deck. He'd sat on
his coffin, and Lion had settled at his feet. Only
then he knew what it meant to lose him. He
couldn't bring himself to look at the corpse, he
said, but he came with me to George Street, and—
(*Each sentence is like a studied act of memory*)
I have never seen such crowds. The length of the
street. They had hung the room in black. And
there was a hatchment daubed with our arms. And
the coffin lay on a bier—with candles—and a
wreath—quite withered—and his face—his poor,
battered face—
(*She turns to Lady Byron who looks suddenly older,
shrunken, cut off from memories in which she can have no
part*)
but you never saw him, did you? It was so cold,
Annabella—inanimate—so altered—the hair gone
white—I could hardly believe it was him.
(*She turns her gaze from Lady Byron*)
I don't even know what I'd thought I should see.
The Byron I'd parted from eight years before, I
suppose. But he was gone. Dead. And I'd done my
bit, along with all the rest of you, to kill him. That's
what I couldn't bear. What I still can't bear.
(*She goes back to the window and stares out. Her voice low*)
I thought that week would never end. The day of
the funeral, I remember sitting in the dark—the
shutters drawn—hardly able to breathe—listening
as the Abbey bell drifted across to St. James's—
waiting for each toll—following the cortege in my
mind—measuring with every peal the distance
they were taking him from me when I heard the
child's laughter—from another room I heard it,
and it was him, it was Byron, Annabella, and I
knew then I had not lost him, knew they could not
take him away from me so long as I had her—

LADY BYRON   And was I to live on nothing?

AUGUSTA   (*Ignoring her*)
She can have been no more than ten, but she was
so different from her sisters too,
(*She turns and moves across the room, animated by the
memory*)
so much quicker, more alert than they had ever
been. Even when she was scarcely more than a
baby, she could make them do whatever she
wanted, would have them running after her—
ready to do whatever she demanded. I used to fear
sometimes that poor Georgey would grow to resent
her, but I don't think she ever did—
(*Her voice is quiet, ruminative*)
Feared her maybe—wary of her as something she
could not understand—or resist—but was as much
under her spell as I was myself.

LADY BYRON   (*Her voice quiet too, anger dissolved in the shared memory*)
And do you think I was not?—Do you think I
could look at her and not see him? Hear her and
not hear him—do you think I couldn't feel his
coils tighten round me with every look that child
gave me?
(*She crosses the room, and begins mechanically shifting
papers around on the table*)
I can still see, too, the first time that I ever saw him
with her. Only weeks after our marriage. I
remember him taking her up on his knee, and the
expression on his face—a look I'd never seen there
before—and I remember telling him that I'd like to
have him painted with just such an expression as
he had at that moment—
(*There is a slight pause before she goes on again*)
Do you know I prayed that when Ada was born she
might bring him back to me. But he could never
have loved her, because she was too like me to love,
too like me—
(*She gives a cold, humourless laugh*)
even for me to love.

(*She turns from the table, her voice weary*)
He'd hoped she would be born dead, you know.
He'd come into my room during those last weeks,
and stand by the bed, brandy on his breath, staring
down at me. "It's already dead," he would say.
"And if you could die with it then—"

AUGUSTA   Dear God, can you think he meant half of what
he said—even knew what he was saying—

LADY BYRON   (*On her own single-minded track*)
He was ready enough to use her against me if he
could—exploit her—but I don't think he could
ever see anything else in her but me. I remember
only days after she was born, resting with the door
half open, and hearing him speaking to Mrs.
Clermont. He was looking at the child. "Let me see
its legs," he said. And then—I can hear the
bitterness in his voice—"What a sweet temper it
will have. There is no Byron there."

AUGUSTA   (*Almost with pity*)
How can you have known him so little—or your
own daughter?

LADY BYRON   And the misery of it is, that he was right too.
When she was still a child crowds would gather
outside hotels if the word got out, fighting to catch
a glimpse of Byron's daughter as if she were some
fair-ground show— and I used to look at her—
such a plain thing—and wonder what they hoped
to see in her—compare her to Medora and . . .
But what a fool I was!—ever to have wondered
why she seemed so much more a Byron than his
own daughter did, why—God help me!—I found
myself drawn to her in a way I wasn't to my own
child,
(*There is a slight pause as she brings herself under control.
She takes a long slow breath*)
Drawn to her as I had been to you.

AUGUSTA   (*Quietly, to herself, as she stands looking intently up at the Manfred picture*)
Ah, but if you'd had to watch her grow up, too—watch her as I had to. You can't imagine what it is to love and fear your child at the same time, to hope and dread that others will see in her what you can see—to watch as every day she becomes more and more like him—more reckless and wayward—more demanding—more wilful—to hold your breath and wait for it to start all over again—the rumours—the scandal—
(*She breaks away from the picture, and walks across to the caged bird, putting a finger through the bars*)
That was why I was so relieved when her sister could get away—so—so grateful almost to Trevanion when he asked for Georgey's hand. The poor child had always been so much under Medora's shadow at home, was so timid—so—
(*She glances round at Lady Byron*)
so like me at her age, that I hoped at last that she could grow—

LADY BYRON   Then why in Heavens let the child live with them?

AUGUSTA   (*Turning back to the bird. Wearily*)
Let her? Whenever did anyone say no to Medora? Even at fourteen. You know as well as I how she could make us all do what she wanted, but Georgey—
(*She again puts a finger through the bars*)
Poor, soft Georgiana was wax in her hands.
(*For a moment she seems more engaged with the bird than Lady Byron*)
It was Georgey, you know, who wrote begging that she should live with them.

LADY BYRON   I don't believe you.

AUGUSTA   (*Still intent on the bird*)
Which only shows how little you ever understood

of Georgey—of what a child she was still—even at
seventeen—so clinging—so afraid of leaving
behind everything she knew—
(*She glances round*)
And God knows there was little enough joy for her
at home but at least there—
(*She turns back to the bird with a sigh*)
At least in her family there was no more to fear
than her father's temper. I think perhaps that was
what attracted her to Trevanion, too, the fact that
he was her cousin, someone she could almost
believe she had known all her life.
(*She moves away from the bird, pausing in front of one of
the sporting prints*)
And then I remember the morning of her
marriage—the poor child's face—the look on it
when she realised that Leigh was not even there—I
don't think she had ever really loved him—she'd
always been too afraid of him for that—but I don't
think until that moment—until she saw that she
had no one with her but Medora and me—did she
realise the step she was taking—

LADY BYRON   (*Menacingly*)
Ah, but you knew well enough—

AUGUSTA   (*Ignoring her*)
I think after the marriage, too, it only made it
worse when you lent them Bifrons. We had all
hoped his father could find them something closer,
but alone with him in that great barrack—
(*She looks round at Lady Byron*)
Without even the face of a maid she could
recognise—with no one to speak with—no one to
turn to—no one at all from morning till night
except a man she was only just learning to know—

LADY BYRON   And who had kept her ignorant—

AUGUSTA   (*She turns back to the print*)
I think I was even glad, too, when she wrote to ask
for Medora. Glad for both of them by that time.
Because you can't think what it became those
months after Georgey was gone—

LADY BYRON   I don't recall that I was ever allowed to forget.

AUGUSTA   (*Wearily*)
Ah, you won't understand, will you—won't ever
hear what you don't want to. Now any more than
then. How hopeless it was. How completely
hopeless. And lonely.

LADY BYRON   You had a husband, didn't you?

AUGUSTA   (*With a slight laugh and an ironic gesture towards the print*)
Ah yes, I had a husband! For the first time in my
life I had a husband! Do you know that I hardly
ever saw him when he could afford to be anywhere
else, but one of the great blessings of poverty was
that I found that after all I did have a husband—a
husband who never left his rooms except to rage at
me for defying him over Georgey—a husband to
blame me for everything that had gone wrong for
him, for every horse that had ever gone lame, every
jockey who had cheated him, for every imagined
slight, every sound the children made—Oh yes,
(*Her tone is more ironic than bitter*)
I had a husband.

LADY BYRON   Which was more than you ever left to me.

AUGUSTA   (*As if she had not heard. Her voice softer*)
Not that I could ever blame him for being what he
was. Then or now. Byron could never understand
how I had ever borne with such a helpless creature,
but he was not a bad man—just—
(*She looks at Lady Byron*)

just never made to be poor—to hold up under the
debts—the failures—the indignities—the
rejections at court—
(*She breaks off*)
until the only revenge on life left to him was to take
it out on me—turn my sons against me—cut
Georgey off from me—terrorise even poor,
helpless Charlotte into her fits and tantrums until I
could no longer even hold on to her—
(*She pauses at the window, lost in her own thought, tracing a
rivulet of rain with her finger across the glass pane*)
And that was the only time, I think, that I ever
grew close to hating him. Charlotte was so
defenceless. So easily hurt. Even as a little child she
could never bear to see anything in pain, and he
knew that—and would rage at me in front of her
until she could stand it no longer—would throw
herself on the ground—harm herself—scratch at
her face—tear at her hair.
(*She turns back to Lady Byron*)
Oh yes, I was glad to have Medora escape. If it had
not been for Emily I think I would have done so
myself. If I could have ever found the strength. But
there were times—
(*She turns away, her voice weary*)
times I thought I should lose my mind. Times I
think when I did—

LADY BYRON   And is that all you can think of? What it did to
you?

AUGUSTA   (*Her voice leaden*)
It's all I can bear to think of. But do you imagine
there's a thing you can say that I haven't said to
myself, a day that's passed when I haven't gone
over it again in my mind—wondered what I could
have done—what if I'd only known—

LADY BYRON   And how could you alone have not known—

AUGUSTA   (*Bitterly*)
             Ah, but I never had your spies, did I?—nor even
             the friends who might have helped—you had made
             only too sure of that—
             (*The bitterness goes*)
             And Georgey would never have breathed a word of
             it to me. Would have sooner died. I don't think her
             sister had been with them a month, though, when
             she discovered it was Medora he had wanted, but
             by that time Georgey was so—I've never
             understood what it was—not quite fear but
             something worse—
             (*She struggles to make sense of it*)
             so completely in his power—so completely under
             the influence of the two of them—that she would
             have done anything they wanted—borne any
             humiliation—said anything—hidden anything—

LADY BYRON   (*Moves menacingly forward*)
             Only what was there for the wretched child to hide
             from you? What could she have told you that you
             had not always known? Hadn't planned?
             (*She closes on Augusta, standing behind her*)
             And to think how I once pitied you for what Byron
             had brought you to, made excuses for your
             weakness, blamed him when—
             (*She moves around so she can see Augusta's face, only inches
             from her own*)
             when there's never been anything you won't do—
             when there is no one who is safe—not your
             brother—not even your daughter's husband—

AUGUSTA   Good God! What are you saying?

LADY BYRON   (*Her voice filled with hatred*)
             When you'd sacrifice your own children to your
             lusts—as you once sacrificed me.
             (*She turns away in disgust, pacing the room, her hands
             clenching and unclenching*)

And to think I was weak enough to give you the
money for Georgey to marry him!—fool enough to
be your dupe a second time—
(*She whips round on Augusta*)
And what did you have to promise Trevanion—a
wretch half your age—what did you have to give
him to have him for yourself? Was it just Georgey
or was it both daughters from the start?

AUGUSTA   (*Crumpling into a chair. Almost inaudible*)
How could even you—

LADY BYRON   (*An unbalanced edge to her voice*)
I should have known that there was no depravity to
which you wouldn't sink—nothing you wouldn't do
to cling on to what you wanted. Do you think all
those years ago, I didn't see the way you'd let
Byron look at Georgey—

AUGUSTA   (*In horror*)
Are you mad?

LADY BYRON   (*To herself*)
As if he couldn't wait to corrupt his niece as he
corrupted everything he touched.
(*She stops in front of Augusta and stares down at her*)
It's in your blood, isn't it? Your whole serpent race.
Byrons. Trevanions.
(*She leans down, her hands resting on the arms of the chair,
her voice low*)
How could I have thought that you could ever
change? And did you imagine I didn't know? Do
you think Trevanion didn't boast of it? Of his hold
over you? Do you imagine, too, that I have not seen
your letters? Love letters to your daughter's
husband?

AUGUSTA   (*Pushing her way out of the chair. Fiercely*)
No, no!

LADY BYRON   Promising him your love—whatever he did to
               Medora—

AUGUSTA   (*More pitifully*)
               No. Yes, no, no—I loved him—but loved him as a
               son—

LADY BYRON   Yes, as you had loved Byron as a brother—
               (*Continuing to pace the room*)
               and just as you once gave Byron your blessing to
               have me, you stood by and watched Trevanion
               seduce your child—his wife's own sister—stood by
               in silence while she was smuggled out of the
               country—a fifteen-year-old girl in a foreign
               country—

AUGUSTA   No!

LADY BYRON   Hid his crimes from the world—rid yourselves of
               the baby—lied to your husband for him—prosti-
               tuted your own daughters

AUGUSTA   (*Almost unable to speak*)
               No, no—how in Heaven can you think I ever
               knew—ever knew any of it—ever guessed what I
               was sending them to—what kind of man
               Trevanion was?

LADY BYRON   Your husband did.

AUGUSTA   (*With sudden anger*)
               Oh no, no he didn't. Oh he was against the
               marriage true enough, but don't think that was for
               any reason but money—if Trevanion had only
               been rich enough—
               (*There is bitterness in her voice*)
               Colonel Leigh would willingly have given him all
               his daughters.

LADY BYRON   And were you any different? Wasn't it to be Emily
next—as soon as she was old enough? Isn't that
what you promised him?

AUGUSTA   (*Exhausted, her voice and movement sluggish as she turns
away*)
What can I say now if you can believe that of me?

LADY BYRON   And what else should I believe?

AUGUSTA   (*Beyond caring if she is believed or not*)
Believe? Oh, you'll believe what you want. You
always have. But if you had ever known Trevanion,
listened to him, seen him—
(*She glances round*)
and there was a time when you were not so
immune to the Byron charm—
(*She looks round again, staring into the fire*)
and he was like him too—or so, at least, I thought
then. When he first appeared. When, God knows, I
needed someone's kindness. Someone who
wouldn't look at me as if I were a pariah. I was
already learning to live, too, with the knowledge
that my own sons were going the way of their
father—
(*She picks up a poker and prods weakly at the fire, as if
physically punctuating the words*)
arrogant—thoughtless—
(*She turns to look at Lady Byron*)
and Trevanion had seemed so much the son I had
wanted, that when he at last confessed about
Medora—begged my help—then—yes—
(*Her tone suddenly bitter, challenging*)
But whom would you have blamed, Annabella,
with all you know—all you believe? A man who
could appear everything a mother could have
hoped for—or a "child of sin"—a Byron "Ape"?
(*She breaks off and turns back to the fire, jabbing feebly at it.
The bitterness has gone when she continues*)

And even then I had no idea what he was doing to those girls. It was not only Georgey, either, who was too frightened to breathe a word against him. I could never have dreamed that anything could cow Medora, but by the time she found out what he was like—discovered that she could not master him as she had everyone else in her life—she was too far under his control to escape even when she had the chance.

LADY BYRON   (*With a slow, righteous anger*)
And yet you let her back to him. Even when you knew she was carrying his child again—encouraged them to elope—

AUGUSTA   (*Dully*)
And what else was there to be done? Do you think I could have stopped Leigh killing him had he found out—and God knows he hated him enough to do it!—hated him as he'd hated Byron—as he hated anything he couldn't understand—

LADY BYRON   And after what they had done to him, he should have embraced them both I suppose?

AUGUSTA   (*Ignoring her. Obstinate*)
I did what I had to.

LADY BYRON   Oh yes, you did that—you did that well enough,
(*She moves towards her*)
even as far as trying to force her to destroy the thing—

AUGUSTA   (*Her voice flat*)
Is that what she told you?

LADY BYRON   And I'm to suppose she was lying—

AUGUSTA   (*Quietly, without rancour*)
When did you ever hear Medora do anything else?

(She turns away from Lady Byron, walks to the table, picks up one of the letters, and drops it without looking at it)
(Almost to herself)
When did anybody? I don't think the poor creature could even help it. She had been so open when she was a child, too—

LADY BYRON   She was a child!

AUGUSTA   But once Trevanion had got hold of her, twisted her—I think she would have said anything he told her and believed it—
(She breaks off)
Even after she had ruined herself for him she found out that he no more loved her—not for herself—than he had done Georgey—
(She moves over to the window, and stares out into the rain)
Or any of us. I remember when he first came up from Caerhays, the passion with which he would always talk of Byron,
(She glances round)
and he was the only one, you know—the only one from our whole family—to have been there at his funeral—
(She turns back to the rain)
But it was something more than passion—more than loyalty—more as if he wanted to possess him—to possess everything that had ever been his—sister—niece—child—and—above all—the thing that only that child could give him.
(She moves away from the window)
I don't think I have ever seen a man take anything so hard as when her infant died. I don't think he ever gave a thought to poor Georgey's children, but it was as though he could not let go of Medora until she had given him the living child he craved—until he had linked his blood with Byron's own—possessed him in her and her child—

LADY BYRON   And when she'd served her use—did you think of
              her then?—when he'd ruined and abandoned
              her—barely more than a child herself still—eaten
              by a shame that should have been yours—

AUGUSTA   (*Her voice scarcely audible*)
              Can you have so little mercy?

LADY BYRON   (*The words are almost hissed*)
              And did you have mercy on her?
              (*She seizes Augusta's wrist, forcing her to look at her*)
              You talk of her lies. Did you ever confess what she
              owed to you—warn her of what she was—a
              creature doomed to madness from her birth,
              polluted by the blood that ran in her veins,
              corrupted by her mother's and father's sin?
              (*She drops her wrist in disgust and moves away, turning
              again from the other end of the room her voice clear and
              hard*)
              And do you ever wonder what state I found her
              in—when I learned of it and tracked her down to
              her French garret—brought her home with her
              infant child—

AUGUSTA   Stop it.

LADY BYRON   Do you ever hear in your dreams her racking
              cough, and see the blood on her pillow?—Do you
              ever see her so thin and worn that her own rela-
              tions could not recognise her? So beside herself
              with misery that she scarce even knew herself?

AUGUSTA   (*Almost unable to breathe*)
              Stop it, stop it!
              (*Then with a sudden burst of energy, her question half a
              challenge, half plea*)
              And what could I have done? Do you think there
              was no one else? Who do you think had to look
              after Georgey, and her children? Who had to

scrape together every penny to support them? Her
husband? Her father? His family? Do you think,
too, I didn't send her what I could—to keep her
alive—to keep her safe—for her sake to keep her
away—

LADY BYRON   (*With contempt*)
For her sake, was it?—her disgrace you feared,
(*She closes on Augusta again, her tone insidious*)
Or your own Augusta? Did you hear the whispers
starting once more? The world closing in on you,
only now without me to stand between you and its
hate—

AUGUSTA   (*Weary*)
And what, anyway, could I do—
(*More heavily still*)
What had I ever been able to do? Do you think
that Medora would have listened to anything I
said?—Do you think that if she did not care what
happened to herself—to her sister—to her
family—do you think I could have said or done
anything to reach her? There was nothing—
(*Her voice quavering*)
Nothing I could do—no way I could see—nothing
ahead but ruin if any of it should come out—ruin
if she ever came back to England—
(*She suddenly breaks down, each word punctuated by sobs*)
the ruin I had dreaded every day for twenty years.

LADY BYRON   (*As Augusta is convulsed with sobs, Lady Byron watches
her, rigid and implacable*)
Ever the coward.
(*There is no answer*)
Afraid, as always, for yourself.

AUGUSTA   (*Quieter now, wiping at her eyes, her voice low and dull, she
walks to the window where she stands, her back to Lady
Byron*)
What would you know of fear? You don't know

what it is to walk into a room and be cut on all
sides—to have friends turn from you—to hear the
whispers behind your back—to feel the rumours
spreading—have your letters returned unopened—
your gifts for a child's birthday sent back
unwanted—
(*She stops and turns to face her*)
Oh yes, I was afraid, afraid of the world, of you all.
Afraid for myself. Afraid for Medora. Afraid that
you would tear her apart as you did Byron—

LADY BYRON (*A break in her voice*)
I would have loved her if she had let me, saved
her—

AUGUSTA (*Wearily*)
As you had tried to save him, to break and control
him and only made him hate you? Did you think
that when you saw him in her, that it would be any
easier to tame her? Did you imagine she would end
by hating you less? You could turn her against her
mother, as you once turned me from him, but
when she had rounded on her own kind,
Annabella—when you had taught her to hate her
very self, did you think that she would love you for
it?—

LADY BYRON (*Coldly*)
It was not her love I asked for.

AUGUSTA No, only her submission.

LADY BYRON (*Self-justifying*)
And was that so wrong?
(*She gains in power as she speaks*)
So criminal to want to save her from herself?
When I found her she was on the point of death,
but I dragged her back from illness and despair—
watched over her as she strengthened—watched
the colour come back into her pinched face—

watched the life come back into her eyes—taught her to know herself, to fear and hate that sickness that was at the core of her being—like a disease of the blood—the blight and curse of her birth. I prayed then when I found her and brought her back to England—

(*There is an evangelical fervour to her*)

united her as a sister with my own child,—spared you adding the guilt of her death to that of her birth—I prayed that God would give me the strength to watch over her, uproot the evil that was in her being—to triumph—

(*The evangelical fervour dies away, her voice quiet*)

to triumph where I had failed her father.

(*She moves across to the Manfred, and stares up at it*)

And oh, she was beautiful like him too. When she was strong enough she had her likeness taken for me—had it inscribed to her "Dearest Pip." She asked me if she might call me "Mama," told me she had no one else to love but me—

(*Her voice is unsteady*)

And—do you know—I let her—let her call me Pip as he had done—let her nurse me when I was ill—believed her—believed her as I believed that he could love me—believed once that you might—

(*Her voice is scarcely audible*)

Believed that so much grace and beauty could not be bad.

(*She pauses. When she continues her voice has a harder, ironic edge*)

What a slow learner I have been! Do you know that as a girl when I first saw Byron—

(*She checks herself*)

No, no before that, before ever I had seen him even, I could not believe—could not believe of the man who could have written such things as he had done—

(*She looks across at Augusta as if the sight of her is still baffling*)

that the beauty and the sin were not separable—

could not see that with you all they are one—your
evil only the more dangerous and insidious for its
beauty, more sickening in its hypocrisy—the same
hypocrisy that was your child's birthright.

(*She breaks off, and paces the room nervously. She stops at
the table and picks up a paper and puts it down without
looking at it. Her voice is querulous, bitter*)

There was nothing I would not have done for that
child. I had never been able to reach Ada, but with
Medora I prayed—

(*She falters*)

I gave her everything she could want. I gave her
my roof to live under. I showed her goodness and
she chose sin, gave her freedom and she chose
servitude—lied to me—traduced me—took and
took and took from me and then went back to the
life of vice from which I had saved her.

(*She controls herself, the dominant note sadness*)

Gave her my love—

(*She looks across at Augusta*)

as I once gave it to you, to have it thrown back in
my face.

(*Softly, musing, looking at the ring on her hand*)

Dear God, when I think what a dupe I have been! I
often tell Robertson that I will have my own signet
made, with a gull upon it—a gull impaled upon the
Byron arms.—Crede Byron—believe in Byron!

(*Incredulously*)

My God how I have paid for doing that!

(*She looks at Augusta*)

How the three of you have made me pay for loving
you.

AUGUSTA   (*Quietly*)

And haven't we paid too?

(*Lady Byron turns away without answering*)

Haven't we suffered enough to satisfy even you?

LADY BYRON   (*Her back to Augusta, her voice low but clear*)

Do you think any of you can suffer enough for

what you have done? For what you have made me
become?

AUGUSTA   (*With a soft surprise*)
Ah, how you do hate us!

LADY BYRON   (*Her back to Augusta still, her tone detached*)
Do you know those were my mother's words, after
I fled Byron—How Augusta must hate you, she
warned me, how she must hate you for everything
you are!

AUGUSTA   (*A tired recognition in her voice, as she stands at the table, a
hand on Lady Byron's open travelling case*)
Hate you?
(*She half pulls a letter out from the case and drops it back*)
Hate you, Annabella, when all these years now I
have belonged to you? When I have never entered
a room without wondering who you had shared
your secrets with—
(*She draws out another letter and looks at the envelope*)
When everything I have ever said or done—every
letter I have ever written—every friend I have had
is here—neatly filed away—ready to be used—
ready to be held over me should I ever try to
escape you.
(*She puts the letter carefully back in its place, closes the lid,
and looks vaguely around the room for something, as if about
to leave*)
Hate you? How could I ever hate you, Annabella,
when everything I am and have is yours to dispose
of as you like—my name—reputation—
(*Her voice drops*)
Even my child.

LADY BYRON   (*Turns away in disgust*)
Your child! Ah! She's that again now, is she—now
she's past harming you—now you think yourself
safe again—

Dynastic alliances and cultural certainties:
the Milbanke and Melbourne families

Metamorphosis—from Annabella Milbanke to Lady Byron: "I've seen her of an evening in the most amiable, cordial and sunny humour, full of interest and sympathy, and I have seen her the next morning come down as if she had lain all night not on a feather bed, but on a glacier—frozen as it were to the very soul . . ."

Augusta Leigh:

Her eyes,
Her hair, her features, all, to the very tone
Even of her voice, they said were like to mine;
But soften'd all, and temper'd into beauty.

Newstead:

Hail to the pile!
  More honour'd in the fall
Than modern mansions in
  their pillar'd state;
Proudly majestic frowns the
  vaulted hall,
Scowling defiance on the
  blasts of fate.

Too dangerous to look at: the image of Byron
kept from his daughter until her marriage

Manfred on the Jungfrau:
The rawest of all Byron's confessional verse

Above left: Lady Melbourne: "The best, the kindest and ablest female I have ever known, old or young."

Above right: Lady Oxford, the "grande horizontale" of Whig London. "She recalled a landscape by Claude Lorraine with a setting sun, her beauties enhanced by the knowledge that they were shedding their last dying beams."

Left: Lady Caroline Lamb: "Correct your vanity," Byron told her, "which is ridiculous; exert your absurd caprices upon others; and leave me in peace."

AUGUSTA   (*Her hand stretches out to a chair for support, her eyes on Lady Byron's back, her voice almost inaudible*)
What?

LADY BYRON   (*Contemptuously*)
Your child! And ah, how she loathed you! If you could only have heard her—if you could have seen her face at the mention of your name! Do you know she told me how she used to pick flowers for you, how every year she'd search until she'd found your favourite violets for your birthday—and that how after everything you'd done to her—how every extra year of your life sickened her—how the mere thought of you out there, shuffling on with your secrets—growing older—wickeder—more ugly by the day filled her with horror!—Horror. And fear.
(*She swings round on Augusta*)
Your child! When you had no place for her when she was alive—when you had kept the money that was hers from her—when you'd abandoned her to her lovers—with no one but her own daughter—
(*There is an edge of hysteria in her voice*)
And what would Byron have made of her, do you think, his Medora's bastard a nun—his prayers for the extinction of your serpent race answered within the walls of a French convent—

AUGUSTA   (*Her eyes on Lady Byron, but hearing nothing, her voice soft*)
Medora. Dear God—

LADY BYRON   (*Savagely picking up on the last word*)
God? Do you think God will hear you—think you can ever undo what you have done?

AUGUSTA   Medora.

LADY BYRON   (*Remorseless*)
And do you think you can wash away your crimes

with your tears now? When she died cursing you—
cursing you for everything you'd done to her?

AUGUSTA   (*Looks at her, the tears flowing down her face, the voice
mild*)
Tears? No, no tears—none that is—
(*She shuts her eyes in a half-smile of release, her hand
closing over a small closed locket at her throat*)
None but relief—gratitude—that it's at last over—
because, because you see Annabella
(*She looks at her with a slow shake of the head*)
I didn't know—didn't know she was gone.

LADY BYRON   (*She is stopped in her tracks, an old woman suddenly, her
voice shrivelled with horror*)
What?

AUGUSTA   (*She moves to the window, and as she stands there looking
out, the sun comes out bathing her in light*)
Didn't know she was beyond your reach at last—

LADY BYRON   (*Slumping heavily into a chair, her voice small*)
Dear God.

AUGUSTA   Safe from you all.
(*She opens the locket at her neck, looks down at a double
miniature, addresses it with a note almost of surprise in her
voice*)
But dead? Is it possible, child—and I not know?

LADY BYRON   (*Collapsed in the chair, in the shadow that cuts the room
into two, her face hidden in her hands, her body shaking
with the attempt to control herself*)
Didn't know? Didn't know? Dear God, what have I
become—what have I done—

AUGUSTA   (*To herself*)
Together, and without me?

LADY BYRON   What have I become.

AUGUSTA   (*Still looking at the miniature, oblivious to Lady Byron's presence*)
I remember when they wrote from the asylum, to say that poor Charlotte had died. The release. The thankfulness that she was out of pain. That nothing could touch her again. Touch any of you now—

LADY BYRON   What have I done—

AUGUSTA   (*She glances round, as if only just aware of her, her voice strangely serene*)
Done? God knows how often over the years I've wondered if you would ever ask yourself that, whether you'd ever understand what it might feel like to have your child taken from you—not even to know where she was—to weep over letters and have nowhere to send them—to glimpse the back of a stranger turning a corner and wonder if she is your daughter—to know that changed and bruised beyond all recognition she is out there still— somewhere—
(*She looks across at Lady Byron, Augusta outlined against the bright sunlight*)
Do you know last night I couldn't sleep, and I got up, and went into the room she had when she was a child—and I looked at her bed—and her things still there—her ribbons—a drawing she had done for me—and I could hardly bring myself to think of her—to think what you would know of her— what you would tell me—but now, now—
(*She snaps the locket shut*)
Now you have given her back to me—given them both back.
(*She moves from the window towards the table, and picks up her gloves as a cloud covers the sun, darkening the room*)

LADY BYRON   (*Without looking up*)
How could I have known?

AUGUSTA   (*Putting her gloves on, her voice calm and low*)
Known? No. When did the child die?

LADY BYRON   (*Low*)
The winter.

AUGUSTA   (*After a pause*)
In pain?

LADY BYRON   (*Her face still turned away*)
How could I have known you had not been told—

AUGUSTA   (*She moves towards the door, and pauses, speaking without looking back*)
And was there any word?

LADY BYRON   (*Pulls herself to her feet, and walks slowly towards the other end of the room, beneath the Manfred print. Her voice is leaden*)
No. Only—only that she forgave those that had harmed her.

AUGUSTA   (*Her voice unnaturally quiet*)
Ah!
(*She pulls on her second glove*)
Mr. Robertson will have my fly.

LADY BYRON   (*Without looking round*)
All I have ever wanted of you—of any of you—all I still want—

AUGUSTA   (*Quiet but unbending*)
I will be late for my train.
(*She half opens the door, and pauses, looking across the room without rancour or feeling*)
There was a moment even today when I might still

have been yours, but no more. When I think of all
these years I have struggled to appease your
hatred, afraid of you—afraid of my own
weakness—afraid that one day I would have to face
Byron with the knowledge that I had let you take
that child from me—
(*She lets the door half-close again*)
But not now, not when you can no longer touch
her—no longer avenge yourself on him through
either of us—
(*She stares intently at Lady Byron, as if to fix her face in her
memory for one last time*)
Because you were right, Annabella—you did not
need to say anything, but I could see it in your look
when I walked in—I am dying. It's over between
us. Over. We will not meet again.

LADY BYRON (*Her tone flat and dull*)
We will not meet again. Those were his last words
to me, too. "We will not meet again," he wrote, "in
this world—
(*She pauses for effect*)
or the next."

AUGUSTA (*With a kind of sober bravery as she confronts what is
being said*)
No.

LADY BYRON (*Looks at her*)
And have you no fear?

AUGUSTA (*She smiles slightly*)
Of death?

LADY BYRON Of your Maker?

AUGUSTA (*Her voice calm*)
Why should I fear Him when I no longer fear you?

LADY BYRON

(*Wearily, without hostility, she turns away from the picture and moves to the window, her back to the room, as the rain blows against the glass. Her voice is slow and lifeless*)
And do you think that can be the end of it? That the world will leave you alone? Any of you? Him. You. Medora.

(*As she is talking, Augusta opens the door, pauses for a moment to take in the room in all its cluttered gloom for one last time, looks over to Lady Byron and, silently and unnoticed, leaves. Lady Byron goes on, in the same flat voice, to an empty room*)
You're all the same. He always believed he could do as he liked with the world's love—take it and despise it at the same time—despise the very beings he had quickened into life.

(*She looks fixedly out through the window*)
Do you have any idea what it means to be taught to feel and then be abandoned? To be left with nothing but your own self? Your littleness? And do you imagine I don't know what I am? That I have never looked in the glass? Seen myself? Heard myself? Do you think, though, there was ever any choice? Any choice but to destroy you—or be destroyed?

(*Her voice takes on a grimmer note*)
And do you think it's for you now to say that it's over? When you have shadowed my whole life? When before I even knew you, you were there, between us. When there has not been a day in all these years when I have not tried to think of him and seen only you? Do you think now that I will let you go? Or the world will be any kinder? When it knows you as I do? Knows how it has been duped? When it sees everything it has admired is corrupt—listens to everything it has loved and hears only the lies—do you think when your own child grew to hate you for what you'd made her, that the grave—

(*She turns, to find Augusta gone, and Robertson standing in the open doorway, watching her*)

will protect Byron's Astarte?
(*For a long moment she holds Robertson's shocked look, and then turns away, and walks over to Manfred. Her voice when she speaks is without emotion*)
I didn't hear you come in.

ROBERTSON   (*Awkward*)
I'm sorry, but I heard Mrs. Leigh leave, and wondered if there was anything I could do—

LADY BYRON   (*Without turning*)
No, nothing.

ROBERTSON   Then perhaps—

LADY BYRON   (*She raises a hand to silence him*)
Nothing.
(*There is a pause*)
She is gone then?

ROBERTSON   (*Apologetic*)
Yes.

LADY BYRON   (*To herself, a note of quiet bitterness that makes a mockery of the words*)
Then "Fare thee well—and if for ever—still forever fare thee well"—
(*She moves into the middle of the room, her movements automatic. She stands at the table, staring into space, compulsively twisting her wedding ring round and round on her finger*)
(*Her voice is defensive*)
I know what you are thinking—

ROBERTSON   I would never dream, dear lady—

LADY BYRON   I know what you are thinking. You've no idea, though, what she is. Even now, on the edge of the grave.

(*She stares down at the wedding ring on her small, delicate hand*)

It has never fitted. I had to tie it with a black ribbon, the first day I wore it. He said it was an omen. He would have come back to me though. If it had not been for her. He would have come to see it. That I was his only true friend. The only one who could ever have protected him against himself. The only one who—

(*She turns away, her hands clenching and unclenching*)

ROBERTSON   (*He moves anxiously forward*)
Lady Byron?

LADY BYRON   (*She holds up a hand, her back to him, her voice remote*)
It would be a kindness if you would collect up these papers for me, and send for my carriage—

ROBERTSON   Yes, of course.

LADY BYRON   And Mr. Robertson—one more thing.

ROBERTSON   (*About to go out*)
Lady Byron?

LADY BYRON   (*Without looking at him*)
I shall need pen and ink before we leave—I do not want there to be any—misapprehensions—about today. Lies.
(*There is a slight pause. Her voice is firm again, unyielding*)
And I shall be wanting, too, your signature.

ROBERTSON   (*For a moment he stands in the door, looking across at the figure standing rigid and isolated, her back to him, staring up at the Manfred. His voice carries a note of defeat*)
Yes, yes of course.
(*Lady Byron is left standing alone. Outside the rain beats against the window panes*)

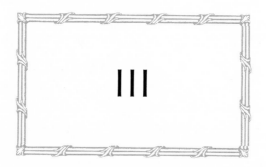

III

A SENSE OF FAILURE

Look! The beautiful Daughter of Albion sits naked upon her Stone,
Her panting Victim beside her; her heart is drunk with blood,
Tho' her brain is not drunk with wine; she goes forth from Albion
In pride of beauty, in cruelty of holiness, in the brightness
Of her tabernacle, and her arc and secret place . . .
O beautiful Daughter of Albion, cruelty is thy delight!

Blake, *Jerusalem*[1]

On the north wall of the chancel of St. Peter's, Croft, a few miles south of Darlington, a royal coat of arms proclaims the indivisible union of Shelley's hated trinity of "God and King and Law." There is nothing about the painted board that could not be found in a hundred other parish churches, but the inscription at the bottom of it gives it a peculiar interest here. "Given to this church by Sir Mark Milbanke," it reads, "1702."*

A world of theological and social difference lay between the idiosyncratic faith of Annabella Byron and the early Milbankes of Halnaby, and yet there is a feeling that as she parted from Augusta for the last time, she had returned to her Milbanke roots. For the best part of a lifetime Annabella had flirted with the dangers of Byronic romanticism in one incarnation or another, but never again after the misery of Reigate would she risk her moral or emotional well-being outside the safety of Lawrence's "walled city."

"Crede Byron"—Believe a Byron—was the family motto and the bitterness Annabella felt was in direct proportion to the passion with which she had embraced that faith. From Trelawny to George Eliot,

---

*The church is particularly worth seeing for the Milbankes' monuments and family pew, a grotesque red curtained and canopied celebration of position and power. It is possible that Byron sat in it with Annabella on their honeymoon, and if so throws an interesting sidelight on the apocrypha that surrounds his wedding night. "Good God," he is supposed to have recorded in his memoirs, as he woke to see candles flickering through the red of his bed curtains, "I am surely in hell." Far more likely in the pew.

the history of the nineteenth century is littered with men and women who could never forgive Byron for "failing" their expectations or needs, but in Annabella's case it was not just Byron himself, but sister and child who had rescued her only to throw her back to drown in the shallows of her own emotional inadequacy.

It is impossible to believe that anything that Augusta could have said at Reigate would have appeased Annabella, but it was the finality of this last disappointment that was so bitter. For almost forty years she had fought to save the Byrons from themselves, and as she felt Augusta slipping through her fingers—"impenitent" to the last as she told Robertson—she knew that the crusade that had begun in the summer of 1812 had ended in failure. "Feeling broke loose," she recorded her frustrations after Augusta had left, in a "Memorandum of my Interview with Mrs. Leigh at Reigate" that runs to six and a half angry sides,

> & I said something about it all having been in vain—I felt utterly hopeless—and asked to be left alone to comfort myself.[2]

It was not only the frustration of failure that Annabella felt, however, but the heavier knowledge that with this meeting she had lost all chance of a peace she had been craving since she had first heard the news of Byron's death. Twenty seven years earlier she had pleaded with his servant Fletcher to recall any message Byron might have left her on his deathbed, and more than anything else she had wanted a confession from Augusta that it was she who had prevented his return. "Elizb [Medora]—how. where—my line of conduct," she had scribbled in an almost illegible hand on the tiny scrap of paper that she had carried with her to the meeting, and then—

> 3. Question—*you* kept up hatred—you put things in a false &[?] point of view.[3]

Against all evidence and probability, she had managed to convince herself that Augusta had withheld—and even forged—letters to keep Byron from her, and it was an accusation she had repeated at the meeting. "I told her I had become convinced that it was not in human nature for any one to keep up such animosity as Lord Byron had shown to me," she noted, sounding a theme that had grown over the years since his death into an obsession,

> unless it had been *fed*—that for *his* sake, that he might not be blamed more than he deserved, I sought to know the truth about this . . . A L could not have been fair, or he could not have continued to feel bitterly so long.4

The irony of it was that if there was one charge against which Augusta could comfortably defend herself it was this, as it had been as much a matter of self-interest as affection to bring about a reconciliation between Annabella and Byron. She denied that she had ever said anything to alienate him from his wife, and when Annabella—convinced of "her smooth way of making mischief"5—retorted that "there was a difference between exasperating and not softening," Augusta appealed to Hobhouse's testimony. "She said that she had recollected a proof that she had acted justly to me," Annabella continued, outraged that the name of one of Byron's hated "Piccadilly crew" should be dragged in as a witness against her,

> for Sir J. Hobhouse had said to her, in speaking of what she had said of me to Lord Byron: "You risked his affection by doing so."
>
> At such a testimony I started up, and all but uttered an ironical answer—but she had *trusted me unconditionally*, and I replied: "I don't understand it." From that moment there was a mingling of indignation with the intense pity I had before felt—and I was afraid of myself. I said, I believe, that I should always wish her the blessing I could not give her, or something kind if my tears did not prevent me uttering it—but the strongest desire to be out of her presence took possession of me, lest I should be tempted beyond my strength.6

It was the paradox of her attitude, however, that even while she believed that Augusta had withheld and forged letters to keep Byron away, she could never quite obliterate an image so closely involved with all the aspiration of her youth. "I thought Mrs. Leigh my friend," she had told Robertson only months before Reigate, "I loved her—I love her still! I cannot help it."7

If that was no more than the truth, in the bitter aftermath of the meeting it only served to fuel her sense of betrayal. On her return to Brighton she dictated a brief note announcing her safe arrival, but when at the end of April, Augusta attempted one last defence of herself the letter was returned unopened. "I had not, and never implied that I had anything to reveal to you with which *you* were not previously acquainted," Augusta had written—a final and moving plea for justice that, even when she sent it back again, with a covering letter to Robertson asking to see him, Annabella refused to look at.

> Nor can I at all express to you the regret I have felt since those words escaped you, showing that you imagined I had encouraged a bitterness of feeling in Lord Byron towards you. I can as solemnly declare as if I were on my death-bed that I never did so in any one instance but that I invariably did the contrary.[8]

"Madam," Frederick Robertson wrote back on Annabella's behalf to Augusta at her apartments at St. James's, on 21 May 1851—the last communication, bar two words, the women would ever share,

> I regret to say that I feel it impossible to accede to the proposal that you have made, viz. to favour me with an interview in which you might substantiate your assertion made to Lady Byron.
>
> In the meeting at Reigate Lady Byron expressed a conviction that your influence on Lord Byron's mind had been unfavourable to his coming to just conclusions respecting himself.
>
> This you denied strongly and distinctly; and you quoted a speech of Sir John Hobhouse, one sentence of which appeared to shock and startle Lady Byron exceedingly.
>
> No-one but myself was witness of this conversation. I am a stranger to you, and my opinion can be of no importance. I need scarcely say that the topics of that interview are sacred, and that they will never pass my lips. The proofs which you desire to give me could only be given in Lady Byron's presence, and she will never consent to another meeting. The last was final ... If your own conscience is free and clear, and

Lady Byron is no way injured by you, the sense of innocence in God's sight will make the opinion of any human being a matter of small importance. If on the contrary there was anything for the sorrowful acknowledgement of which that meeting was the last and final opportunity which you can ever have in this world, then, of course, no opinion of Sir John Hobhouse, written or expressed, nor of Lord Byron to himself, can reverse the solemn judgement upon the whole matter, which must be heard very, very soon, when you meet God face to face.

I remain, Madam, your obedient servant,
Fred. W. Robertson

P. S.—I ought, perhaps, to add that I did not transmit your letter to Lady Byron and therefore return it. She is resolved that the communication was ended with the last letter she wrote; and, indeed, the result of that interview has been a dangerous illness.

I trust you will not look upon the plain words I have spoken as expressing harshness of feeling. I would gladly, now or hereafter, as a minister of Christ, do what might be in my power to alleviate sadness, but I am quite sure that it is not my duty to receive any evidence of the nature you propose.9

If it would have come as a surprise to Frederick Robertson's congregation to know that he would go down in history for his uneasy role in the Augusta affair, the tone of this letter perhaps suggests why. To many contemporaries who had heard Arnold and Newman preach, Frederick Robertson was simply the greatest orator of his day, and yet if he is remembered at all now it is as one of those emasculated Victorians whom women of the stamp of Annabella or Florence Nightingale could reduce to the hopeless bondage of the superior "bagman."

Were it not a *donnée* of the whole Byron story that Byron has "devoted friends" and Annabella "hangers-on," Robertson might yet enjoy a better press than he has, but he is too firmly established now as a Brighton *Slope* to make rehabilitation much worth trying. Annabella and Robertson had first met when her restless, wandering life took her to a house near the Pavilion at Brighton in 1848, and within a year she had begun to confide her history to him, graduating over their meetings and letters from theological discussions of Byron's childhood Calvinism to the full revelations of his incest with Augusta.

There were twenty-five years between them, and Robertson was a married man, but it was still a relationship of supreme importance to both. For most of her middle age Annabella's closest friendships had been with women, but with the charismatic and theologically maverick Robertson she rediscovered a capacity for spiritual and emotional ardour that she had not known since her courtship of Byron. "I must thank you for the greatest gift that a human being can make to his fellow," she wrote to her cousin, Robert Noel, in 1848 after he had introduced them, "the means of intercourse with a great soul— Robertson's."[10] "Between the widow of the greatest poet of his age and the fervid young priest," wrote Frederick Arnold,

> there had gradually grown up an intense and famous friendship worthy of comparison with the renowned friendships of antiquity.[11]

For Frederick Robertson, brought up like all his generation on Byron, there was an obvious excitement in the revelations, and yet nothing else we know of him suggests a man easily seduced by the frisson of scandal. There was invariably an element of patronage in Annabella's friendships, but if it was never entirely absent from her dealings with Robertson, it should at least make one pause that a man of his instinctive independence and generosity could have found in her character and history so compelling a cause for sympathy.

Even when that is said, however, it seems there was a gap between what Robertson felt and what Annabella demanded that can be accurately measured by the fact that when he copied that letter out for her he carefully omitted his postscript. There was a quixotic streak in him that would always be vulnerable to a woman like Augusta, but no one who had ever dealt with Annabella for any length of time could have had any illusions that impartiality was an option.

The hand that wrote that final letter to Augusta may be Robertson's, but the presence looming behind it with all the force and sanction of the Victorian age, is unmistakably Annabella's. For the best part of a lifetime she had been justifying herself in terms of moral and religious "duties," and in the implacable and ruthless certainty of rejection, in its demonstration of a will strong enough to bend a man of Robertson's generosity to the unforgiving dogmatisms of Evangelical righteousness, we come face to face with the Annabella Byron of old age.

It is one thing, however, simply to register the fact, but it is quite another to understand what could have turned the Regency Magdalene Hayter painted in 1812 into the woman capable of dictating that letter to Augusta. With anyone but Annabella a life of rejection and disappointment might seem answer enough, but if one reads that letter again or looks into the face—sexless and joyless as an old Boer trekker's—that stares out of photographs of her in old age, it is clear that whatever else might be said of her, she was *not* the natural stuff of victims.

It cannot simply be the operations of revenge or jealousy, either, that explain a lifetime's self-laceration in the cause of a family she never ceased to love. After all she had suffered at the Byrons' hands it would have been extraordinary if such feelings had not played their part, but as one contemplates the emotional wasteland of her life, something more complex and elusive—more *tragic* in the fullest sense of the word—is needed to explain what could have driven a woman of her intelligence and aspirations to consume her health, energies and ultimately humanity in a campaign of self-justification and moral tyranny that ended only with her death.

It is that question that is explored here, and while Annabella would never have recognised the terms in which it is couched, she would have acknowledged the emptiness it describes. Until the end of her life she was always able to restock her immediate circle with new acolytes and admirers, but with that brief, vivid exception of Brighton and Robertson nothing in her whole life began to fill the void that opened before her when her marriage to Byron failed.

And wherever eventually they might lead, every question ever asked of Annabella—or any question she asked of herself—always begins with Byron and marriage. She once described herself as "embalmed by a name,"[12] and if to the outward eye the only thing that connected the wealthy philanthropist of old age to her younger self was that name, no one knew better than Annabella that the only "life" that had ever mattered was the one that had opened and as suddenly closed when she swapped the name of Milbanke for that of Byron almost forty years before.

MARRIAGE

There is possibly no marriage about which we know so much as that of Byron and Annabella, but still after the best part of two centuries of partisan controversy the mystery at its heart remains as elusive as ever. From the day it collapsed in rumours of cruelty, sodomy, rape and incest there has not been a single moment unexplored, and yet the paradox is that it is the very weight of surviving evidence that exposes those areas of emotional and sexual truth and human vulnerability at which we can do no more than guess.

The same could be said, of course, of any relationship that can only be viewed from the outside, but it is the nature of the accounts that we have in this case that makes any "truth" much harder to find. In the weeks after the separation servants, doctors, family and friends all left a mass of testimony, but it is almost exclusively on the word of a wife determined not just to fight her public cause but also to mask the truth from *herself* that we still have to rely for any sense of the texture of their married year.*

Even when every caution is taken, however, and the obvious embellishments of subsequent years discounted, the profound misery of those twelve months still has a power to shock that no repetition can blunt. There is such a deceptive and lulling air of normality about the wedding itself too, that the sudden descent from the comforting mundanity of a world defined by such details as family,

---

*Byron also left his own memoir—one that Annabella refused to look at when he offered it to her—but that went up in flames in John Murray's offices and the different fragments the various incendiaries "remembered" need to be treated with extreme caution.

gloves, pelisse and kneeling cushions to the secret and sudden misery of an enclosed carriage has a Gothic quality about it that cannot merely be the product of Annabella's imagination.

"At the altar she did not know that she was a sacrifice," Harriet Martineau wrote of Annabella's wedding day, "but before sunset on that winter day she knew it."[1] "As soon as we got into the carriage his countenance changed to gloom and defiance," Annabella remembered in one of her many versions of events,

> He began singing in a wild manner as he usually does when angry and scarcely spoke to me till we came near Durham, when he said amongst other things calculated to excite mistrust, "You had better have married—, he would have made you a better husband." On hearing the Joy-bells of Durham ringing for us, he appeared to be struck with horror, and said something very bitter about "our happiness" . . . He called me to account for having so long withheld my consent to marry him, signifying I should suffer for it, and had better not have married him at all.
>
> At the Inn at Rushford he turned to me with a bitter look & said, "I wonder how much longer I shall be able to keep up *the part I have been* playing"—or some equivalent expression, decidedly expressing that he had worn a mask which he now intended to throw aside.[2]

It is impossible to know whether or not that first wedding journey had the nightmare air it later assumed in her imagination, but the butler's memory of Annabella's face as he handed her from the carriage, "agonised and listless with horror and despair,"[3] suggests that she was not exaggerating Byron's antipathy. It is clear from his own admissions that Byron thought that he had suffered some kind of nervous attack in these first days of marriage, and if Annabella's memories of the journey demonstrably changed with time there is evidence enough of Byron's capacity for the kind of mental cruelty she charged him with to believe the substance of her account.

It was not Byron's anger that crushed her, though—the well-rehearsed details of those first days at Halnaby, the ravings, the loaded pistols, the daggers, the oblique confessions, have a curiously "stagey" quality about them—but the hopeless realisation of the desert that lay ahead. In the whole period that Byron had courted Annabella they can have spent no more than a week in each other's company, but now with no one but servants in the house, she found herself cut off by the dreary, ice bound landscape of the West Riding, immured with a man beyond her reach—two people mutually ignorant of each other, divided by temperament, expectations, history, faith and, above all, that invisible "third" who from the first day of their marriage had always been with them.

There had been a letter to Byron from Augusta, addressed to the "Dearest, first and best of human beings,"[4] on the first day of their "treaclemoon," and his constant lament was that she was the only person who could ever love or understand him. In later accounts Annabella dated her first "blasting" suspicions of "something most dreadful between him and his sister"[5] to these weeks at Halnaby, and if that is true, there can be no more eloquent testimony to her loneliness, than the fact that within three days of marriage she had turned to Augusta herself for help.

The two women had seen each other—without meeting—across the crowded rooms of a London season in 1813, and although they had exchanged properly affectionate letters after the engagement, it was from these first weeks of marriage that their lifetime's intimacy dates. From the first day that she re-entered Byron's life Augusta had been able to laugh him out of his *Wertherish* moods in a way that no one else could, and with a generosity tempered by self-interest she did her best now to advise his new wife, forging between them in the process a kind of solidarity that had Byron at its heart—a wayward, consuming, demanding presence that was simultaneously the rationale and fatal flaw of their improbable sisterhood.

Even by the time that Annabella received Augusta's first letter, however, pledging as Annabella had begged of her, to be her "ONLY friend,"[6] Byron's mood had begun to lift. In a later confession to Hobhouse he admitted to a "melancholy" that had descended on his wedding night, and while "attack" was the only way in life or art Byron ever knew of assuaging guilt or anger, he was too instinctively generous to remain unmoved by Annabella's desolation.

It was, in fact, his "unrelenting pity"[7] rather than any histrionics that had brought Annabella's misery home to her, but gradually a sort of exhausted calm seems to have settled over Halnaby. "You would think we had been married these fifty years," he wrote to Lady Melbourne,

Bell is fast asleep on a corner of the Sopha, and I am keeping myself awake with this epistle—she desires her love—and mine you have had ever since we were acquainted.[8]

"Bell and I go on extremely well," he reported to her again, and as they settled into a domestic rhythm, with Byron working while Annabella transcribed his Hebrew Melodies, the first stirrings of hope appear that the mutual horror of the opening days was behind them. "I don't dislike this place," he wrote on 7 January—

it is just the spot for a Moon . . . I have great hopes that this match will turn out well—I have found nothing yet I could wish changed for the better—[9]

It was an optimism that survived even a return to Seaham, where in spite of Byron's reluctance, they went on 21 January. For the next month Byron found himself at the centre of a domestic world of which he had no real experience, and if familiarity made him no fonder of his mother-in-law, he endured the boredom of Sir Ralph's interminable prosing with a decent good humour. "My spouse and I agree to—and in—admiration," he wrote to Tom Moore after ten days of Seaham,

Swift says "no *wise* man ever married"; but, for a fool, I think it the most ambrosial of all future states. I still think one ought to marry upon *lease;* but am very sure I should renew mine at the expiration, though next term were for ninety and nine years . . .

My Papa, Sir Ralph, hath recently made a speech at a Durham tax-meeting; and not only at Durham, but here, several times since, after dinner. He is now, I believe, speaking it to himself (I left him in the middle) over various decanters, which can neither interrupt him nor fall asleep,— as might have been the case with some of his audience.

Ever thine,
    B.

I must go to tea—damn tea. I wish it was Kinnaird's brandy, and with you to lecture me about it.[10]

And after the claustrophobic weeks at Halnaby, incarcerated in a featureless landscape, the sight of the sea lifted his spirits as it always did. During the breaks in the rain and family games Byron and Annabella would scramble over the rocks she had known since childhood, his sensitivity to his lameness eased by her kindness and tact—the Childe, as Annabella contentedly reported to Augusta, a wild and boisterous boy again.

And yet even at their happiest together it was significantly images of freedom and escape—of Biscay and Aegean squalls—that the desolate north-eastern shoreline stirred in Byron and there was scarcely a day when Annabella was not left in tears by some cruelty. More than twenty years later her old servant Mrs. Clermont recalled her anxieties at this time, and if there seemed to her some fear running through the whole Milbanke household that stopped anyone naming their apprehensions even Sir Ralph was not blind to the danger. "Her father during their stay saw what he did not like," Dr. Bence-Jones recorded Mrs. Clermont telling him,

> & one day said to Mrs. C., He persecuted her to marry him
> & I believe he only married her to persecute her—if it is so
> he shall have my dying curse.[11]

If Byron had had any hopes that marriage might bury his obsessive need for Augusta, he already knew that it had failed. On the day after they reached Seaham he had written to allay his new "*tante's*" anxieties, but ten days later he was writing again, as he had done so often in the year before the marriage, to confess his helplessness. "I suppose your 'C- noir is +,'" he wrote to Lady Melbourne—his "Corbeau blanc"—on 2 February, employing his habitual "+" symbol for Augusta,

> but if + were a raven or a griffin I must still take my omens
> from her flight—I can't help *loving* her though—[12]

With negotiations for the sale of Newstead underway, Byron had wanted to leave Annabella at Seaham while he found a house for them in London, but when finally they left on 9 March for Augusta's home near Newmarket she insisted on accompanying him.

It was the second time in just over two months that Annabella had
to give up the security and sympathy of family life to be alone with
Byron. In many ways—emotionally and physically—Seaham had
been a greater success than either of them could have hoped, but
from the moment she stepped into the carriage she might have been
on her way to Halnaby again, with Byron railing bitterly against her
parents or flinging her own physical helplessness in her face.

On their second night south they stopped at Wandsford, and as
Byron's mood briefly lifted, Annabella enjoyed probably the last
unalloyed moment of happiness of her married life. In the early
evening his behaviour had seemed as capricious as ever, but later,
Annabella recalled, "he said to me the kindest words I could ever
wish to have heard.

> "You married me to make me happy, didn't you"—I
> answered with some expression of attachment—"Well then,
> you *do* make me happy!"—with passionate affection, I fan-
> cied. I was silent, and he saw not, but felt the tears of joy
> which rose from my heart.[13]

There is something so pathetic in Annabella's gratitude here—so
humiliating in the poverty of her expectations—that it brings home
her misery in a way that no story of Byronic violence does. It is difficult to read the self-justifying accounts she later wrote with much
sympathy, but whatever Annabella eventually *became* should not disguise the courage and genuine goodness she brought as a young
bride to these first weeks of married life.

The tragedy of Annabella Milbanke is of wasted humanity, and
the selflessness of her behaviour during these beleaguered months
makes one wonder what kindness and love might have made of her.
The passionate affection she showed Augusta during the first days of
her separation from Byron underline a capacity for loyalty for which
she has had little credit, but if she had learned anything in two
months of married life it was that there was nothing she could do—
and no one she could be—that could avert the fate Byron had *willed*
for her.

In many of her accounts she dated her first suspicions about
Byron and Augusta to the honeymoon, but it was the fortnight at the
Leighs' house at Six Mile Bottom that left little room for doubt. From

the first evening Byron seemed determined to force the knowledge of it on her, packing her off to bed early while he stayed up alone with Augusta, only finally appearing in a black rage in Annabella's room, to make his loathing for her clear.

Evening after evening the same pattern repeated itself, but, as Annabella herself saw, Byron was equally bent on making his sister's life a misery. During the last weeks at Seaham Augusta had written as often as ever to the new couple, but for all her friendliness there had been an ambivalence of tone that Byron could not have missed, a sort of tactical—even occasionally ironical—withdrawal from intimacy that opened up for him a prospect of loss that he could neither accept nor forgive.

For the only time in his life his treatment of Augusta seemed to be actuated more by an urge for power and ownership than by love. It is impossible to know if he had ever fully envisaged the consequences of marriage on his relations with her, but as they were now brought home by Augusta's reluctance to resume their old intimacy, she seems to have become as much an object of his hatred and revenge as his unwitting wife. He would sit between the pair of them, comparing their kisses, and talk in front of Annabella of Augusta's underwear. "His delight was," Annabella later wrote,

> *to work us both well.* (he kept her in a state of misery beyond mine I thought)—that she was in his power from some cause I could not often doubt—with all my endeavours to do so— and that he made the most cruel use of that power. I pitied her from my heart if Guilt had brought her thus low, and would not have aggravated her oppression of mind by a single look.[14]

It never seems to have occurred to Byron, however, that his attempt to play one woman off against the other would simply drive them into an alliance of their own. During her long courtship Annabella had seen herself in the role of Byron's redeemer, but as she began to realise that he was beyond her control, her emotional commitment shifted to the thing closest to him, embracing Augusta with the same romanticising and possessive ardour that she had expended on him.

It is one of the bizarre paradoxes of this fortnight that while it signalled the death of her marriage, it sealed Annabella's compact with the Byrons for good. At the centre of the strange *ménage à trois* still towered the figure of Byron of course, but as Annabella and Augusta grew closer together, other emotional currents and connections developed from which he was inevitably excluded.

Augusta might obediently wear the brooch, complete with his lock of hair and coded "+"s, that Byron had ordered from London, but it seemed more a badge of emotional slavery than love. Whenever the weather permitted, the two women would walk in the garden and talk, and if the great issue that lay between them remained unspoken, its mere existence brought them closer together, binding them into that dangerous and unstable inter-dependence that would only end with their lives.

As their carriage pulled away from Augusta's home, however, and Byron turned on Annabella to demand what she had thought of *her*, there seemed nothing in front of them but the blank misery of marriage. During their stay at Six Mile Bottom Annabella had shown the first signs of "Symptoms which look a little gestatory,"[15] but even the prospect of an heir apparently filled Byron with no pleasure. "It is a subject upon which I am not particularly anxious," he told Moore,

> Except that I think it would please her uncle, Lord Wentworth, and her father and mother. The former (Lord W) is now in town, and in very indifferent health. You perhaps know that his property, amounting to seven or eight thousand a year, will eventually devolve upon Bell. But the old gentleman has been so very kind to her and me, that I hardly know how to wish him in heaven, if he can be comfortable on earth.[16]

Not for the first time in his letters as a married man, Byron strikes here a note of financial anxiety that was to be the constant background to all their troubles. Through the early months of 1815 negotiations over the sale of Newstead dragged on in their usual frustrating fashion, and the house that Lady Melbourne had rented on their behalf from the Duchess of Devonshire only exacerbated problems that not even Lord Wentworth's death could avert.

If anything, in fact, it made their position even worse, because as the news that Annabella was now an heiress spread, Byron's creditors closed in. Sir Ralph's own difficulties had meant that Byron had seen nothing of the money owed him under the marriage settlement, and as settlement of the Wentworth will was delayed by litigation, Byron found himself facing the real possibility of the bailiffs and the compulsory sale of his possessions.

In the letters and recollections of contemporaries, there is an occasional glimpse of a happier and more stable life at 13 Piccadilly, or of a benign and solicitous husband hovering over Annabella's chair at the theatre, but a little has been made to go a long way. For Byron there was a literary and public life beyond the straitening confines of his home to divert him, and yet there seems something oddly unsettled even in his letters from this year, something in the patching of old quarrels or frenetic activities at the theatre or the drinking bouts with old friends that carries a faint valedictory flavour.

After a relative calm of ten days, Augusta was with them again, in London to prepare for her new duties as lady-in-waiting to Queen Charlotte. An apartment in St. James's Palace went with the position, but Annabella had written echoing Byron's invitation to stay with them in Piccadilly, and on 30 March an uncertain Augusta wrote back to accept. "Dearest Sis," she replied,

> . . .You will perhaps be a better judge bye & bye whether I shall not be a plague—& you must tell me *truly* if I am likely to be so—you know I should not be "affronted."[17]

Almost immediately on Augusta's arrival with her eldest daughter, Georgey, it was as if they were all again at Six Mile Bottom, though to add to the humiliations, Annabella was in her own home and in the first stages of pregnancy. In her defence Augusta seems to have done whatever she could to shield her from the worst excesses, but with Byron's mood swings getting ever wilder his sister's mere presence seemed goad enough.

"You were a fool to let her come," he told Annabella the first night that the three of them were reunited, "You will find it will make a good deal of difference to you *in all ways*,"[18] and he was as good as his word. During the next two months Annabella again found herself driven upstairs in the evenings, forced to listen to their voices below, waiting in a frenzy of misery for the sound of their footsteps, learning by bitter experience to read into the weight and speed of his tread his mood and intentions as he came to her room.

There is a genuine horror to her descriptions of these vigils, an unconscious echo of Macbeth's vision of murder approaching with

"Tarquin's ravishing stride," that more than anything catches the psychological and sexual violence that filled the household at 13 Piccadilly.* She never seems to have felt herself in any physical danger from Byron at this point, but for a woman who had committed herself to him with such hope and belief only months earlier, the brutal alternations of conjugal demands and physical abhorrence were in their way even more degrading.

Even the one consolation of the fortnight at Six Mile Bottom, the friendship of Augusta, seemed polluted. "I must not (having so far spoken of myself as to imply that I preserved, generally, self-possession and forbearance)," she confessed many years later,

> omit to state that my feelings were once—in London—so worked up by the continual excitement of horrible ideas . . . that in a moment when one of them became to my imagination a *fact*—I turned round to use a deadly weapon lying by—not against him, but against one whose treachery seemed at that instant revealed . . . There are moments of one's past life before which one stands in awe.[19]

And yet it was only now, alone in face of what seemed a double betrayal by brother and sister, that Annabella showed the extraordinary strength—part courage, part absolute inner certainty—that was to characterise her behaviour through the rest of her life. It would be possible to read her letters from this period and gain no sense of misery at all, but if that has been held up as proof of later exaggerations it more likely stems from a pride that made her determined to see that family or strangers should never guess the truth. "She is pretty, not beautiful," the American George Ticknor described her after visiting Piccadilly in June,

> has a large fortune, is rich in intellectual endowments, is a mathematician, possesses common accomplishments in an uncommon degree, and adds to all this a sweet temper.[20]

---

*It is fascinating to catch literary echoes in Annabella's writing because it shows how her mind worked as she set about shaping experience into dramatic form. It has often been pointed out how her descriptions of the honeymoon have the flavour of a gothic novel, and among her papers from 1812 survives a lengthy analysis of Mrs. Siddons's views on Macbeth that eventually seems to have provided the language to understand and articulate her own loneliness.

"She did not seem to me as pretty as she did the other day," he wrote again after a second visit,

> but what she may have lost in regular beauty she made up in variety and expression of countenance during the conversation. She is diffident,—she is very young, not more, I think, than nineteen,—but is obviously possessed of talent, and did not talk at all for display. For the quarter of an hour during which I was with her, she talked upon a considerable variety of subjects—America, of which she seemed to know considerable; of France, and Greece, with something of her husband's visit there,—and spoke of all with a justness and a light good-humour.[21]

Annabella was not only determined to maintain appearances, but to fight her corner too, and in the middle of June, after almost two months vacillating between thoughts of murder and spasms of guilt, she asked Augusta to leave. In a poignant comment on her feelings Annabella later described the way that she had sublimated revenge into a cult of "romantic forgiveness,"[22] and yet if that tells part of the truth it conceals a subtle shift in the balance of power between the two women that is perfectly caught in all the loaded connotations of that word "forgiveness."

It is only in retrospect that one can see it, perhaps, but that request for Augusta to go also signalled the first step in an emotional withdrawal from Byron that would only end with their separation. In their letters Annabella and Augusta had talked of "Baby" Byron as though they were dealing with some errant child, but for the first time since her marriage Annabella now seemed secure enough in her own judgement to regard her husband with the eye of the Seaham moralist as well as the wife. "My head is better," she told Augusta,

> And I wish to make a few observations respecting the nature of my greatest fears for B.—and I think I daily understand the case better. His misfortune is an habitual *passion for Excitement*, which is always found in ardent temperaments, where the pursuits are not in some degree organised. It is the ennui of a monotonous existence that drives the best hearted people of this description to the most dangerous paths, and

makes them often seem to act from bad motives, when in fact they are only flying from internal suffering by any external stimulus. The love of tormenting rises chiefly from this source. Drinking, Gaming &c are all of the same origin. How far it may depend on body or mind it is difficult to ascertain. I am inclined to think that a vitiated stomach, particularly if it arises from habits of excess, is a chief cause of the sensations of Ennui; and that change of scene, air, & exercise are more efficient to its removal than any efforts of Reason.[23]

In a curious way marriage had both matured and arrested Annabella, forcing her to grow up, and yet confirming her in all the rigidity of her old beliefs. For a few brief months she had succumbed to the temptations of Byronism, but under the provocation of his hate she had been forced to fall back on herself and assert in the face of his abuse and contempt the dull verities of her stable, moral world.

With their finances in ever deepening crisis, and Byron unable to do anything about it, and too proud to accept money for his verse, he had also failed her in the simplest terms that he had spoken of when he first proposed. It was to her great credit that she never resented for herself the financial anxieties he had brought on her, but with Annabella protectiveness and patronage were never far apart, and it is possible that Byron saw his own sense of impotence reflected back in her eyes.

More important than anything, however, even for so un-maternal a woman as Annabella, was the simple fact that as she moved into the last stages of her pregnancy other duties and imperatives asserted themselves. In its first weeks she had hoped that a child would bring Byron closer again, but long before the birth both instinctively saw that it was an end not a beginning, the flash point that would bring those fundamental divisions on which their marriage had foundered—divisions between orthodoxy and rebellion, continuity and change, licence and control, convention and originality, between the natural outsider and that deep "human compact by which we all live together"[24]—to open war.

With bailiffs now in the house, his books for sale, and Byron drinking more and more, the weeks before the birth saw him at his savage worst. He talked constantly of separation or escape, or of his hopes that Annabella and her baby might die. At the end of October, too, he took a mistress in a joyless revenge on both Annabella and Augusta, now equally to blame in his eyes for the hell in which he was trapped. "He leaves the house, telling me he will at once abandon himself to every desperation," Annabella wrote to Augusta,

> speaks to me only to upbraid me with having married him when he wished not, and says he is therefore acquitted of all principle towards me, and I must consider myself, *only* to be answerable for the vicious courses to which his despair will drive him. The going out of the house & the drinking are the most fatal. He was really quite frantic yesterday—said he did not care for any consequences to me, and it seemed impossible to tell if his feelings towards you or me were the most completely reversed; for as I have told you, he loves or hates us together.[25]

On 15 November, at Annabella's own desperate request, Augusta returned to Piccadilly for the approaching confinement, to find Byron smashing furniture and letting off his pistols beneath his wife's room. Within the household there were now genuine fears for her safety and even for Augusta there could be no other issue but the protection of mother and child. Under her improbable leadership the forces of normality and retribution began to mass, closing ranks against the outsider in the classic rhythms of tragedy. To the Milbankes' old servant, Mrs. Clermont, invited to help by Augusta, was added the figure of Captain George Byron, Byron's impeccably ordinary cousin and heir. In the middle of November Annabella's mother—Lady Noel as she now was by the terms of her brother's will—arrived in town, and on 9 December, the first of those professionals who would eventually preside over Byron's ruin, Sergeant Heywood, was consulted on the advisability of removing Annabella from Byron's reach.

It was decided, however, that it was safer that she should stay at Piccadilly, and the following day, Sunday 10 December, a girl was born and named Augusta Ada—Ada in a piece of Byronic family flummery, Augusta after the sister expected to be the child's godmother. A "horrid story" reached an appalled Hobhouse that Byron had demanded to know whether the child was dead while Annabella was still in labour, but whether that is true or not another comment recorded by an old family friend of the Milbankes, captures the air of gothic nightmare that had enveloped the household. "When her lovely little child was born," Lady Anne Barnard wrote,

> and it was laid beside its mother on the bed, and he was informed "he might see his daughter," after gazing at it with an exulting smile, this was the ejaculation that broke from him, "Oh! What an instrument of torture I have acquired in you!"[26]

For two people who had driven each other to such a pitch of mutual despair, however, neither Annabella nor Byron seemed fully conscious that with the birth of Ada they had crossed some invisible line. Throughout the whole period of his marriage it would seem that Byron was in fact only ever half aware of what he was doing, as if the man who sat on the Drury Lane committee and helped fellow writers like Coleridge, Godwin or Maturin with such tact and grace had nothing to do with the tyrant and drunk he had become at home.

With the deepest part of his personality, though, with that part of him that found both its relief and profoundest expression in his poetry, Byron had *willed* the rupture that Ada's birth made inevitable. The sufferings of Annabella during their year together have rightly dominated judgements of their marriage, and yet if they constitute no excuse for him, Byron's own miseries were just as acute, his sense of suffocation and impotence driving him to the brink of what he himself called madness.

The only two major poems of this period, *Parisina* with its theme of incest and death, and *The Siege of Corinth,* a tale of banishment and revenge, underline too just how constant was the call to exile. From his earliest childhood there had been something oppressive in English life to Byron, but marriage and Piccadilly had intensified dislike into a claustrophobia that had a physical urgency to it, lending a Wildean poignancy to the images of escape and freedom that haunted his imagination. "This is but a dull scrawl, and I am but a dull fellow," he wrote plaintively to Moore after the birth of Ada,

> I am absorbed in 500 contradictory contemplations, though with but one object in view—which will probably end in

nothing, as most things we wish do. But never mind—as somebody says, "for the blue sky bends over all." I only could be glad, if it bent over me where it is a little bluer, like the "skyish top of blue Olympus," which, by the way, looked very white when I last saw it.[27]

Byron was wrong, though, if he thought that life in Piccadilly would simply drift, because whether or not he knew it, the marriage was now beyond redemption. While there was no one else but herself to think of, Annabella had been able to sustain herself with images of self-sacrifice, but with anxieties for her child—the fear above all that Byron might remove her abroad with him—there was no longer room for the luxury of romantic delusions.

The birth had done nothing to calm Byron's rages either, and as he fed himself on de Sade's writings, it seemed for the first time that Caroline Lamb's "mad, bad and dangerous to know" might be no more than the truth. There is nothing in his letters from these weeks to suggest the slightest trace of mental instability, and yet under the influence of drink he seemed increasingly incapable of controlling himself, driven by some compulsive *necessity* to the destructive outbursts that mark the last phase of his marriage. "The principal insane ideas are—that he *must* be wicked," Annabella noted for Doctor Baillie, who was consulted on Byron's possible insanity,

Undoubtedly I am more than anyone the subject of his irritation, because he deems himself (as he has said) a villain for marrying me on account of former circumstances—adding that the more I love him, & the better I am, the more accursed is he.[28]

With Byron littering his rages and remorse with hints of some unforgivable sin, the attractions of insanity to Augusta are obvious, but it had no less profound an appeal for Annabella. There was a clear tactical advantage to such a diagnosis if it ever came to a struggle over Ada, but more importantly it enabled her to cling to the last vestiges of self-respect, allowing her not only to blind herself to Augusta's role in her misery but to the raw intensity of Byron's hatred.

By the time that Annabella turned to Dr. Baillie, however, it was too late for any medical advice to save the marriage. On 6 January— almost exactly a year after her wedding—she was handed a note by

Augusta from Byron. "When you are disposed to leave London," he had written,

> it would be convenient that a date should be fixed—& (if possible) not a very remote one for that purpose. Of my opinion upon that subject you are sufficiently in possession— & of the circumstances which have led to it—as also to my plans—or rather intentions—for the future. When in the country I will write to you more fully. As Lady Noel has asked you to Kirkby, there you can be for the present—unless you prefer Seaham.
>
> As the dismissal of the present establishment is of impor- tance to me, the sooner you can fix on the date the better— though of course your convenience & inclination shall be first consulted.
>
> The child will of course accompany you—there is a more easy and safer carriage than the chariot (unless you prefer it) which I mentioned before—on that you can do as you please.[29]

It was Byron's last written communication to her of their married life together. For another week Annabella held on at Piccadilly, taking soundings on his mental health, but one last burst of rage decided her. Early on the morning of 15 January 1816, she got up with the five-week-old Ada, and without saying goodbye, walked past Byron's room and out to the waiting carriage. She confessed later that she had to steel her will against throwing herself down at his door on the mat on which his Newfoundland used to lie.

The temptation lasted only a second, and was gone. That night was spent at Woburn, and the following day she was with her parents at Kirkby. She had seen Byron for the last time.

SLEEPING WITH THE VAMPIRE

I f anyone had asked the ageing Annabella to flesh out this skeletal account of her married life, it is unlikely that after all the years of introspection she could have done so with any honesty even if she had wanted to. At the height of the separation battle that followed her departure Byron had generously declared that she was "truth itself," and yet as her life had spiralled out of her control and the most intimate details of her marriage became the lawyers' and the public's property, truth soon became a luxury she could less and less afford.

The process began almost from that day in the middle of January 1816, when thin, ill and exhausted from her journey, she arrived with Ada at her family home at Kirkby. For twelve months of married life she had somehow succeeded in disguising from herself the ambiguities of her relationship with Byron and Augusta, but confronted suddenly by her parents' indignant interrogation she felt, as she told Augusta, as if she "were going to receive sentence from the Judge with his black cap on."[1]

Even after all that she had gone through, she confessed, there were times when she would have forgotten self, child and principles to devote herself to the "being who cast me off," and there can be little doubt that she had no idea of leaving Byron when she first arrived at Kirkby. "Dearest Duck," she wrote to him the following day, the second of two loving letters that would come back to haunt her over the weeks and years ahead, undermining all she said of Byron's unmitigated brutality to her through their marriage,

We got here quite well last night, and were ushered into the kitchen instead of the drawing-room, by a mistake that might have been agreeable enough to hungry people. Of this and other incidents Dad wants to write you a jocose account, & both he & Mam long to have the family party completed . . . If I were not always looking about for B., I should be a great deal better already for country air. *Miss* finds her provisions increased, & fattens thereon. It is a good thing she can't understand all the flattery bestowed upon her, "Little Angel." Love to the good Goose [Augusta], & everybody's love to you both from hence.

> Ever thy most loving
> Pippin . . . Pip . . . Pip[2]

In the weeks ahead it became Byron's bitter conviction that Annabella's family had turned her against him, and if that was not true in the way he imagined it, it was in another and more important sense. In the last days of her marriage Annabella had clutched at every excuse from madness to drink to explain away Byron's loathing, but as one by one the revelations were prised out of her, as suspicions of incest were added to accusations of cruelty, unspecified suggestions of sexual deviance to legal charges of adultery and insanity discounted by the doctors, it became a matter of absolute self-preservation to distance herself as far as possible from the Piccadilly menage and the "Pip" who had written that letter.

The harrowing irony of her position, too, was that it was still at Piccadilly that she felt at home, because in a curious anticipation of the Stockholm syndrome, it was with her tormentors and not her rescuers that she most closely identified. In the eyes of her parents there could be no room for compromise or forgiveness of Byron's conduct to their daughter, but if Annabella had learned anything from her marriage it was that life was more complex than Milbanke morality would allow. "Independent of Malady," she wrote to Augusta, still at Piccadilly and sending off daily bulletins on Byron's behaviour to her "sis" at Kirkby,

> I do not think of the past with any spirit of resentment & scarcely with sense of injury—God bless him.[3]

These were emotions, too, that she could share only with Augusta. "Dearest A," she addressed her again from her parents' home, writing almost as if from an enemy camp, guarded by supporters she refers to as "them," her mind "overstrained and my body weak in compassion,"

> Do not wish anything *for me*, except that I may fulfil my duties whilst I am amongst them—and render me more thankful in performing them, by the comfort of being dear to one who feels for me as you do . . . You can not know the feelings with which I receive every mark of your affection . . . No, if all the world had told me you were doing me an injury, I *ought not* to have believed it.[4]

Whatever Annabella's feelings under her parents' roof, however, the conduct and progress of the separation had slipped for the time being out of her hands. On 20th January her outraged mother had set off for London to consult a lawyer, and armed with the advice of Sir Samuel Romilly and a statement from Annabella detailing Byron's "dismissal" and his "settled aversion" to marriage, the Milbankes made their first overtures to him for a quiet and amicable separation.

At this early stage in the process, the charges against Byron were of so unspecified a nature that in his reply to Annabella's father he was able to hide behind a blanket of mystification. In his long and evasive answer to Sir Ralph, Byron conceded "a morbid irritability of temper"[5] over the last year, but while he was prepared to admit that Annabella had sometimes seen him gloomy or violent under the pressure of illness and financial worries, he insisted that they had parted in such "apparent harmony,"[6] that he could not believe Sir Ralph was acting with her sanction.

A letter from Annabella to Augusta, followed by a second dogged letter to Byron himself, left little room for doubt of that, and not even a stream of appeals from Byron at his most contrite or insinuating could reach her. It was Byron's and Augusta's belief that if he could only have *seen* her they could have made it up, but from the opening manoeuvres it had been a deliberate part of the Milbanke strategy to keep her out of his way, and with every day that distanced Annabella from her old self and Piccadilly, his hold on her weakened.

There can never be any doubt, though, that the tragedy which now began to unfold was of Byron's making, or one that he could have escaped, but to do that would have been to renege on those very instincts that had pushed him into the marriage in the first place. By the middle of February even his most loyal friends had recognised that a separation was inevitable, and yet with a self-destructive recklessness that is either the most baffling mystery or the key to the whole business, Byron refused to grasp the chance while the stakes were still relatively low.

The moment, however, that the issue is posed in such a way, "mystery" or "key" cease to be viable alternatives, for when in the whole of Byron's life were the stakes anything but high? From the first day of his married life he had seen Annabella as the incarnation of a world of which he wanted no part, and the brutal truth is that he had not married the most unsuitable woman in England to let her quietly escape him now on the grounds of mental cruelty or mutual incompatibility.

There is, in fact, for all its apparent contradictions—his attempts at reconciliation, the gestures of penitence, the legal stalling—a terrible and remorseless logic to Byron's behaviour that links it directly back to those months before his proposal to Annabella Milbanke. In his journals and letters at that time he had tried to convince himself that marriage was a last hope of "salvation," but if at some superficial level he did manage to delude himself, his choice of anyone so supremely unfit as Annabella betrayed a deeper compulsion to make it the pretext for the battle that now finally beckoned.

In Lawrence's vision there is always this suicidal element in the fall of the aristocrat, but it is important to remember too that for Byron social destruction and creative survival were one and the same thing. In the supreme masterpieces of his exile he would show what he could do when freed from the stifling restrictions of English life, and in his blind determination to turn the separation from a private into a public issue, from a matter of domestic difference into the great test of principles that it became, he was simply obeying imperatives that he could no more resist than he could have become Bob Southey.

And if it was a battle that he wanted, a tactical error from the Byron camp made sure that the Milbankes were more than ready to oblige. Through the last days of January Annabella had continued to receive almost daily reports from Augusta on the state of Byron's physical and mental state, and on the 30th his cousin, George, brought another lengthy letter from her to Kirkby. "I shall tell George in a few words what I wish which is nearly as I expressed myself yesterday," Augusta had written, desperate to avert the separation for her own sake as well as Byron's and Annabella's,

> That you would *pause* a few days, consider the *probable* and *possible* consequences of this letter from ye effects on B—for they *must* affect *you & your child*. I am very strongly of opinion *revenge* will be uppermost & this from my late observations. What revenge could he take so effectual as depriving you of the child! & *who* could prevent him. Can *we* all say that a man who is not deranged *sufficiently* to admit of being *controuled* is unfit to have the care of his own child! & what would be the consequences to that child & your own feelings![7]

If Augusta imagined that she could frighten Annabella into compromise with this threat, she had fatally miscalculated. By her own admission there was scarcely a maternal bone in Annabella's whole body, but the mere thought of losing Ada was enough to trigger off among the Milbankes all those paranoid social anxieties Byron had been born to provoke.

The threat was also enough to bring Annabella more directly into the drama, and on 22 February, leaving Ada behind, she joined her father in London and for the first time told her lawyer, Stephen Lushington, of her suspicions of incest. Lushington had hoped before this first meeting that he might bring about a reconciliation, but with such an accusation in the air he knew that this was impossible, and over the next weeks Annabella composed under his direction the series of statements that collectively form the historical case against Byron and Augusta.

The separation drama had now taken on an independent life of its own, and if Augusta had any lingering hopes that she might still have some influence, those were destroyed when on 5 March the two "sisters" finally met for the first time since Annabella's departure. Annabella was "*perfectly determined* NEVER to return to him, happen what might," a shocked Augusta reported to Byron's friend Hodgson the same day, in a letter that tells us more about Annabella than all the legal documents of the separation put together,

> that if *her own* friends even *knelt* to her to do so she felt herself bound by every moral and religious duty to refuse . . . I never can describe Lady Bs appearance to you—but by comparing it to what I should imagine that of a Being of another world. She is positively reduced to a Skeleton—pale as *ashes*—a deep hollow tone of voice & a *calm* in her manner quite supernatural. She received *me* kindly, but that really appeared the only SURVIVING *feeling*—all else was *death like* calm. *I* never can forget it—never![8]

It was not just Byron's fate Augusta should have read into that icy calm, but her own too. In the weeks before this meeting Augusta had clung to her faith in the strength of Annabella's affection, but with the pressures from Lushington mounting and rumours of incest common currency now even among Eton schoolboys, she had become as necessary a casualty as Byron of Annabella's overwhelming need for respectability.

Through the rest of the month the two women continued to meet occasionally, but unknown to Augusta, Annabella had already begun that exquisite campaign of innuendo and muted half-confidences that she was to sustain for the next forty years. At the end of February she received a letter from an old friend of Augusta's begging her to scotch the rumours circulating London, but in the gap between what Mrs. Villiers asked and what Annabella was prepared to say, Augusta stood as exposed as if she had been openly denounced. "I deeply regret the reports which have been circulated relative to the causes of Separation between Lord Byron & myself," she wrote back,

> and none can occasion me more sorrow than that which you mention as reflecting on Augusta's character—but as I can *positively* assert that not one of the many reports now current, have been sanctioned or encouraged by me, my family, or my friends, I cannot consider myself in any degree responsible for them . . .

In the state of circumstances you must be aware that a publication of the real grounds of difference between Lord B. and myself would be extremely improper—and in conformity with the advice I have received, I *must* abstain from any further disclosure.9

It was not in the end, though, the pressures from her lawyers or parents that finally released Annabella from the ties of gratitude and affection, but an intervention of a very different sort. At the end of March Annabella was on the point of returning to Kirkby and Ada, when she received a note from Lady Caroline Lamb, asking to see her in secret for a moment before she left town.

There could scarcely be a more perfect demonstration of Byron's genius for uniting the most disparate elements of English society in a common cause against him than this meeting of polar opposites. In the first days of the separation Caroline had written to offer him her passionate support, but when her letter went unanswered she was determined to make him pay for the confidences and indiscretions that had left him dangerously in her power.

When Annabella met her at George Lamb's house, she found Caroline in a state of apparent agitation at the thought of breaking "solemn promises,"10 but with the interests of revenge and higher morality in such perfect conjunction the consciences of both were soon comfortably squared. "Oh I never knew what it was to love before," Caroline reported Byron confessing to her,

> there is a woman I love so passionately—she is with child by me, and if a daughter it shall be called *Medora*—11

Judging from Annabella's notes, it was Caroline's subsequent denunciations of Byron's homosexuality, his perversion of his page, Rushton, and his "unrestricted practice" in the east, that most jolted Annabella at the time, but it was the revelations over Augusta that lodged deepest. Caroline told her that from the time Augusta had arrived at Bennet Street in 1813 Byron had hinted at an illicit passion, and when Caroline had piqued him with the comment that whatever she might believe of him she would not credit it of Mrs. Leigh, he had brutally retorted that "the seduction had not given him much trouble."12

It did not matter whether the accusations were true or not, or that the source was so wildly unreliable, the meeting proved the final blow for Augusta, because it allowed Annabella to bend to her lawyer's demands without any apparent sacrifice of principle or consistency. Up until this point she could plausibly argue that so long as there was any doubt as to Augusta's guilt Christian duty dictated kindness, but in the name now of the same morality her obligations were plain.

On leaving Caroline she wrote to Lushington, telling him that her suspicions had now hardened to *"absolute* conviction."[13] Through an intermediary, she broke the news of a change of heart to Augusta, explaining that neither her spirits nor health would allow them to meet again. "I hope you will approve the purport of the accompanying letter to Mrs. Wilmot," she wrote in a prophetic covering note to Robert Wilmot, a cousin of Byron's,

> which is intended to convey to Augusta, with the least possible pain, the line of conduct that now appears necessary—for whatever a solitary moment of indignation may have prompted me to express, my permanent feelings will always be to soften, as far as my principles will permit, the misery that awaits her—[14]

It was a moment of tragedy for both of them, a moment when under the pressures of social necessity and self-preservation, their respective characters began to mutate into the forms of their later lives. There is no need to sentimentalise Augusta into a sort of wronged Hermione, but in these weeks either side of the separation, when she had first defied Byron to protect Annabella and then against all advice and self-interest stayed loyally at his side at Piccadilly, the pliancy at the heart of her character acquired a quality that has a kind of grandeur about it. "When all around grew drear and dark," Byron wrote in a celebration of her almost reckless selflessness,

> *And reason half withheld her ray-*
> *And hope but shed a dying spark*
> *Which more misled my lonely way;*
>
> *In that deep midnight of the mind,*
> *And that internal strife of heart,*

When dreading to be deem'd too kind,
The weak despair—the cold depart;

. . . .

Thou stood'st, as stands a lovely tree,
That still unbroke, though gently bent,
Still waves with fond fidelity
Its boughs above a monument.

The winds might rend—the skies might pour,
But there thou wert—and still wouldst be
Devoted in the stormiest hour
To shed thy weeping leaves o'er me.[15]

For someone as innately shy as Augusta, there could have been no crueller proof of the cost of her loyalty than the notorious incident just over a week later when she and Byron were both publicly cut at Lady Jersey's. From the very start of the crisis her courage had been of the private sort that shirks exposure, but as the separation battle entered its last days and Byron prepared to sign the papers and leave England for ever, it became the public contest he had always sought. "Lady Jersey had a party a few nights ago, at which *he* appeared to the surprise of the company," Annabella reported the incident to her mother with a shallow triumphalism that shows how far she had travelled since the first days of the separation,

> Mrs. G Lamb cut both him and Mrs. Leigh—Brougham & some other Gentlemen, *him.* Lady Jersey has since called on me. So have many people—Lady Derby three or four times . . .
> Mrs. Ellison, whose kindness has been most zealous, says that now one has an opportunity of knowing who are bad & good—that there never was a question which disclosed morals so decisively.[16]

When every act of Annabella's during these months is scrutinised, however, every single discrepancy in her different accounts of her marriage pounced on by Byron partisans, the crucial fact so often forgotten is that *she* was as much on trial as was Byron. In its earliest days their courtship might have progressed in the lax world of the "spider queen," but if Annabella had been married off by the rules of the Regency her separation and marriage were to be judged by a morality that we now think of as "Victorian."

And born of the political and religious convulsions of the six-teenth and seventeenth centuries, nurtured by Addisonian morality, held at bay for another century by the vigour and intelligence of the Augustan age, "Victorianism" was a force that only the most inde-pendent mind could have resisted. As the rumours of sexual deviancy circulated through London, England and the nineteenth century had found their true voice. To the old and familiar attacks of the Tory papers was added the snakelike voice of Henry Brougham; to the Manse-born outrage of Joanna Baillie, the slurs of the gutter press. Even Lady Melbourne, mercifully only two years from the grave, felt discretion the better part of valour. In the middle year of Lord Liverpool's premiership—while Thomas Bowdler was prepar-ing his notorious edition of Shakespeare and Shelley and the daugh-ter of Godwin and Mary Wollstonecraft were going into exile—his "corbeau blanc" knew there was nowhere a Byron could hide. "I was accused of every monstrous vice by public rumour and private ran-cour," he later wrote,

> my name, which had been a knightly or a noble one since my
> fathers helped to conquer the kingdom for William the Nor-
> man, was tainted. I felt that, if what was whispered and mut-
> tered was true, I was unfit for England; if false, England was
> unfit for me. I withdrew; but this was not enough. In other
> countries—in Switzerland, in the shadow of the Alps, and by
> the blue depths of the lakes—I was pursued and breathed
> upon by the same blight. I crossed the mountains, but it was
> the same; so I went a little farther, and settled myself by the
> waves of the Adriatic, like a stag at bay, who betakes him to
> the waters.[17]

For all the self-dramatisation of this apologia, not to mention a healthy dollop of equivocation, the hysteria which greeted the publication of *Don Juan* two years later underlines that Byron was essentially right. There would be the odd dissenting voice raised in its praise, but when the radical Thelwall and the apostate Wordsworth can join forces, William Roberts of the Evangelical, Tory-supporting *British Review* and the liberal *Edinburgh*'s Jeffrey share the same platform, one is looking at a country fighting for its moral life. "You will probably see Gifford, the Editor of the Quarterly Review," Wordsworth wrote to Crabb Robinson, a man who would later call Annabella "the most noble woman"[18] he had ever known,

> Tell him from me, if you think proper, that every true-born Englishman will regard the pretensions of the Review to the character of a faithful defender of the institutions of the country, as *hollow*, while it leaves that infamous publication Don Juan unbranded . . . What avails it to hunt down Shelley, whom few read, and leave Byron untouched?[19]

But if in a land of "true-born Englishmen" there was nowhere for Byron to hide, there was still less chance, on this cusp of the Georgian and Victorian ages, of a woman escaping her share of criticism. In his letters and poems Byron had always addressed Annabella in the classic terms of nineteenth century fiction as "angel" or "devil," and as the rumours surrounding her marriage grew louder she could only be one or the other, the "pure woman" enshrined in the fantasies of the coming age or her demonic "other"—Jane Eyre or Bertha Mason, Amelia Sedley or Becky Sharpe, Mina Murray or Lucy Westenra, the "Annabella" that Byron had imagined when he first saw her, or another Caroline Lamb, whose rampant sexuality was already degenerating into the madness of her last broken days. "How could you go on?"[20] Annabella was asked by Lady Ann Barnard, as if somehow the integrity of all womanhood had been compromised by her silence. Why had she not returned to her father's home from Halnaby in the first days of her honeymoon? How could a woman of any purity have remained in that Piccadilly household with her suspicions, Mrs. Stowe needed to know. How could she protect and befriend a woman guilty of Augusta's crimes? How could she have invited Augusta in the first place? Or left her there, with a man she believed deranged, if she suspected the danger? How could she allow any gratitude or scruple of conscience to stand in the way of sterner moral obligations? "The most degraded of street walkers in the Haymarket was a worthier character" than a woman who could have lived with those suspicions, a Victorian journalist wrote. "How weak, and worse than weak," another writer condemned her,

> delicacy should have died, and nature was privileged to show—if such there were—the records of uttermost pollution.[21]

In a sense, Annabella had only herself to blame for this crisis, because it was her decision alone to make incest an issue of the separation. The accounts of her first meetings with her lawyer, Lushington, make it plain how wary he was of any such accusations, but from the moment that Augusta became any part of the equation Annabella could either be sullied with the taint of her own sexuality or begin the metamorphosis from wife to "madonna," and from madonna into that disembodied and sexless spirit from a higher world that became the final, hideous avatar of Victorian femininity.

And only Annabella knew what a long journey that was, how deeply compromised she was by Byronic "sin," just how vulnerable she was to any question of when she first knew of Byron's and Augusta's relationship. Over the years she would shunt that moment backwards or forwards as the varying demands of drama, morality or legal advantage required, and yet if there is one thing that no tampering can disguise it is that in her fascination with the Byrons she had willed herself to an ignorance long past any time that was humanly possible to sustain.

To any neutral, the misery of her honeymoon, the anxieties of a bride imprisoned by the snows of Halnaby, or the claustrophobic misery of Piccadilly would be explanation enough for any equivocation but not to the over scrupulous mind of Annabella. Over the years in public she might justify her passivity as Christian charity or the uncertainty of innocence, but in that complex, morbid conscience of hers she knew that she had allowed herself to be tangled in a web of deception and self-deception subtler and more morally dangerous than anything the "spider" had woven for her.

These scruples have come to seem in many ways so alien, the language in which they are invariably couched so unattractive, that it is easy to forget how seriously they preyed on a young woman of twenty-four whose conscience had been shaped by early nineteenth-century evangelicalism. In the last statement she made about her life with Byron the year before she died, Annabella described the temptations of the kind of moral relativism that she had faced in her marriage, and of the sterner imperatives of religion that had steeled her against them: "I felt a responsibility for him as well as myself," she wrote

> and when my own interpretation of the *natural law* was clouded by my feelings, I referred to the *Revealed* will—in this sense J. Christ may indeed be said to have been my Saviour—I found in his precepts that "immutable morality" which the reason of man is often incapable of discerning.[22]

To anyone who can think like this, it would be no consolation either that there had been no moment of choice, no incident that forced her to see the love of Byron and Augusta for what it was; there had been no balancing of suspicions and probabilities, but only a gradual slide into acquiescence that was so much easier to bear than the alternatives. In the early days of her marriage when she begged Augusta to be her "ONLY friend" she can have had little idea of the unholy compact she was forming, but long before that cold January morning when she left Byron's house for the last time she knew that she had crossed some invisible boundary that separated her married self from the Seaham moralist for good.

After the first desperate week of the honeymoon, too, when Byron emerged from the blackness of his wedding day, there would seem to have been a period of emotional and sexual happiness that left an even deeper scar on her psyche. From the earliest correspondence of her marriage it is clear that she took an almost coquettish pleasure in her own sexuality, but as she was swept up in the public demand for female "purity," this was a truth about herself that had to be ruthlessly suppressed.

During her first London seasons Annabella had earned a reputation for cool restraint—"good, amiable, and sensible," the Duchess of Devonshire had called her, "but cold, prudent and reflecting"[23]—but even before their marriage Byron had recognised something more passionate in his future wife. As early as May 1812 he had read some verses of hers and expressed his surprise at the strength of feeling that lay behind her "placid countenance,"[24] and on the first visit to Seaham after his engagement he had written back to Lady Melbourne confirming his suspicions of a side to Annabella's nature her aunt had never guessed at. "She is as you know a perfectly good person," he wrote with the cynical candor he habitually employed with the "spider," "but I think not only her feelings and affections—but her passions stronger than we supposed . . . for my part I have lately had recourse to the eloquence of action (which Demosthenes calls the first part of oratory) & find it succeeds very well & makes her very quiet which gives me some hope of the efficacy of the 'calming process' so renowned in 'our philosophy.' "[25]

There is no reason to think that Byron's tactics as a husband were any different from those as a suitor and no evidence either that Annabella ever objected. Annabella's own early letters as a married woman are sadly—and perhaps significantly—missing, but an arch remark of Augusta's in reply to a letter from the new bride suggests a sense of physical satisfaction worlds apart from anything she would later admit to. "I am glad B's spirits do not decrease with THE moon," Augusta wrote to Annabella at the end of January—one of a number of comments that reflects the sense of emotional and physical ease that among all the disquiet over Byron's moods or drinking filled Annabella's own bulletins to her "sister" at this time. "I rather suspect he rejoices at the discovery of your 'ruling passion for mischief in private.' "[26]

"Were you then *never* happy?"[27] Byron wrote to her in genuine bewilderment after the separation, and Annabella could no more have answered that truthfully to herself than to her lawyers. There is nothing in her correspondence during her marriage that remotely suggests the unremitting misery of later statements, but in her memory even the briefest flash of fulfilment had to be buried under the visceral horror of Byron's footsteps echoing outside her bedroom door at Piccadilly or Six Mile Bottom.

It is interesting, though, that almost alone in the Piccadilly household—Augusta included—Annabella seemed to know that even in Byron's blackest moods she was in no physical danger from him. In the weeks after the birth it is plain from the servants' testimony that he tried to force himself on her, but that poignant cry from Kirkby that she would prefer even the coal hole at Piccadilly to the safety of her parents' home conjures up an image of emotional servitude more complicated, elusive—and ultimately destructive—than physical brutality alone might indicate.

And if in the end there is nothing that lies so completely or properly beyond the reach of biography than another's sexuality, the obsessive denial that began with the separation process suggests the guilt of the disillusioned acolyte rather than the cruder trauma of the victim.* It is notable that in a literary context Byron's bitterest enemies invariably came from the ranks of his former disciples, and when, as in Annabella's case, the Byronic "contagion" was literal and not figurative—the impregnation physical and not mental—the revulsion was of a different order altogether.

If this must be speculative, there is corroborative evidence of Annabella's disgust and self-disgust in the pattern of physical illnesses that began with her marriage and dogged the rest of her adult life. There has been a lot of savage play made of the "professional" invalidism that became such a feature of her long widowhood, and yet one hardly needs the tools of psychology to recognise in her history of nervous illness, mimetic pains, and bouts of bulimia, the physical symptoms of those suppressive, hysterical disorders that fill the medical textbooks of her age.

The behavioural patterns of her whole life, too—the self-dramatisation, the emotional lability, the "sibling" rivalry with Augusta, the violent alternatives of love and hatred—read like case notes on hysteria and whether her illnesses were psychosomatic or not it is revealing that she herself traced her disorders to the womb and the birth of her daughter. "He is equally positive that all my complaints are dependent upon a disorder of the womb," she passed on a medical opinion to her mother as early as 1819, foreshadowing, perhaps, one reason for the emotional frigidity of her relations with her adult daughter,

> that has existed ever since Ada's birth . . . The vessels of that region are in consequence overloaded and will require continual depletion by cupping and leeches.[28]

---

*In a brave book, written in a very different sexual and legal climate more than forty years ago, G. Wilson Knight was less tentative. In "Lord Byron's Marriage" he argued that the fear and guilt that drove Annabella was that of consensual sodomy, a conviction he largely based on the Don Leon poems, to which he gives a kind of apostolic authority on the subject of the marriage that derived from Byron himself.

That last sentence is particularly revealing, and at times of emotional crisis throughout her life she regularly cupped or "depleted" her abdomen, as if to rid herself of the contagion of her own sexuality, to "drain" herself—as Byron accused her of doing to their daughter—of the Byronic blood that had infected her. "Yet, though dull hate as duty should be taught," Byron addressed the infant Ada in the third canto of *Childe Harold* with a prescience that would only be finally realised in the family vault at Hucknall,

> *I know that thou will love me; though my name*
> *Should be shut from thee, as a spell still fraught*
> *With desolation, and a broken claim:*
> *Though the grave closed between us,—'twere the same,*
> *I know that thou wilt love me; though to drain*
> *My blood from out thy being were an aim*
> *And an attainment,—all would be in vain,*
> *Still thou wouldst love me, still that more than life retain.*[29]

Byron's imagery was unerring, because if one incarnation among all the myths of Byronic corruption might define Annabella's trauma in the months after the separation, it is that of the vampire. In the popular fiction of the century a loose association of Byron and vampirism would come to enjoy a harmless vogue, but for the woman who had blindly accepted him in marriage, the identification of Byron with physical and moral pollution that began with Polidori's *The Vampyre* had a complex and erotically charged significance that was at once more disturbing and liberating. "It happened in the dissipations attendant upon a London winter," *The Vampyre* opens with a macabre reprise of that *annus mirabilis* of 1812—the year of *Childe Harold*, Caroline Lamb and Annabella Milbanke's first sight of Byron,

> there appeared at the various parties, a nobleman more remarkable for his singularities, than his rank. He gazed upon the mirth around him, as if he could not participate therein. Apparently, the light laughter of the fair only attracted his attention, that he might by a look quell it and throw fear into those breasts where thoughtlessness reigned ... His peculiarities caused him to be invited to

every house; all wished to see him, and those who had been accustomed to violent excitement, and now felt the weight of ennui, were pleased at having something in their presence capable of engaging their attention. In spite of the deadly hue of his face, which never gained a warmer tint, either from the blush of modesty, or from the strong emotion of passion, though its form and outline were beautiful, many of the female hunters after notoriety attempted to win his attentions, and gain, at least, some marks of what they might term affection: yet such was the apparent caution with which he spoke to the virtuous wife and innocent daughter, that few knew he ever addressed himself to females. He had, however, the reputation of a winning tongue; and whether it was that it even overcame the dread of his singular character, or that they were moved by his apparent hatred of vice, he was as often among those females who form the boast of their sex from their domestic virtues, as among those who sully it by their vices.*30

It is fascinating, in fact, to see the ways in which expressions of Byronic "evil" that became the stock metaphors of nineteenth century fiction seemed to have an almost *literal* urgency for acolytes who fell under his spell. In the *roman à clef* with which she took her revenge on Byron in 1816, Caroline Lamb likened his impact on England to that of infection, and at the heart of Mary Shelley's *The Last Man*, written in the wake of his death at Missolonghi, lies precisely the same sense of physical contagion that *The Vampyre* and *Glenarvon* both voiced.

There is, of course, nothing new or unusual in the harnessing of "sin" to disease in this way, but in the mythologising of Byron to which these three fictions contributed there was a slightly different process at work. From the Black Death to AIDS, disease and illness

---

*For all its plagiarisms—it was based on an idea of Byron's—and the commercial deceptions with which it was launched, the story has won Polidori, Byron's talented but emotionally unstable doctor, a place in literary history that in one sense at least is deserved. *The Vampyre* is no better or worse than the hundreds of gothic or horror stories that filled nineteenth-century magazines, but with the Byronic figure of Lord Ruthven, Polidori changed the mythology of the vampire for good, rescuing him from his roots in the peasant folklore of eastern Europe, and reinventing him in the guise of the "aristocratic predator" that in popular western culture he has remained ever since.

have been routinely ascribed to moral causes, and yet in the case of Byron cause and effect have always been subtly complicated, the physical and sexual glamour of the living man being first stigmatised as moral threat and then in turn metamorphosed back into images of plague or vampirism that stretch out beyond the grave to endanger the world.

And if three such different, but dependent, personalities as Polidori, Caroline Lamb and Mary Shelley, can have seen Byron in these similar terms, it is unlikely his wife would not also have clutched at the same kind of associations. One of the subtler attractions of the vampire myth for the nineteenth century was that it enabled people to project a sense of inner pollution onto an external enemy, and for Annabella more than anyone, the haunting consciousness of her own submission—the secret fear of her own sexuality—would have given this demonisation of Byron an almost redemptive urgency.

If there was a kind of comfort in the notion of Byron as an *external* threat, however, the fictional rituals of vampirism would come to enshrine a more disturbing aspect of Annabella's predicament as she tried to reinvent the psychological and sexual realities of married life. In the popular mythology of the creature it is always the victim who invites the enemy across the threshold, and the truth that Annabella could never have admitted to herself let alone her lawyers or parents was that it was *she* who had courted Byron—*she* who had renewed their relationship in 1813—*she* who had surprised him even before their marriage at Seaham with her ardour—*she* who had joked of her sexuality to Augusta—*she* (and her subsequent denial and self-denial were so complete that her descendants could not believe the evidence when they saw it) who had invited Augusta into her household and begged her to stay.

As the separation ground towards its conclusion, more mundane arguments over money and procedures also inevitably took their toll, but the sense of guilt that fuelled Annabella's growing intransigence cannot be ignored. If she could have talked to the one person in a position to understand the moral and emotional confusions of her feelings it might have been different, but cut off as she was from Augusta and surrounded by advisers and sympathisers determined to raise her on a pedestal, Annabella abandoned herself to the myth of pure womanhood her public demanded.

Given the pressures on her, the process was probably inevitable, but during these last weeks of the separation battle Byron's own behaviour certainly made her retreat into martyrdom and denial all the easier. On 18 March he sent Annabella a draft version of the first verses he ever wrote for her, and whatever sympathy they temporarily won for him at large—and schoolgirls in America wept over them—their manipulative dishonesty only hardened her resolve. "Fare thee well!," the verses begin and end, with every shade of emotional exploitation and half-truth sandwiched in between,

> *Fare thee well! and if forever,*
> *Still for ever, fare thee well:*
> *Even though unforgiving, never*
> *'Gainst thee shall my heart rebel.*
> *Fare thee well! thus disunited,*
> *Torn from every nearer tie,*
> *Sear'd in heart, and lone, and blighted,*
> *More than this I scarce can die.*[31]

"Serenely purest of her sex that live," Byron wrote of her again a fortnight later, "But wanting one sweet weakness—to forgive."[32] It was not a sentiment likely to mollify Annabella. It was not even a charge that she had yet earned. It did, though, invert a truth that, in one of those flashes of insight which sometimes illuminate her pages of soul-searching, Annabella herself recognised. He had injured her too badly, she noted, ever to be able to forgive her.

He had, also, hurt her too much for the Milbanke camp to forgive or bend. Right through to the middle of April 1816, three months after Annabella had first left Piccadilly, Byron continued to struggle against the inevitable, contesting detail by detail the terms of the separation, and with every delay making his position worse. There had never been any question of Annabella's lawyers using the charge of incest in court against him, but with the swell of public opinion running strongly in their favour and every week spawning fresh rumours, Lushington knew that they had no need.

With the end only a matter of time, Byron prepared to leave the country. On Sunday 14 April, Byron and Augusta said their final goodbyes, brother and sister both convulsed with grief at the certainty that they would never see each other again. A week later his lawyer Hanson brought the deed of separation to Piccadilly, and with a final curse for Annabella's helpless old confidante, Mrs. Clermont, Byron signed it and, two days later, on 23 April—abandoning birds, squirrel and everything else in the house to the bailiffs—set off for Dover and exile.

If there could scarcely be a more symbolic day for the outsider to quit London, or a more defiant way to do it than in his new coach modelled on Napoleon's campaigning carriage, Byron marked his arrival in Dover the next day with a second and less grandiose gesture of identification. The sea was too rough for the Ostend packet to sail, and with Hobhouse and that other exile-in-waiting, Scrope Davies, he made a pilgrimage to the churchyard where Charles Churchill, eighteenth-century satirist and archetypal outcast, lay buried. Byron lay down on Churchill's grave, measuring himself, as it were, for his future role in life. "I stood beside the grave of him Who blazed the Comet of a season," he recalled in a poem that veers uneasily between pastiche Wordsworth and sober self-questioning,

> *And I saw*
> *The humblest of all sepulchres, and gazed*
> *With not the less of sorrow and of awe*
> *On that neglected turf and quiet stone,*
> *With name no clearer than the names unknown,*
> *Which lay unread around it.*
> *And is this all? I thought—and do we rip*
> *The veil of Immortality, and crave*
> *I know not what of honour and of light,*
> *Through unborn ages, to endure this blight,*
> *So soon, and so successless.*[33]

Had Byron left no other hostage to fortune but his fame, he could have afforded his philosophy, but he had fatally done more than that. "I have just parted from Augusta," he had written bitterly to Annabella the previous week, the same day that he had seen his sister off to Newmarket for the final time,

> Almost the last being you had left me to part with—& the only unshattered tie of my existence—wherever I may go— & I am going far—you & I can never meet again in this world—nor in the next—let this content or atone.—If any

accident occurs to me—be kind to *her.* If she is then
nothing—to her children . . . I say therefor—be kind to her
& hers—for never has she acted or spoken otherwise towards
you—she has ever been your friend—this may seem value-
less to one who has now so many:—be kind to her.34

Byron never wrote a more thoughtless letter. Exhausted but triumphant, Annabella had been handed the blue print for her whole
future life. "But first on earth as Vampire sent," Byron had written in
a mood of extravagant self-parody in the Giaour,

> *Thy corse shall from its tomb be rent:*
> *Then ghastly haunt thy native place,*
> *And suck the blood of all thy race;*
> *There from thy daughter, sister, wife,*
> *At midnight drain the stream of life;*
> *Yet loathe the banquet which perforce*
> *Must feed thy livid living corse:*
> *Thy victims, ere they yet expire,*
> *Shall know the demon for their sire,*
> *As cursing thee, thou cursing them,*
> *Thy flowers are wither'd on the stem.*35

It was such a threat that Annabella was coming to see in Byron. "And
shall I take a thing so blind," another apostate Byronist, Tennyson,
would demand in a passage that might have been written for her,

> *Embrace it as a common good,*
> *Or crush it like a vice of blood*
> *On the threshold of the mind.*36

For Annabella, as for Tennyson, there could in the end be only one
answer. She had felt not just the glamour, but the dangerous, liberating, potency of Byronic freedom and would never forgive herself for
having almost succumbed. At the age of just twenty-three, reunited
after almost two months with Byron's sole legitimate daughter, her
course was set. Self-preservation and moral duty pointed her in the
same direction. She owed an obligation not just to herself but to

Byron. She had failed him but she could save those that he had loved from the pollution of his influence. Her life's crusade, prosecuted with all the unquestioning, melodramatic conviction of the saved, would be to redeem the Giaour's blood-line from the curse of its own inheritance.

THE KINDNESS OF SISTERS

O n the same day that Byron sailed from Dover, Annabella left for Kirkby, her job in London complete. For a short time after the publication of "Fare Thee Well" public support might have wavered, but for a month at least the tide had been running strongly in her favour, the sympathy won by Byron undone by the savage sequel he directed against a defenceless Mrs. Clermont. "Good God," Mrs. George Lamb had written after Annabella asked her not to discuss the separation,

> can I sit by and hear him defended when I know him to be the greatest Villain on earth, and you the most injured and excellent of human beings. I really *cannot*. As to the other person, I do not wish to reveal her faults, for I could almost pity her, when I think how unhappy she must be and I look upon her more as his victim than as his accomplice.[1]

As Annabella returned to her family, it was to take possession of the more palpable spoils suggested in a cartoon George Cruikshank drew of Byron's departure from Dover. He stands in a bottle-laden rowing boat taking him out to the Ostend packet, the Drury Lane actress Charlotte Mardyn on one arm, a couple of doxies clinging to a leg apiece, a smirk on his face and his hat doffed in a last gesture of ironic farewell to the receding shore line of England. Out of his mouth, the key words heavily underlined in case the irony was lost on anyone, come those lines from his poem to Annabella,

All my faults perchance thou knowest—
All my madness—none can know;—
Fare thee well! thus disunited—
Torn from every nearer tie,
Seared in heart—& love—& blighted—
More than this I scarce can die!!!!!

It is not so much the richly comic figure in the rowing boat, though, that makes this cartoon so relevant here, as the background. On the left is just visible the stern of the vessel that will take him to freedom. On the right, is a miniature England, church spire rising from the kind of landscape that had so bored Byron, the cliffs of Dover lapped still by a pre-Arnoldian sea of certainty. On the white cliff top, guardian of its morals—half Blakean figure of innocence, half archangel at the gates of Eden—stands Annabella, her daughter Ada in her arms.

It is the presence of Ada in this cartoon, as in another entitled "The Separation," that pinpoints the role that Annabella had found for herself with the end of her marriage and return to Kirkby. It is ironic that both cartoons should have made such insistent capital of a daughter that Annabella had not actually seen for two months, but in an important sense they were right because it was on that child and the future she embodied that Annabella lodged her moral justification to pursue the course that would consume the rest of her life.

When one is talking about the "life" of Annabella, though, one is talking about an inner life that, as with so many men and women touched by Byron, seems to run parallel with an outer existence with which it has little obvious connection. If one charted Annabella's external career in the years after Byron's exile, one might see a woman gradually freeing herself from the legacy of marriage, moving with age and recovering self-confidence from the private to the public sphere, immersing herself in the reforming issues of the day, doing good works, founding schools and raising a daughter, with seemingly nothing but chronic ill-health and something akin to the terminal restlessness of the dying to link her to her secret life that fed off the corpse of her married self.

In a piece of autobiography she wrote at the age of sixty-seven she spoke vividly of the cold unreality of the outside world to her during these years, and if it is the Annabella of Reigate one is after—the frail and driven figure of old age—then it is in the history of that feverish other world with its inescapable realities of guilt and fear that one has to look.

In the first weeks after Byron's departure, however, it was as if even that was dead. During the last phase of the separation struggle Annabella had lived on the adrenaline of battle, but back with her parents and cut off from the excitement of a controversy, the inevitable physical and emotional reaction set in. "I feel more weakness now than during my greater exertions," she confessed at the beginning of June, "Sleepless nights, and head-achy days."[2]

By the time that Annabella wrote that letter, just six weeks after arriving at Kirkby, she had also clearly had enough of the enforced intimacy of home life, and on 8 June she set off on the cross-country journey with Ada to Lowestoft where she had taken a cottage for the sea air. On their journey westwards the crowds came out in force to stare at Byron's wife and child, and yet judging from the easy tone of Annabella's reports, notoriety held fewer fears for her than the oblivion of Kirkby. "The people at Ely and Peterborough Stared at us very much," Annabella wrote, as if recording her infant daughter's impressions, "and Mama said we were 'Lionesses.' "[3]

As Benita Eisler has shrewdly underlined, Annabella's months at Lowestoft mark an important phase in her development, because it was there that she made her first contacts with a group of those "saints" who provided nineteenth-century Evangelicalism with its moral and social leadership. In her early years there had always been an essentially cerebral quality to Annabella's religious convictions, but under the influence now of the rector of Harrow, John Cunningham, whom she met during this Lowestoft summer, Annabella's faith and language began to assume the distinctive tones of her maturity. "I have talked to Cunningham a great deal about Lord Byron," she reported back to Kirkby on 7 August,

> which his Harrow connections with him naturally led to, and found him very accessible to Truth. I have accompanied the Cunninghams to some of the Cottages of the Poor, and have very much admired the way in which they administered the comforts of Christianity . . . I have done as much good as I could amongst the sufferers in this place, & I fancy there will be a general mourning at my departure.[4]

If there is any evidence needed of the dangers of Evangelicalism to a woman of Annabella's temperament it can be found in that letter. In the immediate days after her flight from Piccadilly there was an astonishing lack of priggishness or rancour in her memories of Byron, but one only has to look at the complacent certainty of her use of the word "Truth" to see how far Lowestoft had taken her towards identifying her own cause and that of public virtue as one and the same.

For all the contacts with Evangelicalism, however, the Cunninghams' influence was one of tone rather than substance, because long before Lowestoft she had already begun her campaign of self-justification. In the final separation agreement the question of Ada's future had been left undecided, and although there was never any real prospect that Byron might hand her over to Augusta's care, the threat of it had been excuse enough for Annabella to resume those contacts with her sister-in law that answered to some of the deepest but most unattractive needs of her personality.

To be fair to Annabella, however, it had cost her far more to cut herself off from Augusta in the first place than it ever had from her husband. In the first days after leaving Piccadilly she had clearly felt a real anguish at losing Byron, but more startling is not that she could have still loved him after everything she had suffered, but the speed and determination with which she was able to crush her affections.

It was her great fear, she told Lady Ann Barnard, after the separation, that she would think only too kindly of Byron, but while she genuinely believed that, she had misunderstood an important aspect of her attraction to him. From the first day that she had seen him he had been at least as much a "cause" as a man for her, whereas with Augusta every feeling was real, forged by the strangest of intimacies, tested among the miseries of Newmarket and Piccadilly, and rewarded by an affection and kindness that was genuine on both sides.

If Byron and his wife brought out the worst in each other, the oddity of the marriage is that Augusta and Annabella had brought out the best. There were certainly times during that year when Annabella could have "plunged a dagger"[5] into her rival's heart, but those spasms of jealousy and anger were balanced by months of reciprocal support without which neither of them could have survived a hostility that at times fused them in Byron's mind into a single, composite enemy.

Even during the most antagonistic moments of the separation, too, when the gap between the two women had inevitably widened to an open breach, the most partisan of Annabella's supporters could never forget the protective kindness Augusta had shown her. "[In] regard to Mrs. Leigh," Mrs. Clermont had written to Lady Noel, trying to allay those fears that Byron would remove Ada from her mother and put her in Augusta's care,

> you have I think been very unjust, as I am confident, how-ever maliciously he may act, it never has been her wish to take it from A or ever will be, although I feel she must have felt herself much hurt of late by a change of manner on this side. I know she has acted weakly but I do firmly believe her intentions have been good—nor can I ever forget the kind-ness A experienced from her the latter part of the time she was in Piccadilly; even for her life, I believe we may thank Mrs. Leigh.[6]

Something more than gratitude should have bound Annabella to Augusta, however, because if she needed to free herself of her hus-band, she could not banish Augusta without—in Falstaff's phrase—banishing the world. There was a concentration and destructive intent to Byron that Annabella rightly feared, but with all the messi-ness of her circumstances, with her hopeless husband and ailing chil-dren, her endless pregnancies and financial crises, her mixture of kindness and selfishness, of moral laxity, self-sacrifice and stumbling pieties, Augusta was her lifeline to a fuller sense of humanity.

More disturbingly, though, Augusta was also her lifeline to a fuller sense of her own personality, and as with Byron, it was not so much Augusta's faults as the reality of her *fascination* that turned Annabella against a woman to whose sense and kindness she owed so much. In later life she would tell the novelist Harriet Beecher Stowe that there had never been anything physically or mentally attractive about Augusta, but it was actually she who was the "Byron" Annabella had always wanted, alien but sympathetic, sensuous but unaggressive, fallen but pliant in ways that answered to all her most chronic needs. "Dearest A.," she had written in the first days of the separation,

> I know you feel for me as I do for you, and perhaps am better understood than I think. You have been, ever since I knew

you, my best comforter, and will so remain, unless you grow tired of the office, which may well be.7

"In this at least I am 'truth itself,' " she wrote again, in the same vein,

> when I say that, whatever the situation may be, there is no one whose society is dearer to me, or can contribute more to my happiness. These feelings will not change under any circumstances, and I should be grieved if you did not understand them. Should you hereafter condemn me I shall not love you less . . . I wish you to consider yourself, if you could be wise enough to do that for the first time in your life.*8

This profound and passionate attraction was something that Annabella could never admit to her family during the separation, nor increasingly to herself. Throughout most of her future life her closest friendships would be with other women, but if Annabella had so much as suspected a sexual dimension to her feelings for Augusta it would have only doubled her resolve to crush her.

The story of her campaign for the "redemption" of Augusta in the months after Byron's exile forms as ugly an episode as any in the bitter history of the marriage. It is difficult to think of the ghost-like figure at Mivart's Hotel and forget the tragedy that lay behind it, and yet it is harder still to imagine what circumstances could ever justify the campaign of mental cruelty with which Annabella attempted to stamp out the memories of her own complicity in Byronic "sinfulness."

"Be kind to Augusta and her children,"9 Byron had asked her in a fit of deluded optimism, and there is something awesome in the ferocity with which she interpreted that injunction. Under the repellent guise of duty there was no refinement of moral tyranny that could not be justified, no letters to and from Byron that should not be censored, no retrospective adjustment of fact, no minute advance or withdrawal of affections—held over her like a prisoner's privileges—that was not warranted by the duty of reducing Augusta to that proper "spirit of humility and repentance."10

---

*When these letters—and they are not the only ones—came to light after Annabella's death, her family was so astonished that they thought them forgeries.

It would have been unpleasant enough if this had been a silent and solitary persecution, but throughout her life Annabella's treatment of Augusta was characterised by a mix of public forbearance and private indiscretions. During the days of the separation her suspicions of incest were confided only to her lawyers and parents, but on the day before she left London for Kirkby, and Byron for the continent, she paid a visit to a friend of Augusta's that marked a significant broadening of her campaign.

That friend was the forty-year-old great-great-great granddaughter of Oliver Cromwell, the Hon. Mrs. George Villiers, the former Theresa—or Therese as she preferred to be known—Parker. She had first written to Annabella at the end of February in an attempt to stem the rumours sweeping through London, but from Annabella's first visit she seems to have become a willing convert to her side, united in the pursuit of what she labelled "the *great* object,"[11] and only divided by the tactics that should be used. "My dear Mrs. Villiers," Annabella wrote to her from Kirkby less than two weeks after their meeting, explaining why she had decided not to confront Augusta directly with incest as her new ally was advocating,

> . . .Your argument that the Physician should know the whole of the Malady, would lead me to regret that a natural horror of the subject, and a feeling for her, had kept me so long silent to you—and even when I did speak, the only effect I meant to produce was that of inclining you to forgive whilst you lamented this *impression on my mind*, without at all convincing you of its justice. Nor do I now assert that it is in my power to convince you, though my own opinion is unalterable—but you shall receive any information by which you may be enabled to do her good. My great object, next to the Security of my Child, is, therefore, the restoration of her mind to that state which is religiously desirable. I differ from you in regard to the effects of an unequivocal communication. It is easier for the injured than the guilty to pardon, & I doubt if any woman would forgive to another such an avowal . . .
>
> Perhaps no human being can create the spirit of humility and repentance which I pray God to bestow upon her—If you would do her good, you judge most wisely in appearing

wholly unsuspicious—Let us not be impatient with a "mind diseased"—but wait to assist the effects of Time—Absence—and I hope—Solitude—for it is not whilst reflection is excluded by the engagements of Society, that moral principle can be revived . . . Whatever may be the intermediate circumstances, it will be in her power to reclaim my friendship whenever it can *really* serve her for more than worldly purposes—to speak seriously as I feel, I regard this as a Christian duty—[12]

If this note of Christian oppression seems repulsive enough, Mrs. Villiers was ready to go even further in their bid to rescue Augusta from "the most infernal plot it had ever entered the heart of man to conceive." "Now I cannot but think," she wrote back on 18 May to a further detailed apologia from Annabella, suggesting in her crusading enthusiasm a way to break Augusta's faith in Byron's loyalty,

that if she was told by some proper person, & perhaps no one could do this so properly as Mr. Wilmot, [a cousin of Byron's co-opted to Annabella's cause] how completely he had committed her to you: if she could be told certain facts which could only be known to her thro' him & which perhaps *she* must *feel* to be true—if above all she could be made to believe the fact you mention in your letter of his having betrayed her in writing to two or three women, surely nobody but *Calantha* [the heroine of Caroline Lamb's *Glenarvon*] could remain infatuated after that. With such knowledge absence would essentially save her. Without it I cannot but foresee a probable evil—that from the state of their circumstances he may propose to her to go abroad to him . . . You say she would never forgive you for such an avowal of your knowledge—but who is to suffer for her forgiveness—not you—but her—& this she has sense enough to see after the first *entetement* is over—& her affection for her children will I think prevent her attempting to make any resistance that shd. produce an *eclat* which must terminate in *her* ruin and theirs.[13]

There was clearly a real satisfaction for Annabella in these exchanges of confidences, but as she prepared to leave Kirkby for Lowestoft a war by proxy was no substitute for the real thing. Through the rest of May long and detailed letters did the rounds between Annabella, Theresa Villiers and even Wilmot, but it was Augusta herself Annabella was after and on the 23rd she announced her intention of extending a "limited intercourse"[14] to a woman she could not in truth live without. Her intention was, she told Theresa Villiers,

> to make *herself* acquainted with my real opinions & feelings, without binding me to avow them publicly, should she be so desperate in the first impulse—that it will nevertheless suspend this terror over her, to be used as her future dispositions and conduct may render expedient, whilst it leaves her the power of profiting by my forbearance, without compelling the utterly degrading confession of her own guilt.[15]

Alone and vulnerable at Newmarket, physically and emotionally exhausted by the separation crisis and the birth of her fifth child, dogged by incessant money worries and dependent for her very social existence on Annabella's patronage, Augusta was in no position to resist even the most insulting concession. While Byron was still in England she had stood by him with a wonderful disregard for her own reputation, but Augusta's courage was not of the kind to survive in isolation. "My dear Annabella," she wrote back on 6 June to the first, chilly offer of friendship, superbly dignified in defeat, but defeated for all that,

> . . . I cannot say that I am *wholly surprised* at its contents. Your silence towards me during so long an interval and when all *obvious* necessity for it must have ceased formed so decided a contrast to your former kindness to me—and to what *my Conscience tells me my conduct towards you deserved from you* that it could not but require some explanation . . . To general accusations I must answer in general terms—and if I were on my death Bed I could affirm as I *now* do that I have uniformly considered you and consulted your happiness before and above any thing in this world. No sister ever could have the claims upon me that *you* had—I felt it—& acted up to the feeling to the best of my judgement. We are all perhaps too much inclined to magnify our trials, yet I think I may venture to pronounce my situation to *have been & to be still* one of

extraordinary difficulty. I have been assured that the tide of public opinion has been so turned against my Brother that the least appearance of coolness on your part towards me would injure me most seriously—& I am therefore *for the sake of my children* compelled to accept from your *compassion* the "limited intercourse" which is all you can grant to one whom you pronounce no longer worthy of your esteem or affection.[16]

Even Annabella was impressed by the letter, but it was Augusta's last throw, the last time she ever appealed to the emotional *truth* of a relationship that no one but the two of them could have possibly recognised. For the next three months she would continue to plead her innocence of any *intent*, but long before she and Annabella finally met at the beginning of September the hauteur of this first reaction was gone, the "*pride* of innocence"[17] broken to a complete and increasingly masochistic subjection. "You would pity me did you know what I must *ever* feel," she wrote to the tormentor she called with decreasing irony her "Guardian Angel"

either in your absence or presence for having been *the cause* of one moment's unhappiness to you! But rely upon *one* thing. I will never *seek* to see you while it is *your wish* I should not— One ray of comfort & hope suggested itself in the thought that *we may meet again*—that *my future conduct* may conduce to it—Tell me—pray—of anything in that which could by any possibility atone for the past—in pity—tell it me dearest A. that I may have one more chance of happiness—[18]

There could be no more revealing proof of the despondency and fear that Augusta felt at this time than the depths to which she allowed Annabella to drag her. There was of course a sense in which with a husband and position at court she could do nothing but take friendship on any terms that it was offered, but within four months of Byron's exile she had so completely identified with the image of herself as victim that she was sending his letters on to Annabella and answering to her dictation. "His feelings towards you have varied," Annabella wrote to her on 30 July, from Lowestoft, where alternate bouts of gorging herself and taking out a boat to vomit at sea testify to her own nervous condition,

& they were very seldom suppressed with me—Sometimes he has spoken of you with compassion—sometimes with bitter scorn—& sometimes with dispositions more reprehensible . . . Till you feel that he has in reality been your worst friend—indeed, *not* your friend—you cannot altogether think rightly—yet I am far from thinking any uncharitable feelings are to follow—forgive him—desire his welfare—but resign the pernicious view of being his friend more nearly . . .

There is another reason too of the greatest weight—For the sake of your children—both as respects the world's opinion of yourself and still more from the injury young minds must receive in the society of one so unprincipled—I feel most anxious for your children in this respect, & for dear Georgiana particularly, whom, as you must remember he had every disposition to injure—[19]

It was still almost a month before Augusta and Annabella would meet again, and resume something like their old relationship, but in the meantime Augusta was risking nothing. "I have no idea of his returning," she wrote back on 5 August—just two weeks, that is, after Byron, alone at the Villa Diodati on the shore of Lake Geneva, had celebrated her constancy in his "Stanzas to Augusta,"

& if I gave way to my own forebodings, they wd incline me to think we should never meet again—but to dwell on such is useless—I assure you most solemnly—most truly—I have *long* felt that he has *not* been my friend—but from my heart I forgive him—& pray to God to forgive him & change his heart—to restore him to peace—& there is nothing I would not do which could be done consistently with my duty to God and to others to contribute to his good—how far & whether I may ever be able to do it is I think impossible to foresee—since *futurity* is veiled from us—I perfectly agree with you my dearest A that the *present* presents no hope of the sort—[20]

To be fair to Augusta, though, with the series of verses that began with "Stanzas," and climaxed the following summer with Manfred's vision of Astarte, Byron was giving her as much reason to fear as miss him. She had never at any time in their relationship been remotely possessive or selfish in her love, but from the first coded confessions of the *Bride of Abydos* and *Parasina* she had known only too well that there was an egotism to his that was prepared to engulf them both.

If that had been true while he was still in England, it was even more so abroad, where freedom and distance inured him to any of the consequences scandal might have for her. In his early letters to her from Switzerland there is a tenderness and sense of loss that is profoundly moving, but for all his real grief at losing Augusta, his retreat from England had not been exile but *escape*.

Byron had *needed* to get out of England, as he had brutally, egotistically needed to provoke Annabella into confrontation, and anyone who admires him has to accept that along with the charm, grace and kindness that make him so endlessly compelling. In his letters to Augusta and Lady Melbourne from as far back as 1813 he had spoke of his boredom and disgust with everything in English life, but it had needed the emotional and mental restraints of marriage to give the physical and claustrophobic urgency to his dissatisfaction necessary to propel him into action.

"God bless him for a gallant spirit and a kind one,"[21] Hobhouse had touchingly written in his journal for 25 April, after waving him farewell, and if that was no more than the truth it was truth in a sense that was only fully revealed in exile. It is only too easy to mistake coincidence for cause and effect, but it is impossible not to feel that Byron's growth as a poet and a man is directly linked to his decision to quit England. The triumphs of the years ahead with such poems as *Beppo* and *Don Juan* are of course essentially matters of prosody and technique, of finding in the *ottava rima* a form that could answer to all parts of his personality, a stanza that in its almost infinite flexibility, its ability to undercut itself, could allow the author of *Childe Harold* and *English Bards* to bed down in the same verse together.

And yet even when that is conceded, prosody can only take one so far in any discussion of Byron, because it is hardly an exaggeration to say—rather as with Churchill on the pivotal importance of El Alamein—that before he left England he never did a thing right and afterwards hardly put a foot wrong. There is nothing that apologists can say to excuse the cruelties of his married life, but with the possible exception of a Venetian interlude that strained even Shelley's tolerance, Byron found on the continent a political, emotional, and artistic maturity that he could never have achieved in the straitjacket of English life.

Above all, it allowed him the licence to *live*, and live in ways that marriage to Annabella, or probably anyone else for that matter, would never have done. In one of her interminable analyses of his character Annabella herself recognised how utterly constrained Byron felt by life in his native country, and it is the supreme paradox of his later poetry—and a sad comment on English culture—that it was only in "exile" and a foreign verse form that Byron discovered that rich, generous, subversive and inclusive "Englishness" that makes him one of the greatest comic poets in the language. "As to Don Juan," he wrote to Douglas Kinnaird in October 1818— "Bowdler's Year"—making this point, as almost everything else, better than anyone else could,

> Confess—confess—you dog—and be candid—that it is the sublime of *that there* sort of writing—it may be bawdy—but is it not good English?—it may be profligate—but is it not *life*, is it not the *thing?*—Could any man have written it—who has not lived in the world?—and tooled in a post-chaise? in a hackney coach? in a Gondola? against a wall? in a court carriage? in a vis a vis?—on a table?—and under it? I have written about a hundred stanzas of a third Canto—but it is damned modest—the outcry has frightened me.—I had such projects for the Don—but the *Cant* is so much stronger than *Cunt*—now a days,—that the benefit of experience in a man who had well weighed the worth of both syllables—must be lost to despairing posterity.[22]

The hardship for Augusta was that there was no more room for her in this world than there was for Annabella. In the journal he kept of his Swiss travels he was as desperate as ever that she should share in his experiences, but as he crossed the Alps into Italy and the gravitational pull of English responsibilities weakened, he was ready in his verse to put his passion for Augusta to a more brutal and public use. "She was like me in lineaments," the tortured but defiant Manfred— the most confessional of all Byron's creations—conjures up

Augusta's image in the figure of the dead Astarte, destroyed by his incestuous love,

> *Her eyes,*
> *Her hair, her features, all, to the very tone*
> *Even of her voice, they said were like to mine;*
> *But soften'd all, and temper'd into beauty.*
>
> *Hear me, hear me—*
> *Astarte! my beloved! Speak to me:*
> *I have so much endured—so much endure—*
> *Look on me! the grave hath not changed thee more*
> *Than I am changed for thee. Thou lovedst me*
> *Too much, as I loved thee: we were not made*
> *To torture thus each other, though it were*
> *The deadliest sin to love as we have loved . . .*
> *For I have call'd on thee in the still night,*
> *Startled the slumbering birds from the hush'd boughs,*
> *And woke the mountain wolves, and made the caves*
> *Acquainted with thy vainly echoed name . . .*
> *I have outwatch'd the stars,*
> *And gazed o'er heaven in vain search of thee.*
> *Speak to me! I have wander'd o'er the earth,*
> *And never found thy likeness—Speak to me!*[23]

It was incomprehensible to Augusta's friends and family that Byron should be willing to risk her reputation so callously, but the miseries of Six Mile Bottom and Piccadilly had already taught Augusta the destructiveness that co-existed with the love expressed in his invocation of Astarte. In his verses to her he could speak of that love as something that dissolved the boundaries of personality, and yet if they were united in affection they were united in guilt too, and Byron could no more have freed Augusta from their doom than he could himself. "No avowal can be more complete," an outraged Mrs. Villiers wrote, when she finally read *Manfred* in the summer of 1817,

> It is too barefaced for her friends to attempt to deny this allusion. All that appeared to me practicable I have done with her own family, who have all spoke to me about it. I have said that I had long been aware that his whole object was to ruin

others, and particularly those to whom he owed the most, and I had long been convinced of his wish to confirm the reports of last year to Augusta's prejudice.[24]

The hysteria seems understandable, but other responses to the drama suggest that Mrs. Villiers was over-reacting, and perhaps at least part of the anger that fuelled Manfred was Byron's growing sense that Augusta had uncoupled herself from their common fate. It is impossible to imagine that she could have survived the poem in the immediate aftermath of the separation, but if the lack of public comment in 1817 is anything to go by, her campaign of self-abasement over the previous twelve months had done its job.

And consciously or not, in gaining even the limited recognition that she had from Annabella, Augusta had secured the immunity she craved for herself and her family from Byron's worst revelations. "And so—Lady B has been 'kind to you' you tell me," he had written grumpily to her the previous September, just seven days after the first meeting of Annabella and Augusta had given the final public imprimatur to Augusta's rehabilitation,

> "very kind"—umph—it is as well she should be kind to some of us—and I am glad she has the heart & discernment to be still *your* friend—you was ever so to her.[25]

"*A thousand loves* to *you* from *me*" ended another letter from Milan just over a month later, "which is very generous for I only ask *one* in return."[26] That "*one*," though, he was not prepared to relinquish without a fight. In the first months of exile he had written to tell her that it would kill him if she ever ceased to love him, but as it gradually dawned on him from her increasingly evasive letters that she had sold out to the Milbanke camp the misery of loss took on a sharper, more critical edge. Remember, he adjured Augusta, what they had done to her brother. "I curse her from the bottom of my heart" he wrote from Venice the following spring, after discovering that Annabella and her lawyers had instituted a Chancery suit to make Ada a ward of court and deprive him of his paternal rights,

> & in the bitterness of my soul—& I only hope she may one day feel what she made me suffer;—they will break my heart or drive me mad one day or the other—but she is a wretch &

will end ill—she was born to be my destruction—& has been so—ten thousand curses be upon her and her father and mother's family now & forever.[27]

It seemed, too, that with distance Byron was incapable of seeing the misery to which he had condemned Augusta. "I returned home a few days ago from Rome," he wrote with a breathtaking thoughtlessness to her again from Venice in the weeks before *Manfred* appeared, "but wrote to you on the road—at Florence I believe—or Bologna . . ."

> I have received all your letters—I believe—which are full of woes—as usual—megrims and mysteries—but my sympathies remain in suspense—for—for the life of me I can't make out whether your disorder is a broken heart or the earache—or whether it is *you* that have been ill or the children— *or* what your melancholy—& mysterious apprehensions tend to—whether to Caroline Lamb's novels—Mrs. Clermont's evidence—Lady Byron's magnanimity—or any other piece of imposture;—I know nothing about what you are in the doldrums about at present—I should think—all that could affect *you*—must have been over long ago—& as for me— leave me to take care of myself—I may be ill or well—in high or low spirits—in quick or obtuse state of feelings—like everybody else—but I can battle my way through—better than your exquisite piece of helplessness GL or that other poor creature George Byron.[28]

The key to that letter lies in the drum roll of cities with which it opens, because perhaps more important than anything else in the slow but inevitable estrangement of Byron and Augusta was the fact that while her life had contracted through poverty and loneliness to the domestic drudgery of Newmarket and St. James's, Byron's was taking on a new lease. In his earlier letters he would berate her for any real or imagined neglect of him, but if he never ceased to love or demand *her* love with all his old imperiousness, his correspondence is full of a thousand other things in which she could play no role—of Claire Clairmont and the Alps, of mistresses and rumours of mistresses, of Venice and Ravenna and Pisa, of Ada and the birth of his illegitimate child Allegra, of Teresa Guiccioli, Italian politics, *Don Juan* and, finally, of Greece. "I have never ceased nor can cease to feel for a moment that boundless attachment which bound & binds me to you," he wrote almost savagely from Venice in May 1819—that word "bound" taking on a Dante-esque note of eternal punishment,

which renders me utterly incapable of *real* love for any other human being—what could they be to me after *you?* . . . we may have been wrong—but I repent of nothing except that cursed marriage—& your refusing to continue to love me as you had loved me—I can neither forget nor quite forgive you for that precious piece of reformation. But I can never be other than I have been—and whenever I love anything it reminds me in some way of you . . . it is heart-breaking to think of our long Separation—and I am sure more than punishment for all our sins—Dante is more human in his "Hell" . . . Circumstances may have ruffled my manner—& hardened my spirit—you may have seen me harsh & exasperated with all things around me; grieved and tortured with *your new resolution,*—& the soon after persecution of that infamous fiend who drove me from my Country and conspired against my life—by endeavouring to deprive me of all that could render it precious—but remember that even then *you* were the sole object that cost me a tear? and *what tears!* do you remember *our* parting? When you write to me speak to me of yourself—& say that you love me—never mind commonplace people & topics—which can be in no degree interesting—to me who see nothing in England but the country which holds *you*—or around it but the sea which divides us.—They say that absence destroys weak passions—& confirms strong ones Alas! *mine* for you is the union of all passions and affections—Has strengthened itself but will destroy me—I do not speak of *physical* destruction—for I have endured & can endure much—but of the annihilation of all thoughts, feelings or hopes—which have not more or less a reference to you & to *our recollections*[29]

Byron was neither imagining nor exaggerating; his sense of desolation at the thought of Augusta was real. So, too, was his fear of losing her love. These feelings were, though, only half the truth. "Speak to me!" Manfred demands of the implacable spirit of Astarte, "Speak to me!" but as the years of exile stretched out it was increasingly Byron who was silent. Fifteen letters from him to her in the first months of exile; eleven in 1817, just two in 1818. For all its passion, the letter from Venice was the first Byron had written to Augusta in over eight months. "I have been negligent in not writing, but what can I say?" he began defensively,

> Three years absence—& the total change of scene and habit make such a difference—that we have now nothing in common but our affection and relationship.[30]

"My dearest A.,"—he wrote almost exactly two years later from Ravenna, six months after his last six-line business note,

> What was I to write about? I live in a different world.—You knew from others that I was in tolerable plight—and all that. However write I will since you desire it.[31]

For Augusta, however, that desire had become more a reflex than the consuming need it had once been. After the exhausting months of the separation and the summer of 1816 her life had settled into a quieter rhythm. She still occasionally saw Annabella, and sent on Byron's letters—including that long "Maniac" declaration of love—but for both, the intensity of their relationship had inevitably slackened to a warier stand-off. With the fading threat to Ada, Augusta was less necessary to Annabella than she had first been, and for the time being, at least, her capacity for self-justification was appeased.

In her own way, too, Augusta had also got what she wanted out of the desperate spring and summer of 1816. She and her family had survived. With the eventual sale of Six Mile Bottom and their move to apartments in St. James's in 1818 even the Leigh finances had taken a less parlous turn. Her husband was as useless as he had ever been, the small pension granted them by Lord Liverpool's government was invariably late, her boys were rapidly growing up in their father's image, her second daughter, Augusta Charlotte's mental abnormalities were becoming more pronounced, but these were the domestic problems for which Augusta, with her inexhaustible good humour and bewildering belief in providence, was well designed to cope.

The past too was losing its dangers. A letter from Byron still stirred her to a confused anxiety, but only his sporadic threats to return to England could cause real panic. She had survived the third canto of *Childe Harold*, with its celebration of her love; she had survived even *Manfred*, and if the Lamb family continued a campaign of hostility that stretched back to the notorious occasion at Lady Jersey's, a promise of safety seemed to lie in the fact that Annabella had become godmother to her youngest child, Emily.

If Augusta had survived though, the sad truth is that when she bought security with her complicity in Annabella's tyranny she effectively destroyed something in herself that never recovered. It might be absurd to expect or want anything more of a woman who had already given so much to Byron, but in trading love for respectability in the way she did in the first months of his exile, she lost an honesty and integrity that left her with little more than the farago of pieties, deceptions, compromises, and evasions with which she tried to prop up a shabby and uncertain middle age.

Even Annabella and Byron's grandson recognised that the more honest and least destructive answer would have been for her to follow Byron into exile. "A real reformation," Lord Lovelace, wrote of Augusta in *Astarte*—the fascinating judgement of a man on whom heterodoxy had been forced by first-hand experience of the misery and corrosive consequences of his grandmother's brand of moral orthodoxy,

> according to Christian ideals would not merely have driven Byron and Augusta apart, but expelled them from the world of wickedness, consigned them for the rest of their lives to strict expiation and holiness. But this could never be; and in the long run, her flight to an outcast life would have been a lesser evil than the consequences of preventing it. The fall of Mrs. Leigh would have been a definite catastrophe, affecting a small number of people for a time in a startling manner. The disaster would have been obvious, but partial, immediately over and ended . . . She would have lived in open revolt against the Christian standard, not in secret disobedience and unrepentant hypocrisy . . . Judged by the light of nature,

a heroism and sincerity of united fates and doom would have
seemed beyond all comparison purer and nobler than what
they actually drifted into. By the social code, sin between
man and woman can never be blotted out, as assuredly it is
the most irreversible of facts. Nevertheless societies secretly
respect, though they excommunicate, those rebel lovers who
sacrifice everything else, but observe a law of their own, and
make a religion out of sin itself by living it through with
constancy.[32]

There is another point, too, because for all her vacillations and her
lack of "centre," the paradox of Augusta's life is that it was only in
her complete self-abandonment to Byron that she achieved her
fullest and most vivid realisation. In his Stanzas to Augusta he had
addressed and claimed her as his "other half," and in cutting herself
off from him she cut herself off from that part of her nature that no
other person or love could keep alive, from what Henry James—with
her in mind—would later call that "deep participating devotion,"
that "unspeakable intensity of feeling . . . identity of sensation, of
vibration"[33] that had raised a very ordinary woman to the heights of
generosity and moral courage she attained.

It is not surprising that James should be both moved and shocked
by Augusta's history. Three years after the death of his own sister, he
began, in a suggestive coincidence, to plan a short story on the theme
of sisterly love while in his carriage on the way to dine with that same
Lord Lovelace. That evening he was shown for the first time the—
then—secret letters between Augusta and Byron. There would be,
though, he noted in that engagingly "ninnyish" way of his, nothing
of the "nefarious—abnormal—character"[34] in his treatment of the
theme.

The story was never written, but even so that "nefarious" did neither himself nor Augusta any real justice. The "nefarious," the
"abnormal," were irrelevant to Augusta's love for Byron. It was the
most generous, most natural, most moral relationship of her life and
if his ideas had ever got beyond those first brief notes James must
have come to realise that. No one either could have done finer justice
to the strange greatness of Augusta's sacrifice or the withering consequences of reneging on it. No one either could have been better

equipped than the creator of Gilbert Osmond and Madame Merle to chart the refinements of mental cruelty that had reduced Augusta's life to the emotional lie it became.

If James "on" Annabella and Augusta is the book we need, it is in another novel, sent by John Murray to Augusta after the birth of her last child, Emily, in 1819, that Augusta herself might have recognised the most poignant commentary on her loneliness. Given, too, the element of guilt in her inconsolable grief at the news of Byron's death at Missolonghi—the Bible she had given him eight years earlier still in his possession, her name one of the few intelligible words of his last incoherent ramblings—it was the text by which she might have harshly judged herself. "Do you claim that for your sex?," Captain Harville asks of Anne Elliot at the end of Jane Austen's *Persuasion*, when the two are arguing the respective strength of male and female loyalty. "Yes," she replies,

> We certainly do not forget you, so soon as you forget us. It is, perhaps, our fate rather than our merit. We cannot help ourselves. We live at home, quiet, confined, and our feelings prey upon us. You are forced on exertion. You have always a profession, pursuits, business of some sort or another, to take you back into the world immediately, and continual occupation and change soon weaken impressions . . .
>
> I should deserve utter contempt if I dared to suppose that attachment and constancy were known only by women . . . I believe you equal to every important exertion, and to every domestic forbearance, so long as—if I may be allowed the expression, so long as you have an object. I mean, while the woman you love lives, and lives for you. All the privilege I claim for my own sex (it is not a very enviable one, you need not covet it) is that of loving longest, when existence or when hope is gone.[35]

AN INSTRUMENT OF
DESTRUCTION

I f ever a death marked a beginning rather than an end it was that
of Byron at Missolonghi in the April of 1824. Over the last
months of his life his battle for Greek freedom had already begun
to thaw public opinion in England, and his death not only completed
the metamorphosis from pariah to hero, but radically shifted public
perceptions of widow and sister that the separation scandal of 1816
had seemingly set in stone.

Where once Annabella had been swept along on the tide of
national indignation after the collapse of her marriage, she was now
required to pay the price of England's soul-searching. She still had
her loyal supporters in immediate family circles, but as composers set
his verse to music and his friends paid court to his "sweet sister," the
"Clytemnestra" who had driven him into exile was made to feel all
the chilly loneliness of the moral high ground she had occupied
unchallenged for the last eight years.

It was a deeply disturbing experience for Annabella, still more so
as over the years of his exile there had been less and less to sustain
her fragile recovery but the consciousness of her own rectitude. In its
first months the battle for Augusta's soul and the possession of Ada
had generated their own sense of purpose, but the fruits of victory
on both scores was a loneliness and lack of direction that insidiously
fed the doubts and unhappiness that Byron had left to her.

Almost from the start, too, her loneliness and aimlessness had a
physical dimension, as she began the nomadic existence that would

characterise the next forty years of her life. On her return from Lowestoft in the summer of 1816 she had stayed briefly at Harrow and in London, but once she had seen Augusta again and resumed a limited friendship there was nothing to keep her there or prevent her return to family life and Kirkby.

The problem for Annabella, however, was that an unbridgeable gulf now separated her from her pre-married self, and she could no more stay at Kirkby than she could have returned to Piccadilly. Even during the separation crisis there had been tensions between Annabella and her mother, and with continuing disagreements over the renewed contact with Augusta it was soon clearly "essential to the comfort of all parties," as Annabella put it, "that my mother and I should have separate establishments."[1]

In April 1817 Annabella took a house in Hampstead, but while for the first time since the separation her life took on some of the trappings of normality, her preoccupations remained with the past and not the future. In the middle of June she left her new home again with Ada and a companion, and leaving her child with her parents made a slow progress north to Seaham and on to Scotland, feeling better than at any time since she first became "Lady B" as she told Therese Villiers—so much so "that I begin amongst the associations of my native shore to fancy myself Miss Milbanke again."[2]

But wherever she went, and whomever she met—her lawyer, Lushington, Mrs. Minns, the maid who accompanied her on the Halnaby "treaclemoon"—there were inevitable reminders that "Miss Milbanke" had disappeared into "Lady B" forever. During the Lowestoft journey the crowds had come to look at Byron's daughter Ada, but even without that curiosity of warring heredity in tow Annabella must have been conscious that her one claim on anyone's attention lay in her name and history. "I can safely say that my heart ached for her all the time we were together," Walter Scott, whom she visited in Scotland, wrote to Joanna Baillie, one of Annabella's fiercest champions,

> there was so much patience and decent resignation to a situation which must have pressed on her thoughts, that to me she was one of the most interesting creatures I had seen in a score of years. I am sure I should not have felt such strong kindness towards her had she been at the height of her for-

tune, and in the full enjoyment of all the brilliant prospects to which she seemed destined.3

The dignity and poise were touching—especially in front of someone so naturally sympathetic to Byron as Scott—but back again with her parents and Ada at Kirkby it was harder to preserve appearances. In a diary entry from this period she confessed how frightened she was to go into the "dark" alone, and yet Annabella had never lacked the kind of pride that serves for courage and by the following spring she was again ready to face those places most intimately associated with her loss.

It was almost as if she felt she had to test herself against the reality of the emptiness ahead, to take, as it were, full and complete stock of what she had lost when she left Byron, and in the May of 1818, she paid her first and only visit to the family home at Newstead that had at last been sold. "Just come from Newstead," she recorded on 22 May—an account that must surely owe something to Lizzy Bennett's visit to Pemberley in *Pride and Prejudice*, a novel Annabella greatly admired,

> The sunshine, the blue lakes, the appearing foliage of the remaining woods, the yellow gorse over the wild wastes gave a cheerful effect to the surrounding scenes. My feelings were altogether those of gratification. In becoming familiarised with the scene I seemed to contemplate the portrait of a friend.
>
> I entered the hall—and saw the Dog; and then walked into the dining-room—not used by Ld B. as such. He was wont to exercise there. His fencing-sword and single sticks—beneath the table on which they stood, a stone coffin, containing the four skulls which he used to have set before him, till (as he told me himself) he fancied them animated.
>
> I saw the old flags which he used to hang on the "Castle walls" on his birthday. The apartments which he inhabited were in every respect the same—he might have walked in. They looked not deserted. The Woman who lived in his service regretted that the property was transferred. He should have lived there, particularly after he was married—but his Lady had never come there, and "she, poor thing! Is not

likely to come there now," compassionately and mysteriously. She said that he was "very fond of Mrs. L—, very loving to her indeed," as if this were the only part of his character on which she could dwell with commendation, for she drew a very unfavourable comparison between him and G.B. in regard to charity.4

If the memory of Byron still carried with it a romantic aura, however, her daughter, Ada, provided a permanent reminder of her need to resist its allure. On the previous year's tour to Seaham she had recorded her memories of a shoreline she had last walked with Byron, and however desperate her talents as a versifier there is no mistaking her resolution.

> *But tho' tis not Memory's powers that fail,*
> *I see these moments as thro' a veil;*
> *The veil of sorrow hath passed between*
> *And dimmed the hues of the distant scene . . .*
> *Ada! Wilt thou by affection's law,*
> *My thoughts from the darken'd past withdraw—*
> *Teach me to live in that future day*
> *When those hands shall wipe those tears away*
> *Which flow, as I think on the craggy brow*
> *Where I stood . . . that form is before me now!*
> *That eye is beholding the waters roll;*
> *It seems to give them a living soul;*
> *That arm by mine is trembling prest,*
> *I cherish the dream, he shall be blest!.*
> *Again must I break from the magic bond,*
> *Which Memory fastens with links too fond?*
> *Had I been happy I might have wept,*
> *The resisting nerve of my soul had slept;*
> *But I must not soften beneath the spell,*
> *Nor pause o'er the spot where the tear-drop fell!5*

"Where there is leisure for fiction," Johnson robustly—and wonderfully wrong-headedly—declared, "there is little grief,"6 and the element of emotional narcissism at the heart of Annabella's misery has always provided her critics with the ammunition they need. It is certainly true that the figure of Ada could always be more easily evoked *in absentia* than when she was around, but if her daughter remained an abstraction rather than a reality to Annabella, a call to duty rather than affection, it would be a mistake to underestimate how powerful a motive that was.

With every communication from Byron, too, with each threat of his return, every scrap of gossip from Geneva or Venice, each new piece of verse—the third canto of *Childe Harold, Manfred, Don Juan*—this sense of duty became more acutely defined. Through the years that followed her visit to Newstead, Ada provided in a sense the solitary thread of continuity in Annabella's life, giving the only genuine purpose to an increasingly peripatetic existence that took her to Seaham and from Seaham to Leamington and on to London, Hampstead, Tunbridge Wells and Hastings, while all the time—like some hideous family secret—the portrait of Byron in Albanian dress hung behind a green curtain at Kirkby to remind her of what she was protecting their daughter from.

While it was a duty Annabella never shirked, however, it was one that seemed to have brought her almost no pleasure, and the more successful she seemed in educating the "Byron" out of her daughter, the less she found to love. It was true that in Ada she could control his one legitimate child, but in some perverse way "legitimacy" seems to have been hedged about for her with all the irony it has in *Lear,* a kind of second best state of loveless domesticity that robbed her own daughter of the glamour that time and again drew Annabella to the Byrons.

The misfortune of Ada's short and troubled life was, in fact, that as a Byron she could never be trusted by her mother, and as a Milbanke could never be loved. From her earliest childhood to her deathbed she was watched over with a pathological fear for signs of incipient "Byronism," and yet the truth of it was that the traits Annabella disliked in her daughter as she grew up—her secretiveness, her emotional instability, her wilfulness, even, ultimately, her guilt-ridden sexuality—were precisely those that made Ada her mother's rather than her father's child.

Annabella was far too imperious to brook her own character in a daughter, but even if they had been temperamentally suited, it is unlikely that her small sum of maternal instincts would have survived the misery associated with memories of Ada's birth. In the early months of her pregnancy she might have clutched at the hope that a child would win Byron over, but once that illusion was destroyed Ada was always too intimately associated with her own rejection, too bitterly equated with the physical and mental suffering of her married life, ever to have the romantic appeal of the full-blown Byron for her.

But if Annabella could not love her—or inspire love—she was too fond of control to allow Ada to become emotionally dependent on anyone but herself. "I am sorry that I must take the apparently harsh measures of dismissing the nurse," she had written to her mother as early as September 1817, the first in an insistent pattern of responses to any challenge to her dominance of Ada,

> for I am deeply impressed with the painful & pernicious consequence of presenting myself to Ada in the same secondary part which I have been obliged to play . . . It is a fact too well known, and too bitterly felt by myself that she never saw me without beginning to cry—No wonder when Mamma was made the constant bugbear.[7]

Perhaps none of this would have mattered much if Byron had lived, but when in May 1824 his cousin George—now the 7th Lord—travelled down to Beckenham to break the news from Missolonghi, Ada was all that she had left. For the last two years of Byron's exile communication with him had been limited to enquiries over the child, and with even Augusta now beyond Annabella's reach the misery and hopelessness of the first weeks of the separation returned with a force that she had not felt in eight years.

However different their responses, her situation was, in its way, oddly similar to that in which Shelley's death had left his emotionally estranged widow two years earlier. In her later fiction Mary Shelley would write with a confessional poignancy of a remorse that is frozen by death, and when Byron's servant Fletcher visited Annabella in July he left her convulsed with the same feelings, the self-control and dignity that had so impressed Scott shattered on the reality that any romantic illusions of reconciliation had died with Byron.

There had not even been a last word for her, hard as she begged Fletcher to recall one, and the choice of Augusta and her children as

Byron's heirs further accentuated her sense of estrangement. He had made no secret of his plans for the Leigh family when he had drawn up his will just after his marriage, but even though the deaths of Lord Wentworth that same summer and of her mother in 1822 had left Annabella a wealthy woman, so public an exclusion could have only one effect.

In more subtle ways, too, Byron's death confirmed a shift in the balance of power between her and Augusta that had been coming for some years. In the first months after the separation she had held Augusta completely at her mercy, but for all her pleasure in the exercise of power, Annabella could scarcely censor Byron's letters without confronting the bruising truth that in Byron's love Augusta had the only thing that she herself wanted.

If that thought alone was bitter enough, it was Annabella's misery, as she brooded on her marriage, cut off from either the grief or the celebrity of her husband's death, that in Augusta's third daughter she had already begun to find the physical embodiment of everything she herself had lost. She had first seen the infant Medora Leigh on her wedding visit to Six Mile Bottom in 1815, and though it was the older Georgiana Annabella had seen most of, it was always and dangerously Medora—or Libby as she was more commonly known—to whom she was attracted. "Saw A.L.'s children," she had noted in her journal as early as September 1820, juxtaposing the sense of life and possibilities imminent in their lives with the melancholy of her own,

> felt the most tender affection for—[Medora]. What is the reason?
>
> September 17th, Sunday. Walked early to look at my old house in Piccadilly—saw into the room where I have sat with him, and felt as if I had lived there with a friend long since dead to *me*.[8]

It needs stressing again that there is no conclusive evidence one way or the other for Medora's paternity, but nothing could better illustrate the power of Byronic myth over objective reality than Annabella's obsession with the child. It is almost certain that her belief that Medora was Byron's dated to her meeting with Caroline Lamb after the separation, but Annabella could never have admitted as much even to herself, and in the more exotic legend she made of her life, its most vivid proof had come at Six Mile Bottom when she saw the tenderness on his face as he looked at "his" daughter.

The sight of Byron with Medora on that bridal visit—apocryphal or not—became a pivotal moment for Annabella that linked past and future in a single moral crusade. No one would ever replace Byron or Augusta in her imagination, and yet as Annabella grew older she came to find in Medora a child who by virtue of her vulnerability and pedigree answered to all the conflicting needs of her own loneliness—the daughter Ada could never be, the ultimate fix for her Byronic addiction, and above all, moral "cause" and weapon of revenge wrapped in one toxic package.

For a child who was to carry such a burden of expectation, the little that is known of Medora's earliest years is disappointingly ordinary. She was just two when Byron went into exile and only ten at his death, the fourth of Augusta's seven children and Colonel Leigh's favourite—"the loveliest Infant I ever saw"[9] Annabella brutally told her own daughter, Ada—with nothing more sinister than a look of Byron as a baby and the chaos of life at Six Mile Bottom to overshadow her future prospects.

Nor was it anything more romantic than the chronic state of the Leighs' finances that in the year after Byron's death, indirectly brought Annabella into Medora's life. In the will that Byron had signed in the summer of 1815 he had done everything he could to secure Augusta's and her childrens' futures, but for all the resentment it would generate, the terms of the bequest and the burden of existing debts had left the Leighs as desperately off as ever.

With £60,000 of the inheritance tied up for her lifetime in Annabella's marriage settlement, Augusta had all the discomfort of cutting the widow and rest of the family out of the will, with none of the financial rewards the sale of Newstead should have brought. It had been rightly assumed by Byron that the Wentworth fortune would secure Ada's future, but if Annabella could comfortably afford her public magnanimity at her own exclusion, Byron's separation of fortune from title made Augusta an enemy of the 7th Lord she could have done without.*

---

*In order to compensate the new Lord Byron for his "disinheritance," Annabella also made over to him her marriage jointure of £2000, a gesture that secured his loyalty to her for life.

It is richly typical of Augusta's fortunes that her one prospect of financial security ended up causing nothing but misery, and when the biographical fall-out of Byron's death began, the gap between the two sides inevitably widened further. In the immediate aftermath of Byron's death Augusta and his friends must have hoped that in burning his memoirs they could silence rumour, but as Medwin, Dallas, Lady Blessington, Millingen, Hunt, Kennedy and the rest rushed in to fill the gap it was only a matter of time before a truce that had survived since Annabella and Augusta's first meeting after the separation was finally shattered.

In the end it would be the controversies raked up by Tom Moore's biography—and Annabella's answering pamphlet—brought out six years after Byron's death, which would lead to open rift, but though neither party saw it, the seeds had already been sown. In the year after Byron's funeral there had been only limited contact between Annabella and Augusta, but when a distant cousin of the Byrons' proposed to Georgiana Leigh in 1825, financial necessity and a habit of dependence that she had never quite shaken off made sure that the first person to whom Augusta appealed was Annabella. "The young Man is studying the Law & has the talent to make the most of his profession," Augusta announced, in a letter that is so symmetrically and almost miraculously wrong-headed that it shows better than anything else the state to which the moral bullying and equivocation of the last ten years had brought her. He, she continued

> is exceedingly clever & in other respects the only person I know *worthy* of Georgey . . . I've seen much of him since from liking him & finding him so far superior to the *common herd*, but without the slightest idea till lately that Georgey was likely to attract him or indeed any body—She is such a *quiet* being—with very sound & excellent sense & good judgement, but not brilliant in any way, & I should have said too *awkwardly shy* to be admired. As far as one can judge, it promises all the happiness *this* world can give—& in case of anything happening to me, it wd ensure a sort of protection to her sisters.[10]

From her own experience Augusta had a horror of long engagements, and with the lovers looking like ghosts, as she told Annabella, and George Leigh, who was violently opposed to the wedding, temporarily out of the way she was determined to press forward with her plans. For some reason that has never really been clear Annabella was reluctant to be seen openly helping the couple, but she had never forgotten Byron's injunctions to be "kind" and using the name of one of her future travelling companions, a Miss Chaloner, she advanced the £2000 needed for the marriage. "A line—dearest A to tell you our Marriage thank God! Is happily over," Augusta wrote to her after it had taken place on 4 February 1826 at St. James's Piccadilly, with only herself and Medora from the family there,

> & in parting with dearest Georgey I feel I could not to ANYONE in the world with such perfect confidence *as* to Henry Trevanion. I have seen him *daily hourly* for three months— in Moments of Sickness, Sorrow, anxiety & suspense—all most trying predicaments to the Lords of the Creation—& which Shew the *real* Character—& his has only *risen* in my estimation!
>
> I cannot express *all* I feel to you for your kindness on this occasion to which we owe *so* MUCH! But indeed I *am* grateful—so are they—[11]

It is psychologically fascinating that at seventeen Georgey—a "ringer" for Augusta in so many ways—also shared her mother's attraction to the standard Byronic "model." At the time of their wedding Henry Trevanion was still talking of a legal career for himself, but by temperament and ambition he was a poet *manqué* and not a lawyer, a feebly imitative peddler of Byronic guilt with a strange by-line in religiosity—a Byron gone Celt as it were—with nothing of the energy or talent of his inheritance and everything of its self-indulgence and sexual fecklessness.

The susceptibility of both mother and daughter to this type of man would seem to be an insistent reflex of heredity, but Trevanion's own motives in marrying Georgey are probably more complicated. It is only too possible that he shared the tribal narcissism of so many of the Byrons, and yet if his single volume of verse is anything to go by, the attraction was more pose than "fatality," a conscious determination to live up to the challenge of his birthright, arrogating to himself everything that was closest to Byron in an assertion of equality that seems closer to the possessive psychology of an Edward

Trelawny than it does to the helpless compulsion of Augusta. "The Giant Minstrel ceased to sweep Childe Harold's Harp," he revealingly began one poem, signalling his obsession with the Byronic inheritance.

At length the harp a maiden takes—
We start—and Memory weeps to hear;
As Feeling to the touch awakes
The Music distant echo makes
To music felt more near.[12]

It was not often that Augusta defied her husband, and still rarer that George Leigh was right about anything, but in trusting her daughter to Henry Trevanion she made the one cardinal error of her life. For the first two years of the marriage, however, the only public strains seemed the traditional Leigh problem of money, but when in 1829 Georgey was expecting her third child and her fifteen-year-old sister, Medora, was sent to stay with them at Bifrons, the great barrack of a house Lady Byron had lent the couple outside Canterbury, a new episode in the Byron saga began.

One of the great frustrations of this part of the story is that the only account we have of events is that written by Medora herself fourteen years after they occurred. There are a handful of Trevanion's and Georgey's virtually illegible letters to Annabella surviving among the Byron papers, but for any consecutive narrative we are dependent on the "Autobiography" posthumously published after everyone involved with it who might have challenged Medora's version of things, was dead.

"I am the fourth child of a family of seven," Medora began it, narrating her sufferings with such a lobotomised calm—such a complete absence of conscience or moral consciousness—that they read more like the bloodless synopsis for some Lefanu novel than intelligible autobiography.*

---

*The manuscript on which it was based had been in the possession of a man called only "Mr. S." in the introduction, a London solicitor named Thomas Smith who had befriended the twenty-eight-year old Medora in 1843, persuading her to write down an account of her history in an attempt to escape her financial misery.

My eldest sister, Georgiana, married Mr. Henry Trevanion, a distant cousin, in 1826, when I was eleven years old. The marriage, which had the approbation of no one except my mother, did not turn out very happily, owing to the smallness of fortune, and the uneven temper of both parties. I was frequently called in to keep them company, and in March,1829 (after they had been married three years), it was decided that I should accompany them to a country house which had been placed at their disposal by my aunt Annabella, Lady Byron, during the time of my sister's approaching confinement. The house was in the neighbourhood of Canterbury. The last injunctions and admonitions I received from my mother on starting, were to devote myself in all things to please my brother-in-law, Mr. Trevanion; to get rid of the dislike I entertained for him, and to cease ridiculing him, as I had been in the habit of doing. I was urged more particularly to this course of behaviour in consideration not alone of his delicate health, but of the poverty which made him peculiarly sensitive. I promised compliance, and accompanied them to the country, as my mother and sister had arranged. My sister's illness, before her confinement, was the occasion of my being left much alone with Mr. Trevanion. Indeed, I found myself thrown entirely upon him for society. I was with him both in-doors and out, by day and by night, and was frequently sent by my sister into his bedroom on errands, after every one else in the house had retired to rest. Some months passed in this manner, during which Mr. Trevanion took advantage of my youth and weakness, and effected my ruin, and I found myself likely to become a mother, by one I had ever disliked.[13]

If it is hard to understand their subjection to a man they both despised, the explanation probably lies not so much with Trevanion himself, but with the Leighs and their chronic vulnerability to the dismal tyranny of the "professional" male inadequate of which he was so perfect a type. In his volume of poetry published in the year after his marriage Trevanion had self-consciously staked his claim to the Byron mantle, but in his mix of emotional incontinence and moral cowardice the Byron that Medora's seducer comes closest to is not Augusta's brother but—libertine, charmer, sponge and dependent—her father, "Mad Jack."

The romantic appeal of this kind of figure to Augusta, who as an orphaned child had secretly cherished the image of her disgraced father, is unsurprising, and in a more febrile, unstable form there was clearly the same tenderness in the young Medora. "I remember when a child to have been so much affected and horror struck with the fate of the Wandering Jew," she later recalled, tracing her own intense sympathy for the suffering and dispossessed in every form—from orphans to hunted murderers—to the strange meld of images that had filled her childhood nights,

> the loneliness of his fate—the everlastingness of this world to him—& the uncle who lived and died (I was taught)—deprived of all he loved with none but strangers to love or care for him all worked together (a strange confusion) & many nights have I cried myself to sleep.[14]

It would have gone against Medora's whole nature, though, to accept responsibility, and in the years ahead, she blamed not just Georgey, but also Augusta, who, in the spreading fallout of her hatred, was accused of conspiring in her ruin. In her different accounts of these intrigues Medora would later claim Augusta had traded her for Trevanion's favours, and even if the only source for this assertion was Trevanion himself that would never be enough to protect Augusta from the stigma of the charge.

And if it seems beyond belief that Georgey and Medora were the bait dangled by their mother before Trevanion, as Medora claimed, between such Gothic extravagance and a belief in Augusta's total innocence lies a wide expanse of grey that was her natural habitat. At the time that Trevanion arrived in London Augusta was probably as vulnerable as at any period since the separation, and in her Byron cousin she clearly saw a kind of mirror image of what Annabella would want in Medora—the son that her own loutish boys were not and, more importantly, the reincarnation of the brother at whose funeral Trevanion had been his family's representative.

Whatever the degree of Augusta's complicity in her daughter's seduction, however, the only concern at Bifrons as Medora approached her term, was secrecy. Pleading poverty as an excuse for leaving the country, Georgey asked Augusta's permission to take Medora with them for "H's amusement." "The permission was obtained without much difficulty," Medora recalled in the Autobiography,

> & when within four months of my confinement I accompanied them to Calais—The misery I suffered contributed to bring on a premature confinement which took place clandestinely in the house. My child lived & was taken care of by the Medical Man who had attended me . . .[15]

In later life Medora came to believe the baby had been stolen by Lady Byron, but in fact it did not survive long, and three months after the birth, the trio returned to England, Georgey and Trevanion to an aunt's house in Cadogan Square, Medora to her mother's apartment at St. James's Palace. Even in Medora's version of these events Augusta clearly had no idea of what had happened in France, and when Trevanion again became a daily visitor at St. James's, Augusta and Georgey were equally happy to leave the two alone together. "During the whole autumn & winter," Medora went on, blameless as ever in her own eyes,

> I was constantly & daily left in H's society & often till a late hour of the night . . . & early in the following year I found myself likely again to become a Mother. When by H's entreaties & prayers I consented to confide in my Mother, or rather to seek her assistance—for which purpose I copied & signed a letter he wrote to her charging her with all she had exposed me to & invoking her assistance—she burnt it as soon as read—was kind to me at first but became most cruel afterwards to me—though to H. the only difference she made was to increase her kindness.[16]

It is hard to imagine how Augusta could have been blind either to Medora's physical state after her return from France or to Trevanion's attentions, but there was no faking her shock. "It would be impossible for me in the *first* instance to speak to you my dearest," she

wrote immediately to him, the first of two notorious letters that eventually found their way to Annabella—letters that, whatever gloss one
puts on them, mirror the "labyrinth," as she called it, of pieties, penitence, and delusions Augusta found herself wandering lost in during
the years after Byron's death,

> Without such emotion as would be painful to us both—and I
> therefore take up my pen, but only to break the ice!
>
> You know how I have loved and regarded you as my own
> Child—I can never cease to do so! to the last moment of my
> existence you will find in me the tenderness, the indulgence
> of a Mother—can I say more? If I could, tell me so! Show
> me only how I can comfort and support you—confide in me,
> dearest—too much suffering has been caused by a want of
> confidence. What *might* not have been prevented could I have
> known, guessed, even *most* REMOTELY suspected!—but I
> would not breathe a word if I could help it to give *further*
> pain! . . .
>
> I am convinced, dearest, that as I have opened my heart
> and feelings to you, you will comfort me! I need not point out
> to you the means! Your own heart will dictate them—and as
> you are most dear! MOST dear! *Much*, MUCH is in your
> power.
>
> Heaven bless, comfort and guide you![17]

"Your note just received is to me *inexplicable!*" she wrote again the
next day,

> *When* and *how* have you "*witnessed my acting upon a system of
> distrust?*"
>
> When you answer this, I may be able to meet your accusa-
> tion—certainly a most unjust one! I will not say *unkind*, for I
> can make allowances for the effects of your present state of
> mind upon feelings so sensitive as yours! Dearest—I wish I
> *could* comfort you!
>
> I was so completely worn out last night from the effort I
> made to subdue my feelings and to appear cheerful before
> both the subjects of my agonising solicitude, that I *could not*
> write to you after you left me—if I had, I might have caused

you pain from the uncontrollable state of my feelings . . .
Dearest, do not mistake me by supposing that I have so little
consideration for the weakness of human nature as to think
of "a TOO *precipitate* execution of my purpose"—a purpose
on the accomplishment of which depends my only hope of
consolation! You say, *you do not respect me*—you would still *less*
respect me if I did not entertain such a hope, and do my
utmost by the most judicious means I can think of to
accomplish that on which the *eternal* welfare of that unhappy
Being depends! And the PRESENT welfare—(nay, I may say
existence and *sanity*) of so many others depends! . . . Consult
dearest G. on the *most judicious means* of proceeding in such a
cruel predicament. I have explained my ideas to her on
some minor points of *prudence,* which are perhaps more
essential than you think for—it is a hateful word where more
important interests are at stake, but where the ruin of many
may be the alternative of its observance it becomes a serious
consideration.

Now Dearest—let me implore of you to be comforted—to
do your utmost to make the best of circumstances—to trust
in my affections. That you are tried, SEVERELY tried, I feel—
and I pray God to support you and comfort you and guide
you! And I feel confident he will never abandon you if you
trust in Him!

Do not accuse yourself, dearest, and make yourself out
what you are NOT![18]

At the same time Augusta wrote to Medora.

I cannot describe with what pain I observe much that is passing before me; and, my beloved and unhappy child, I
implore you—*on my knees I implore you!* To use every *effort of
your soul* to cope with those temptations which assault
you! . . .

Reflect that you are—no, not now—Great God avert it!
That (how shall I write it) you have committed *two* of the
most deadly crimes! Recollect who you have injured!—and
whom you are injuring—not only your own Soul, but that of
another, you think *more* dear than yourself. Think *whom* you
have deprived of *his* affection! Think of the others upon

whom *shame* and *disgrace* must fall, if even now you are not *outwardly circumspect* in your demeanour! Think of his Family—of *yours*—of your unmarried and innocent sister—of the broken heart of your Father, for that THAT would be the result, I am *convinced*—you know not his agonies for the loss of that poor Angel who was from cruel circumstances comparatively an alien to him—think what *this* would be!—and more than that, of the DREADFUL consequences to HIM—to *another still more*—that no time or place would shield him from their vengeance! Think of what might and *most undoubtedly* WOULD be the consequences even in THIS world! And think of those more important interests, the *eternal* ones of all those Beings dear to you.[19]

Although these letters would come back to plague Augusta, they seem to have had no immediate effect, and when Trevanion and Georgey moved to Colerne, near Bath, Augusta was impotent to stop Medora joining them. If Medora is to be believed Augusta had done her best, in fact, to persuade her to have her child destroyed, but even in the chaos of the Leigh household there was no permanently disguising a second pregnancy, and when Georgey threatened to return alone to St. James's, Colonel Leigh had to be told. "In June of the same year," Medora recalled,

> Colonel Leigh unexpectedly arrived at the country house, preceded by an attorney and sheriff's officer. These parties having gained admittance, Colonel Leigh drove up to the door in a travelling carriage. His old coachman was on the box, and a woman, intended to represent a lady's maid, sat inside. What ensued was great misery to me. I then believed, *though I had been told the contrary by my sister and her husband,* that Colonel Leigh was my father. I wished to spare him the knowledge of my shame. We were never, any of us, taught to love and honour him. But, strange to say, I was his favourite child, and had greater influence over him than any one when he was violent, and would have done anything to hide his faults or spare his feelings.[20]

However naturally violent George Leigh was, a terrified Augusta had clearly persuaded him to see the necessity of discretion, and Medora was able to win herself ten minutes alone with Trevanion before she joined Leigh in his carriage. She had only agreed to go in the belief that she would be returning to her mother's apartments, but on their midnight arrival in London she was transferred instead to a hackney coach "somewhere near Oxford St." "We were driven I know not whither," Medora continued her story, more Lefanu-like than ever,

> until we arrived at a house where I was given into the charge of a lady. The windows of the room into which I was put were securely nailed and fastened down, and there were outside chains and bolts, and other fastenings to the door. There was every show and ostentation of a prison. During my confinement in this place, Colonel Leigh came to see me three times, when I declined to see him any more. My mother came once. Some religious books were sent to me by one of my aunts, I forget which.[21]

The house where Medora was held was in Lisson Grove—"a private lunatic asylum" in Charles Mackay, her editor's, gloss—to the west of the Regent's Park. In the few minutes conversation she had managed with Trevanion he had promised to follow her to London, however, and after two weeks imprisonment Medora saw him and Georgey driving past her barred window. For the next fortnight the same pattern was repeated almost every day.

> Notes were sewed in my linen when it came from the wash, I did not know by whom, but I suspected by my sister. By this means I was enabled to understand the signs he made to me when he drove past the house. One day the lady to whose care I had been entrusted told me that if I liked to walk out of the house nobody would stop me, and showed me how to remove the chains affixed to the door. I did not hesitate in any choice between two evils, but at once put on my bonnet, followed her instructions, and found Trevanion outside waiting for me. We left the street with all possible haste and secrecy, which we might have spared ourselves, as nobody attempted to follow us.[22]

The evidence for the next stages is fragmentary, and after the strange gothic dramas of Lisson Grove, we have only the skeleton of what

A sense of belonging: St. Peter's Croft,
the Milbanke family pew

how Mardyn. Ld Byron

FARE THEE WELL.

FARE thee well! and if for ever—
 Still for ever, fare *thee* well—
Even though unforgiving, never
 'Gainst thee shall my heart rebel.
Would that breast were bared before thee
 Where thy head so oft hath lain,
While that placid sleep came o'er thee
 Which thou ne'er canst know again:
Would that breast by thee glanc'd over,
 Every inmost thought could show!
Then, thou would'st at last discover
 'Twas not well to spurn it so—
Though the world for this commend thee—
 Though it smile upon the blow,
Even its praises must offend thee,
 Founded on another's woe—
Though my many faults defac'd me,
 Could no other arm be found
Then the one which once embraced me
 To inflict a cureless wound?
Yet—oh, yet—thyself deceive not—
 Love may sink by low decay,
But by sudden wrench, believe not,
 Hearts can thus be torn away;
Still thine own its life retaineth—
 Still must mine—though bleeding—beat,
And the undying thought which paineth
 Is—that we no more may meet.—
These are words of deeper sorrow
 Than the wail above the dead,

Both shall live—but every morrow
 Wake us from a widowed bed.—
And when thou would'st solace gather—
 When our child's first accents flow—
Wilt thou teach her to say "Father!"
 Though his care she must forego?
When her little hands shall press thee—
 When her lip to thine is press'd—
Think of him whose prayer shall bless thee—
 Think of him thy love had bless'd,
Should her lineaments resemble
 Those thou never more may'st see—
Then thy heart will softly tremble
 With a pulse yet true to me.
All my faults—perchance thou knowest—
 All my madness—none can know;
All my hopes—where'er thou goest—
 Wither—yet with *thee* they go—
Every feeling hath been shaken,
 Pride—which not a world could bow—
Bows to thee—by thee forsaken
 Ev'n my soul forsakes me now.
But 'tis done—all words are idle—
 Words from me are vainer still;
But the thoughts we cannot bridle
 Force their way without the will.
Fare thee well!—thus disunited—
 Torn from every nearer tie—
Seared in heart—and lone—and blighted—
 More than this I scarce can die.

PUBLISHED BY J. JOHNSTON, CHEAPSIDE.

Escape not exile:

Oh! What a snug little island,
A right little, tight little island.

Ada: "The impression she generally makes upon strangers is that of a lovely child . . . the pertinancy of her remarks and the accuracy of her descriptions are sometimes beyond her years."

Right: One cage for another. Aged nineteen, shortly after her marriage to Lord King

Below: "The greatest of all mercies has been her disease—weaning her from temptation & turning her thoughts to higher and better things." On her deathbed, sketched by her mother

"Unreasonable—most excited—most
irritated": Medora Leigh, c. 1843,
aged about twenty-eight

Medora's last home, Lapeyre, on the banks of the River Sorgue, near St. Affrique. TOMBE DE MEDORA LEIGH (FILLE DE LORD BYRON) the sign announces.

"I must thank you for the greatest gift that
a human being can make to his fellow,
the means of intercourse with a great
soul—Robertson's."

Reverend Fredrick Robertson

Inseparable even in death: the coffin of
Augusta, next to that of George Leigh,
in the catacomb, Kensal Green; and—
a hundred yards away—the grave of
Lady Byron

Yet, through dull hate as duty
*   should be taught,*
I know that thou will love me;
*   though my name*
Should be shut from thee,
*   as a spell still fraught*
With desolation, and a broken
*   claim;*
Though the grave closed
*   between us, —'twere the same,*
I know that thou will love me.

Left: Prophesy fulfilled. Byron
and Ada, Hucknall

Charles Mackay called "the saddest story . . . that was ever laid to the scrutiny of a harsh and unforgiving world."[23] For the first two years after escaping George Leigh's control and abandoning Georgey, Medora and Trevanion lived on the Normandy coast under the names of Monsieur and Madame Aubin, but as her health declined and it seemed that she would never "bear a living child," his interest died and he agreed to the separation she claimed she had always wanted.

During these first, nomadic years of Medora's exile, between July 1831 and June 1833, as she and Trevanion drifted from Normandy to Brittany, her mother had no idea of where she was or even whether she was still alive. In a deposition Augusta later made for Annabella she wrote that she had received news of her daughter's condition for the first time in 1833, and that after every plea for her to come home had been "resolutely and contemptuously refused," agreed an allowance of £60 on condition that Medora should leave Trevanion and take refuge in a convent.

Medora—a Catholic since 1831—had already, in fact, entered a convent in Treguier in September 1833, but discovering within days of her arrival that she was once again pregnant, left before Augusta's offer reached her. United again with Trevanion, the couple moved first to Carhaix and then in the following year to a decrepit old chateau near Plouneour Menez. There, in May 1834—after living together as brother and sister as she put it without a shade of irony— she gave birth to the child Trevanion had always craved. "Henry at this time gave himself up wholly to religion and shooting," Medora added, "I to my child."*[24]

The respite was only temporary, however, and as Trevanion brought a second mistress into the house, Medora's health began to fail. By

---

*Augusta has often been criticised for her inertia, but it needs remembering that she was already trying to look after not just her own family but Georgey and her three children too. "Her income is £800 per annum," Mrs. Villiers later wrote in her defence to Annabella, giving a vivid insight into the background to all Augusta's dealings with Medora during these years,

> Out of this she has to board her husband when at home, and her son Henry always, to maintain herself, Emily, and her servants entirely. She gives her eldest son George £100 per annum—her son Frederick has never cost her less (if so little) as £200 per ann: and she has *entirely* to provide (as far as she can) for the wants and really necessaries of Georgiana Trevanion and her three growing up daughters.[25]

the spring of 1838, it seemed that she had not long to live. "The hardships I had endured caused me to fall dangerously ill," she wrote,

> and after some days my life, contrary to all expectation, was saved, though I was declared to be in a consumption, without hope of living beyond a few months. The medical man who attended me was very kind, and the little experience of kindness which I had during my lifetime, made me, at his solicitation, confide to him my real history. I asked his aid to free me from the cruelty of one whom I had never really loved, and who by his conduct every day convinced me more and more of his worthlessness. My greatest wish was to die away from him. Through Mr. C's [Victor Carrel] means I wrote to my mother, and my aunt, Lady Chichester, informing them of my position, and imploring the means to free myself. I obtained £5, left Trevanion's roof, and went to the neighbouring town, where I continued to receive most affectionate letters from my mother, but very little money.[26]

With a new reign and Annabella's cousin—William Lamb, the second Lord Melbourne—Prime Minister, even the Leighs' pension had been stopped, and if there was little money going to Medora, that was because there was none to give. As Byron's heirs, however, there was the prospect of the £60,000 tied up for Annabella's lifetime in her marriage settlement, and with every bulletin coming from France sounding as though it might be the last, Augusta executed a Deed of Appointment in Medora's favour for £3000 to protect the future of her three-year-old child, Marie.

It was that Deed of Appointment—an act of generosity on the mother's part but a sniff of independence to the daughter—that over the next years finally and permanently metamorphosed Augusta in Medora's eyes from "Dearest kindest Mama"[27] to the hyena she became. Within months of its execution Medora had tried to sell the reversion on the Deed, but so long as her mother held the original she was helpless. "I endeavoured to persuade her to allow me regularly £120 per annum," Medora remembered, with her characteristic disregard for the realities of her mother's desperate finances, the small sum I could live on in a very cheap place. She promised, but did not perform; so that after a year and a half I found I should be compelled, as I was advised to do, to sell the reversion to £3000 which I had, with some difficulty, obtained as a provision for my child, after my death, if I did not wish to be forced to return to Mr. Trevanion. During some months the correspondence between myself and my mother continued as affectionate as ever, I endeavouring all the while to obtain from her the means of existence, and she retaining the Deed. At length I wrote to my aunt, Lady Chichester, who had sent me the £5, begging her influence to obtain the Deed for me, and to Sir George Stephen, to whom I had applied to sell the reversion, stating that I was sure my aunt, Lady Noel Byron, would use any influence she might possess with my mother, to induce her to give up to me that which was my right.[28]

In one respect, at least, Medora was right about her aunt: Lady Byron was never going to pass up the chance of so perfect an opportunity of revenge.

THE END OF THE AFFAIR

E ven if Medora was unaware of it, her aunt had, in fact, known her story ever since she had first gone to live with Georgey and Trevanion at Bifrons nine years earlier. Old friends in the neighbourhood had kept Annabella abreast of the scandal, and through her old ally George Byron, she had provided the money that took them to Calais at the time of Medora's first confinement.

On the face of it this might seem an act of spontaneous generosity—the fulfilment of her pledge to Byron—but a coincidence of dates and the involvement of anyone so antipathetic to Augusta as George Byron, suggest there were other motives involved. From her first sight of Medora, Annabella had felt a bond that gave Byron's injunction to "be kind" a special force, and yet if that certainly played its part, the controversy in the same year over Tom Moore's biography makes her assistance seem as much an act of revenge on her as a kindness to her daughter.

The row over Moore's book could not, either, have come at a worse time. In the previous year there had been a bitter argument over the trusteeship of the Byron marriage settlement, and if the dispute was ostensibly a legal one, both Annabella and Augusta knew that the real issues were questions of freedom and control that went to the heart of their relationship. For almost a decade Annabella had felt her grip on Augusta gradually weakening, and the anger with which she had rounded on her when Augusta contested her choice of trustee is an index of the frustration she felt. "I have had a great deal to annoy me lately," she wrote to one of her confidantes at the end of 1829,

> Think of Mrs. Leigh's having, after all my endeavours to serve her, accused me of the unfriendly conduct. She cannot, I think, believe what she says, after all the reason to know how sacred I have held the promise to be "kind still to Augusta." I grieve that she deprives me of the opportunities of *acting* up to it in future. It is impossible for me to admit of personal intercourse with her after such wilful misconstructions.[1]

"I can forgive and do forgive freely," Augusta wrote in her turn, after Annabella had demanded not just her complete submission, but an admission that she had always acted in Augusta's best interests,

> all and everything that has agonised, and I may say all but destroyed me. I can believe that you have been actuated throughout by a principle which you thought the right one, but my own self-respect will never allow me to acknowledge an obligation where none has been conferred.[2]

This was an "insolence" that Annabella could not forgive. Later that same year Augusta sent Ada prayer books for her birthday. "I had them nicely bound," she wrote to Byron's old friend Hodgson,

> and *Ada*, in old English characters, engraved on the back, and wrote her name and date inside, put them up directed "To the Hon. Miss Byron, with every kind and affectionate wish," and wrote over this, "With Lady Byron's permission." In another outside envelope directed them to Lady B., sent them booked by coach; and have never heard one word since.[3]

It is hard to know if either Augusta or Annabella quite recognised what they were shedding, or, in the genuine anger on both sides, whether they could even remember the intensity of need and affection that had once bound them, but it is doubtful. It was impossible of course for either woman to give up the other without a spasm of pain, and yet it had been so long since the honesty and generosity had seeped out of the relationship, that for both of them its death seems more a release than a tragedy.

More than twenty years would pass before they met again at Reigate, and for Annabella in particular, the break should have been an opportunity to recover something of the emotional balance that had been lost at the separation. In the last years before their break she had continued the nomadic course begun in 1816, moving from one rented house to another in a restless search for peace and health, from Tonbridge and Brighton to Canterbury, Dover, Switzerland— rather like Seaham, only bigger as she wonderfully put it—Italy, Canterbury again, Swansea, Clifton and the West Country.

This restlessness would never completely cease, but for the first time now in more than a decade the Byrons were not the all-engrossing presence in her life, and in 1832, at the age of forty, she moved with Ada to a house called Fordhook, to the west of London, where the educational interests that she had originally shown in 1818 bore their first real fruit. In the 1820s Annabella had involved herself with both prison reform and the burgeoning co-operative move-ment, but it was only with the Industrial School, inspired by Swiss educational reformers, which she founded at Ealing Grove in 1834, that she could immerse herself at last in a world immune to the aris-tocratic, destructive energies of Byronism.

With maturity, too, had come a calm and reserved dignity—at least where Augusta was not involved—that could inspire the same kind of chivalrous response Annabella had elicited from Scott six-teen years earlier. "Her manner," Thomas Campbell admitted, might be "cool, but is modestly and not insolently cool." "I look," he wrote in the *New Monthly Magazine* when Tom Moore's biography had ignited the old controversies over the separation again,

> with wonder and even envy at the proud purity of her soul
> and conscience, that have carried her exquisite sensibilities in
> triumph through such poignant tribulations.4

For partisan or enemy alike, however, as Campbell's eulogy under-lines, it was still her history and *name* that made her interesting. "I don't know if you have seen the last brochure," *Noctes Ambrosianae* described a portrait of her done at this time, milking the Byron memories as if there were no other terms of reference for a woman establishing her own formidable reputation in the world of early nineteenth-century philanthropy,

> It has a charming head of Lady Byron, who, it seems, sat on purpose—a most calm, pensive, melancholy style of native beauty, and a most touching contrast to the maids of Athens and all the rest of them.[5]

"Her complexion seemed to me rather dark for an English-woman," another observer noted at the end of the decade, harking back to the same theme,

> marble-like, quite colourless, but her features were faultless, and her expression was sedate, serene, with hardly a trace of grief long since buried.[6]

In a sense they were right, too, because while the period that followed the break with Augusta was marked by some of her most productive work, it was never enough to fill the cravings of her passionate and possessive nature. There can be no question of the seriousness or success of her philanthropy, but Annabella was herself the first to recognise that in some vital way it was little more than a substitute to her for what she had lost.

And as long as she had Ada at home—sixteen when they moved to Fordhook, and an increasingly alienated, unstable and secretive adolescent—Annabella could never free herself of her obsessive fear of the Byron inheritance. In 1823 Byron had written to Augusta for information on the character and appearance of the daughter he had last seen as a baby, and the description Annabella reluctantly furnished gives an interesting insight into the child that heredity and discipline were making of the seven-year-old Ada. "Ada's characteristic is cheerfulness, a disposition to enjoyment," Annabella wrote,

> this happy disposition was only partially interrupted when at the most oppressive period of her illness, under which she was patient and tractable. The impression she generally makes upon strangers is that of a lively child. Of her intellectual powers observation is most developed. The pertinency

of her remarks and the accuracy of her descriptions are sometimes beyond her years; she is by no means devoid of imagination, but it is at present chiefly exercised in connection with her mechanical ingenuity . . . With respect to her temper, it is open and ingenuous—at an earlier age it threatened to be impetuous, but is now sufficiently under control.7

There are elements here—the nature of her imagination, the fondness of mechanical pursuits—that would serve equally well for a description of the adult Ada, but if the note of sanguine confidence in that last sentence was genuine, Annabella was deluding herself. "About Ada," she wrote to a friend in 1830, seven years after her pen portrait for Byron,

> Her prevailing, indeed besetting fault at this time is a disposition to *conversational litigation*—I can give it no other name—and she goes to law with me still more frequently than with anyone else. It is very necessary that this habit should be checked, both as disagreeable and inconsistent with feeling of respect. When represented to her she admits the fact; but she does not *strive* to correct the fault. In one of her letters to you I saw that she gave herself credit for being more influenced by a sense of a duty than by the expectation of approbation or censure. I cannot say that there is much evidence of the former *unconnected* with the latter.8

In its own less schematic, intellectually rigorous way, in fact, there is something redolent of the upbringing of J. S. Mill about Ada's childhood, and something not dissimilar in its consequences. There was never at any time in Ada's life the full and articulate realisation of things that Mill so memorably recorded in his autobiography, and yet in its own fashion her whole existence was a conscious or unconscious protest against control, an emotional and physical refusal to bow down to repression that manifested itself in the anger, illnesses, rebellions and deceptions which punctuated her childhood and adult years.

In Ada's own memories, her mother's ruthlessly controlled regime of nurses, governesses, "furies" and "spies" took on a nightmarish quality, and there is evidence enough that the placidity of which Annabella boasted had always come at a heavy psychological price. Among the surviving papers from Ada's early years are letters and narrative fragments suggesting a longing for escape, but if the fantasies of flight that haunted Ada's imagination seem revealing enough by themselves, the illness that struck her down in 1829 points to an even deeper psychological malaise.

It is impossible to be sure of what was wrong with her, but with Annabella's and Ada's own subsequent history in mind, a condition that began with an attack of measles and left the child on crutches for the best part of three years was almost certainly psychosomatic. "At this time she never slept in her bed," her mother's friend, Sophia De Morgan, recalled, in an account that brings out just how temperamentally fragile the adolescent Ada had become,

> but wrapped herself in a rug or blanket outside the bed or on a sofa . . . She had strange fancies about eating, which Lady B told me were a repetition of her father's—indeed all these whims, & others which I have now forgotten were, her mother told me, simply inherited . . .9

It was an illness, too, as this account unwittingly suggests, that had been stalking Ada all her life, because at its root was a confusion of identity that went back to the first time she had asked about her father. In later years Annabella would always claim that she had never prejudiced her against Byron, but Ada's first tentative attempts to understand who she was—to recover that Byronic inheritance she became so vividly, almost mystically, aware of as an adult—was met with such a "fearfully stern and threatening manner," that it produced a feeling of guilt and "dread towards her mother which continued till the day of her death."10

And if there were times when, as she later confessed to Annabella, she hated her, the "furies" were always there to enforce the natural guilt of a child unable to love its mother. "My dear Ada," her governess wrote to her in 1833,

> You have a parent to whom you have at times behaved in a manner unbecoming the child of so invaluable a mother . . .
> Do not, then, lose the time that is now afforded to you, in

doing anything you can to lessen the sufferings and encrease the comfort of your inestimable mother . . . In your dear and excellent mother you have (in my opinion) all that can be offered as an ex[am]ple short of the character of our Saviour, and she is always with you.[11]

Up till the age of sixteen, however, Ada's rebellion was largely confined to the unconscious protest of her body, but in 1833 the rumbling discontents finally burst out in an act of defiance that for the first time openly exposed the yawning gap between appearance and reality in her upbringing.

The details of the incident are still uncertain, but sometime round this period Ada fell in love with a tutor hired to teach her shorthand. By her own later admission they had sexual relations that stopped only short of "complete penetration,"[12] and when the pair were discovered and the tutor sacked, Ada ran after him in an attempt to elope that was not thwarted until his family contacted Annabella and had her daughter taken home.

There is understandably little evidence of this episode amongst Annabella's papers, but while she might successfully suppress it, it brought home to her just how fragile her control of Ada was. In one of the curious anomalies of Ada's character, however, rebellion would invariably be succeeded by bouts of contrition and "self-reform," and the months that followed this aborted elopement ushered in probably the most stable years in her whole fraught relationship with Annabella. "Her daughter is now about sixteen," a visitor to Fordhook, Francis Trench, wrote of her, oblivious to any tensions between daughter and mother or the miseries implicit in his description of the adolescent Ada Byron,

> with a fine form of countenance, large expressive eyes, and dark curling hair. Her features bear a likeness to her father's, but require some observation before it appears strongly. Then, I think, it does. At present her health is delicate, and she is obliged to use crutches.[13]

In May 1833, the seventeen-year-old Ada was presented at court, and within two years this promise of social and emotional conformity was confirmed by her engagement to the 8th Lord King. The two had probably first met through a Cambridge contemporary of his at the home of the great mathematician Mrs. Somerville, and by June 1835 he had proposed and been accepted, writing to her from his Somerset "hermitage" "in a state of continued intoxication of delight"[14] that must have offered Ada her first real glimpse of an escape route from the emotional constrictions of Fordhook.

But if Ada was above all "grateful"[15] to William King, as she told him in her first letter, she might well have taken alarm from her mother's delight and relief at the news of the engagement. For all her egalitarian and radical pretensions Annabella had always been serenely conscious of the advantages of rank and wealth, and in the thirty-year-old, impeccably earnest, improving landowner with estates in the West Country and Surrey, she thought that she had at last found the perfect gaoler for her emotionally wayward daughter.

And in spite of Ada's apparent willingness to reform, Annabella's suspicions and fears went too deep for a marriage to do anything more than signal a shift rather than a suspension of vigilance. For nineteen years she had watched for every symptom of emotional or moral excitability in her daughter, and if Ada had dreamed that marriage was her release from the disciplines of childhood, then the first letter of her new life should have sounded a bitterly prophetic warning. "Had I felt less towards my Son," Annabella wrote to her the day after the wedding,

> I could have *given* my blessing—but he will feel assured of it—and in your own happiness mine *must* be secured whether absent or present. Dear little Canary bird, may the new "cage" be gladdened by your notes.[16]

As far as Annabella was concerned, in fact, Ada's marriage simply represented an opportunity to co-opt her devoted and tractable son-in-law as a new partner in her life's crusade. In later years events would turn her affection for William King to a vengeful and con-temptuous hostility, but through these first years of the marriage they were happy to watch together over Ada's moral welfare as fellow trustees, monitoring her emotional temperature and health, control-ling her reading, friendships, servants and children, equally ready to prescribe claret or mathematics as the danger seemed to demand.

Even in the first heady days of this alliance with her son-in-law, however, there was an emotional void in Annabella's life that Ada could no more fill than could the school at Ealing or her work for the Hastings Co-operative. On the surface of it the years immediately after Ada's marrriage were some of the most sanely content of Annabella's life, but when in 1840 she received through the solicitor, Sir George Stephen, a letter from the child she believed Byron's incestuous daughter she was as vulnerable as she had ever been to its dangerous appeal. "On Sir George Stephen forwarding my letter to Lady Byron," who was at the time visiting Paris, Medora wrote of the first extraordinary contacts with the aunt who had paid for her flight to the continent with her sister and Trevanion ten years earlier,

I received a most kind and affectionate letter from Lady Byron, and money, with offers of protection for myself and child, and the power of quitting a neighbourhood which was most painful to me. This was in August, 1840. I willingly and joyfully accepted these offers, and accompanied a medical gentleman whom Lady Byron had sent, and met her at Tours, where it was first thought I should reside. Lady Byron, however, proposed that I should accompany her to Paris, and remain with her for a time. I did so, being desirous of attending to the least wishes of one towards whom I had reason to feel so grateful.

At Fontainebleau, where she was detained by illness, *Lady Byron informed me of the cause of the deep interest she felt, and must ever feel, for me. Her husband had been my father.* She implored and sought my affection by every means; and almost exacted my confidence to the most unlimited extent. I was willing and anxious, in any and every way I could, to prove my gratitude and the desire I so sincerely felt to repay by my affection and devotion any pain she must have felt for circumstances connected with my birth and her separation from Lord Byron. Her only wish, she said, was to provide for me, according to Lord Byron's intentions respecting me, and according to my rank in life. She evinced much anxiety for my health and comfort, expressed indignation for all I had suffered, spoke of the comfort I would be to her, and of the necessity that I should be a devoted child to her. There was a Chancery suit begun against my mother, to obtain possession of the Deed.[17]

For ten years since their argument over the marriage trusteeship, Annabella had been brooding over Augusta's "ingratitude," and it was soon clear that she had found the instrument of revenge she wanted. As late as 1838 Medora had been affectionately addressing her mother as "My own Dearest kindest Mamma," but now with a new patroness to placate she was shrewd enough to see that the symbiotic demands of revenge and justification could only be satisfied in one way.

There was nothing Medora Leigh was not prepared to say against Augusta, and nothing Annabella was not ready to believe, or pass on to a growing circle of confidantes that soon included her own daughter. Throughout Ada's childhood Annabella had always been ruthless in keeping the Leighs at arm's length from her, but under the excitement of the new cause she now claimed from Ada on Medora's behalf the rights of a "sister."

It was a curious sisterhood—as odd in its way as that of Augusta and Annabella—but for the time at least both were willing initiates. "I have formed a very favourable opinion of her," Ada wrote of Medora to her husband from Paris, where in the spring of 1841 she had gone to join her mother and Medora.

> She impresses me with the idea of *principle* very strongly; and I find from the Hen, [the Lovelace family name for Annabella] (who has now communicated to me *everything*), that her sincerity & perfect *truthfulness* have been tested very completely. I have heard altogether a history *most shocking*. The whole of it must be made known to you, but this can be done only in conversation.
>
> As for the ruin of Medora, it was effected by the *united efforts* of the Mother; the Sister; Mrs. T.; and Mr. T. himself; and by means of drugging the victim, who found herself ruined on coming to her senses. Under the circumstances, Medora herself (who always particularly *hated* Mr. T) must be considered absolutely guiltless. She emancipated herself as soon as possible from Mr. T.; but owing to the cruel conspiracy against her, she was in a manner *forced* to remain in his power during two or three years.[18]

It is to this period that we owe the most lurid extravagances of Medora's history, as piece by piece—the drugging and rape, the collusion of Augusta, her affair with Trevanion, the corruption of one daughter, the pimping of the next—the thin, dreary story of Trevanion and Medora took on its definitive shape in Annabella's vengeful imagination. "Think of Mrs. L. sending word to Mr. T. that her other daughter Emily was *ready* for him whenever he chooses to come to England," Ada wrote to her husband in April 1841, adding one final grace note to the score of Augusta's crimes,

> which being outlawed, he luckily cannot do! What a *Monster* of iniquity! And how her wretched children, who are all victims one way or others, are to be pitied—I hope you burn these letters.[19]

It is hard to see how even Annabella could have brought herself to believe a story so utterly at odds with any of the known facts, but for her it became part of a wider delusion that had been growing with the years, belated proof of the wickedness of the woman who, in her distorted memory, had deliberately kept Byron from reconciliation. "Yet alas! It is *nothing* to what I have learned of circumstances now many years passed away!" Ada repeated this received version of Augusta's wickedness,

> So iniquitous & villainous a tale could never have entered into the imagination of any but the wretched actors themselves.
>
> How comes it that my Mother is not either dead, mad or depraved? *This* is the question that must suggest itself as most obvious.
>
> A new language is requisite to furnish terms strong enough to express my horror & amazement at the appalling facts ! That viper—Mrs. L.—crowned all by *suppressing* letters of my Mother's to my father when he was abroad after the separation, & *forging others* in their place! *She monster!*[20]

With such a history for justification, it was not just a matter of pleasure but duty to keep Medora away from the woman who had polluted the child's life at source. In the first months after her intervention Annabella made sure that there was no direct contact with Augusta, but when in the spring of 1841 she received a letter from London pleading for information about her daughter, all the

bottled resentment of a decade's silence burst out. "I am to be con-
sidered responsible for the safety and comfort of your daughter Elizabeth Medora," Annabella wrote,

> Her malady, the effect of physical & mental suffering com-
> bined, can be retarded, in the opinion of the physician &
> surgeon whom I have consulted, only by extreme care and by
> her avoiding all distressing excitement. The former I can
> secure, but not the latter—I would save you, if it not be too
> late, from adding the guilt of her death to that of her birth.
> *Leave her in peace.*[21]

There is no minimising Annabella's malice towards Augusta, nor the
injustice with which she persecuted her, but it is impossible to follow
her involvement in Medora's story and not recognise its more
poignant sub-text. "I am particularly happy just now," she had written from Fontainebleau to Lady Olivia Acheson after her first meeting with Medora, giving frightened expression to all those more
generous and fearful instincts that were tangled up with the desire for
revenge,

> Feelings that have long lain, like buried forests, beneath the
> moss of years, are called forth, and seem to give happiness to
> one for whom I have something like a mother's affection.
> This is a little gleam in my life—it will not last, but its mem-
> ory will be sweet. The object of my affection is marked for an
> early grave.[22]

It was not the prospect of Medora's death that clouded this happiness, though, but as letter after letter makes plain, the fear of one
more rejection at the hands of the Byrons. "Do you remember Dear
E" [Medora had become Elizabeth by this time], Annabella asked a
year later, by which time the underlying strains of their relationship
were already taking their toll,

> that I asked you early in our acquaintance not to use affec-
> tionate expressions towards me? I then felt the possibility of
> a change in your feelings. You did not regard my request,
> and I suffered myself to believe that you had conquered the

early impressions to my disadvantage which were made upon your mind, and were able to love me. But I ought not to have let you deceive yourself and me (much pain would then have been spared) and should not have accepted your expressions of entire confidence and affection.[23]

"From some of your recent letters," she continued the theme in a second letter,

> you have appeared to suppose, contrary to my repeated assertions, that I wished for *expressions* of affection. Far from it. My bitter experience of them in your family has made me almost shrink from them . . .[24]

The relationship was perhaps more complex than this suggests, however, because if Annabella had allowed herself to be emotionally ensnared, the same was true of Medora. Her main concern was always with the Deed and the independence it could give her, but from the day she came under Annabella's care parts of her nature that had been virtually extinguished were suddenly, confusedly and painfully brought back to life.

It is in fact only from this period, when Medora was twenty-eight, that we can gain any sense at all of the personality that lay behind her *Autobiography*. The strongest impression the published version of the story produces is of a self-justifying selfishness, but in the letters she wrote to Annabella over the next two or three years—literally hundreds of them, many six, eight pages long—one gets for the first time some glimpse of a complex nature that from earliest adolescence had been warped by events and expectations beyond its control.

They are extraordinary letters, written in a hand that changes not just from letter to letter, but from paragraph to paragraph, vivid, restless, impulsive and contradictory, humble and self-justifying by turn. They are the letters of someone who feels everything with a frightening immediacy. They often seem written under the influence of alcohol. They are full of the moment—of flowers coming into bloom and dying, of weather, shifting clouds, sunsets, pets, servants, and strangers—and all felt and *lived* with an empathetic intensity that hovers on the edge of mental imbalance.

Above all, though, in her correspondence with Annabella, one can begin to see the appalling cost of the life of sexual and emotional abuse that she had suffered from the age of fifteen. They are not letters that can make one *like* Medora any more than the autobiography does, but for all their self-dramatising egotism there is a terrible pathos in their cry for a lost innocence, a shocking and unanswerable validity in both their infantilism and rage against the childhood she had never had.

She addressed Annabella as "Mama," as "Pip," as "Pippin," as "My old Porpoise," and signed herself "your loving child," "your own dear child." She berated herself for being a bad child. She pleaded forgiveness for her temper, her hatreds. "Oh I have been a good child tonight," she told her, "I have been kind and gentle as you like me." "If you only take care opening this" she sent off another letter, "you will find such a nice kiss." "My dearly beloved Porpoise" she wrote to her, in a letter which fuses all these emotions into one,

> My mother is sixty years old tomorrow—how well I remember my anxiety to procure her violets for that day—now it can pass by occasioning *only* a shudder of horror—almost fear—why was I born to love so dearly . . . Forgive me if I am naughty I do not mean it, your child.[25]

For all the genuine emotional needs the relationship satisfied on both sides, however, there was always going to be enough of the warder in Annabella's attitude to create its own inevitable tensions. While they were in Paris together Medora had been welcomed into the family as Ada's "sister," but back in England and installed at Moore Place— the new house Annabella had bought near her son-in-law's Surrey estate—a certain ambiguity entered into her status, leaving her stranded somewhere between celebrity victim and "madwoman in the attic," a charge too romantic to be abandoned and a weapon too inherently unstable to be deployed with any security. "I find the mind in the state you described," reported Annabella's friend Mrs. Jameson—a kind of Grace Poole at Moore Park to Medora's dark skinned, dark eyed hispanic-looking Bertha Mason,

> Unreasonable—most excited—most irritated—changing however from storm to sunshine at every moment . . .
> There is the wish to be & do right—with an utter blind-

ness to the right—which is inexpressibly painful to contem-
plate . . . I am at moments embarrassed and provoked as
with a perverse but charming child—& when I think that this
child is a woman—[26]

Mrs. Jameson had put her finger on it with that last remark, because
at the age of twenty-eight, with a seven-year-old daughter of her
own, Medora was in no mood to endure the control that had
blighted Ada's childhood. In the early days of dependency it may
have suited her to pander to Annabella's emotional and moral
demands, but as she sensed the power inherent in her birthright it
was her financial "rights" as Byron's child and not moralising charity
she demanded.

For all Medora's desire for independence, however, the final crisis
in their relationship was emotional and not financial. She had originally turned to Annabella in an attempt to secure the Deed designed
to guarantee Marie's future, but when in May 1842 Augusta at last
backed down rather than face the inevitable scandals of a court
hearing, Medora reacted with a fury not even Mrs. Jameson could
have predicted.

Medora's response to her victory is still difficult to understand, but
over the last year she had felt both the frustrations and the power of
her position too vividly to be placated by anything short of her
mother's humiliation. It is impossible to know if she had come to
believe the stories she had told against Augusta in France, but
whether she did or not she was no longer prepared to be the mere
instrument of someone else's revenge and in a bizarre twist rounded
on the patron who had financed her legal battle. "In May, 1842," she
wrote of Annabella in her *Autobiography*,

> my long anxiety in the matter of the Chancery suit was
> ended. The suit was concluded in a way, without consulta-
> tion with me, which showed that all that had been promised
> to me, unsolicited and unsought, was not sincere, and that I
> had been in a manner sacrificed in my mother's interest.[27]

"You cannot imagine the scenes of fury she exhibited," Annabella
later wrote to Selina Doyle,

I had *never* seen anything like it—She told me I was her bitterest enemy and threatened every kind of revenge—I not
having from first to last uttered an unkind word to her . . .
She obliged me to quit my house some weeks before she left
England, by rendering it intolerable to me—but I loved her
still.[28]

That last phrase was not simply for show, but after two volatile years
there was a recognition on both sides that their friendship had
exhausted its usefulness. At the beginning of July Annabella offered
Medora an annual income of £150 if she would live quietly abroad
with her daughter Marie, and after contesting every condition in a
bid for more money, a defeated Medora finally gave way to terms
that left her securely in Annabella's financial control and the Deed in
the safekeeping of Lord Lovelace. "After consulation with Ada and
Lord Lovelace," Medora recalled a year later, conveniently forget-
ting the rage with which she had turned on Mrs. Jameson on her last
day or the threats to Ada that she would throw herself "down the
throat" of the first man who would marry her,

> it was thought best I should leave, and Ada promised, and I
> thought I might trust to such, to watch over and protect me,
> assuring me her mother was deeply attached to me. I trusted
> to this, and left England on Friday evening, the 2nd of July,
> 1842. And partly in order to prove to Lady Byron my earnest
> wish to leave her still, and on my maid's solicitation on
> account of their importance, in the event of my death, left a
> box of letters and papers with Lady Noel Byron's house-
> keeper, to be given to Lady Byron on her return to Moore
> Place; and the Deed of appointment to Ada on her leaving
> me at 6 o'clock that evening, to be deposited with Lord
> Lovelace's papers at Ockham.[29]

Even at the death, though, their relationship was shot through with
other emotions, and by the sense of a shared enmity stronger than
any internal feuds. Before leaving for France Medora went up to
London to have a daguerreotype taken for Annabella, and driving to

Ada's house in the north-west corner of St. James's Square, saw her mother for the last time. "Dearest Pip, I have this instant met my Mother," she wrote to Annabella, in a hand that over the course of the letter degenerates with rage and drink into virtual illegibility,

> I instantly recognised her—she is unchanged in face—& turned my head as if waiting for William who was ringing at the door. She could not have seen my face—my veil being down—& I saw her before she saw me . . . She turned round & looked at the carriage—for I observed her from the little back window—probably from curiosity or thinking it might be you. She was followed by a dirty-looking rascally kind of servant out of livery who was playing with his glove, & was dressed in a dark muslin gown with white pattern, & black silk shawl with long fringe and gathered round her as if she was afraid of losing it & a straw bonnet trimmed with white satin ribbbons. Her large eyes are ever & indeed *unchanged,* her walk is most altered & looks WICKED. Oh, were there a thing I had hoped to be spared it was this . . .
>
> This has shocked me—pained me, but it is over. I have drunk quantities of wine since, & now there is nothing left for me to suffer that I dread. Oh how dearly fondly I loved her, & had she only stifled the existence her sin gave me—but God *is* there—& I will do my best to bear as I have ever done but it is so long, so constant—God forgive her. Oh how horrible she looked—so wicked—so hyena—like—That I could have loved her so! Bear in mind one feeling the sight of her has given me yet more strongly—if for my good or that of Marie—intimidate her—she will grovel on the ground, fawn, lick the dust—all—all that is despicable & bad . . . Oh could I only have loved the memory of my mother, but had death passed over me the chill—the horror—could not have been so great. Pity & forgive me if I involuntarily pain, I do not mean—but I *do* suffer.
>
> Dearest Pip, I have come up to-day early on purpose to get you a Deguerotype done of me—I have heard you say that it would please you to have one—but the Sun is clouded over but you shall have one & as little ugly as possible. I do not contradict what you say about affection—time will best

show you. I no more wish for a "farewell than you"—we have parted—if we meet not again here we shall only meet in happiness hereafter & if we *do* meet again as we *shall* when I am happy and well—we shall not be the sadder for having had an agony less.[30]

If Annabella looked at this letter and saw what a good job she had done with Medora, she ought to have been shrewd enough to know that there was no way she could ultimately control a woman capable of such hatred. In the bargaining that preceded Medora's departure, she had insisted that Medora should be dependent on her alone, but within months Medora had reneged on that and almost every other clause of their agreement, abandoning the anonymity of the provinces for Paris where she canvassed financial and legal help, before returning to England the following year to get her own hands on the Deed. "In the summer of 1843," Charles Mackay began his introduction to the published version of her *Autobiography*, completely ignorant of that streak of self-destructive wildness that had become a mania of defiance in Medora,

> twenty-seven years after the separation of Lord and Lady Byron, and nineteen years after the death of Lord Byron at Missolonghi, there arrived in London from Paris and the South of France, where she had resided for some time previously, a young lady, with a pretty little daughter, nine or ten years old . . . She was good-looking rather than eminently handsome, had dark eyes and hair, and a dark complexion, and was altogether a very lively and agreeable person. She was not, however, in strong health, and worst of all to her at the moment, she was without the means of subsistence for herself and daughter, the little girl Marie, to whom she was passionately attached, and whom she had brought with her from Hyeres. She had come to England to urge a claim which she had, or fancied she had, upon the generosity and kind feeling of Lady Byron; and her expenses from Paris to London had been defrayed by Captain De B[arralier], a gallant veteran of the British army, who had served through the Peninsular war in the 71st Regiment, and had received sev-

eral severe wounds at the battle of Waterloo, for which he
enjoyed a pension of £100 per annum. This officer had long
been resident in the South of France, had found Miss Leigh
in Paris in a state of utter destitution, had heard her sad
story, had relieved her to the extent his limited means
allowed, and had defrayed the charges of her return to
England, in order that she might plead her cause in person
with her wealthy and powerful relatives, and especially with
Lady Byron, who had long treated her with motherly affection, and paid for her maintenance, but had suddenly with-
drawn her favour, and left her and her child to perish of
neglect and hunger.[31]

For all the violence and hatred with which she could turn on people,
there was a pathos and plausibility about Medora that could impress
strangers, and the English solicitor, Thomas Smith, to whom Bar-
ralier introduced her, proved no less vulnerable than the Waterloo
veteran. On 21 July, Smith went to see Annabella's old lawyer from
the separation battle, but Lushington was as ready now as he had
been then to defend his client's interests, and nothing Smith could
say could bridge the gap between Annabella's insistence on control-
ling the Deed and Medora's equal determination to have her fate in
her own hands.

It was an impasse to which there was no solution, because contrition had ceased to be enough, and Medora was not ready to submit
to the absolute tyranny that was Annabella's immovable position.
"You have but *one* course to pursue," Ada had warned Medora in
March, in a letter that with its unpleasant echoes of her own
mother's emotional and moral bullying is "Milbanke" all over,

> submission to your benefactress; and if you have one spark of
> good feeling or of prudence, you will at once recognise your
> rash and ungrateful conduct and regret for it . . . Do not
> make *me* regret that I have not myself been what, let me tell
> you, many in my particular position would have been, viz:
> esteeming it *much* to behave to you with condescension and
> toleration, and beyond all measure and reason, to extend to
> you *affection* and *equality* of intercourse. Remember what you

were at Paris—Grateful for any countenance from me. You
had scarcely dared to hope it. Remember too that there are
circumstances, disgraceful circumstances, connected with
your *birth and position,* which, with many in my relationship to
you, would have made you an object of contempt.[32]

The threat was useless. For thirty years Annabella had tried to control the Byrons in one incarnation or another, but whether it was a
matter of incestuous genes or not she had found in Medora the phenomenon in its most virulent and untramelled form, a life-force
ready to consume itself in its own defiance, a reckless independence
of spirit and will that in the end is Medora Leigh's most valid claim
to the Byronic lineage the world had foisted on her.

Given the fierce defiance of Medora and the obstinacy of
Annabella, there is an inevitability about the rest of the negotiations
that is so deeply rooted in the characters of the two women that the
only surprise is that the final split did not happen earlier. Through
the end of July and the beginning of August, Smith did all he could
to find some way out of the impasse, but while Annabella was prepared on Lushington's advice to buy off Medora's servants when
they threatened to go public with her story, all contact with Medora
herself was over.

Medora had fatally overplayed her hand. Even as late as the
spring of 1843, when Annabella sent her old friend Dr. King to Paris
in an attempt to induce reason, she could still have had £300 a year
in return for her submission. Now she had nothing. She had alienated, too, anyone who might possibly help. One final savage letter to
her mother was her last contact with either Augusta or Annabella.
After that, there was nothing left for her to do but raise what money
she could on the Deed that had at last been given to her, and leave
England.

The rest of her story, too, has the same air of inevitability about it,
and for all its poverty and obscurity, a sadly Byronic fitness. From the
age of fifteen Medora's existence had been shaped by perceptions of
her birth, and exile was simply the logical conclusion of that, the
inevitable destiny of a girl who for all her vividness of being had pri-
marily existed as the construct of others' imaginations—the heroine
of a Byronic drama, the solipsistic product of the bloodline, the violent, unstable embodiment of Byronic sin in all its forbidden glam-

our—that had to be wooed, watched and finally banished to the obscurity of a foreign grave.

The end was not long in coming either. Two years later while working as a servant in Saint-Germain-en-Laye, she became the mistress of a French hussar called Jean-Louis Taillefer, and was soon pregnant. Moving near to his native village in the south, she gave birth to a son in 1847 under her old name of Madame Aubin, and on Taillefer's discharge from the army the following year, married. But Medora was no more born for respectability than she was for security. Almost exactly a year later she went down with smallpox, and died on 28 August, 1849, aged thirty-five, leaving behind her a husband, two children and a strong-box of papers which—in a strangely circular irony—went the same way in her solicitors' fire that Byron's memoirs had gone at John Murray's almost forty years earlier.

She has, however, left a mark on her adopted country. A reliable oral tradition preserved for a generation the memory of a popular and exotic figure in her husband's village, and at the entrance to the tiny hamlet of Lapeyre, huddling in a bend of the River Sorgue a few kilometres to the south of St. Affrique, a sign now announces without any equivocation the "TOMBE DE MEDORA LEIGH, FILLE DE LORD BYRON."

The *tombe* itself lies across the river, shallow and fast here except for the deep pool below the bridge, where the woman who believed herself Byron's daughter did her washing. It is on a hillside overlooking the grey spire of the XII century church and terracotta roofs of the village. The earth of the cemetery has been banked, and buttressed at the front with a stone wall, but the graves still lie on a gentle incline, the rows of dead seemingly tilted towards their old homes in the valley below.

There is something unmistakable about every country's cemeteries, and it would be hard to imagine anywhere less English, or a scene more remote from the big, bleak skies and flat expanses of Newmarket, where Annabella first saw Medora in 1815. At one end of the graveyard the ruins of an old church tower rise from a cluster of tall cypresses and fruit trees, and behind it is a tiny chapel, the beaded skeletons of funeral wreaths mouldering in the quiet cool within.

There is nothing to disturb the peace of Medora's grave except the noise of the river and the sound of the Angelus bell floating across the valley from the village church. She lies towards the southern end of the small cemetery, her grave marked by a stone cross cannibalised from the old church, and a newer plaque recording her name. It is less confident than the notice at the road side, but in its blend of English and French, of speculation and fact, it does—quite literally—set in stone a self-fulfilling myth of alienation that links the end of this thirty-five-year-old exile to another death among strangers a generation earlier at Missolonghi. "Elisabeth Medora Leigh-Byron," it reads.

Épouse Taillefer
28 Août 1849
"Strangers not regardless pass
Ling'ring like me to gaze and sigh 'Alas' "
              Gordon Lord Byron.

A PREPARATION FOR
INVISIBILITY

A t the time that the news of Medora's death reached England in the autumn of 1849, Annabella was fifty-six years old, a mother of a successfully married daughter, the grandmother to three children, and her eye already fixed on the world to come. For as long as her daughter or son-in-law could remember her health had been a source of endless worry and talk, and although she still had another ten years to live, her appearance was already beginning to hold out to her admirers some ethereal suggestion of the "other side." "Her form was slight," Harriet Beecher Stowe wrote of her first sight of her, just a few years after this,

> giving an impression of fragility; her motions were both graceful and decided; her eyes were bright, and full of interest and quick observation. Her silvery-white hair seemed to lend a grace to the transparent purity of her complexion, and her small hands had a pearly whiteness. I recollect she wore a plain widow's cap of a transparent material; and was dressed in some delicate shade of lavender, which harmonised well with her complexion.
>
> When I was introduced to her, I felt in a moment the words of her husband:-
>
> > *"There was awe in the homage that she drew;*
> > *Her spirit seemed as seated on a throne."*

Calm. Self-poised and thoughtful, she seemed to me rather to resemble an interested spectator of the world's affairs, than an actor involved in its trials.[1]

"I sit as God," one less charitable observer, quoting Tennyson, put it, "holding no form of creed But contemplating all,"[2] and there had always been those who found this Olympian certainty less than attractive. As early as the separation Byron's great champion Hobhouse had declared that she was simply a woman that no man could have lived with, and over thirty years later neither age nor illness had done anything to slacken her minute control over the lives of those around her. "I found Lady Byron in her sick-room," Mrs. Stowe described another meeting with Annabella, brilliantly—if accidentally—capturing the mix of tyranny and untouchable certitude that characterised her last years,

> that place which she made so different from the chamber of ordinary invalids. Her sick room seemed only a telegraphic station whence her vivid mind was flashing out all over the world.
>
> By her bedside stood a table covered with books, pamphlets, and files of letters, all arranged with exquisite order, and each expressing some of her varied interests. From that sick-bed she still directed, with systematic care, her various works of benevolence, and watched with intelligent attention the course of science, literature, and religion; and the versatility and activity of her mind, the flow of brilliant and penetrating thought on all the topics of the day, gave to the conversations of her retired room a particular charm . . . All the new books, the literature of the hour, were lighted up by her keen, searching, yet always kindly criticism . . . Her opinions were always perfectly clear and positive, and given with the freedom of one who has long stood in a position to judge the world and its ways from her own standpoint.[3]

With so much of Annabella's energies also absorbed in monitoring the lives of the Lovelace family, and a fresh emotional outlet for her opening up in Brighton with her friendship with Frederick Robertson, it is doubtful how much the death of Medora impinged. Among her papers is preserved a letter from Medora's daughter from Toulon in 1843, but whether Annabella retained any memory of the endearments penned in a painfully neat child's hand, they were not enough to extract an answer when an orphaned Marie added herself to the list of Leighs who had written to Annabella for help.

From at least the 1830s Annabella had been perfecting the tactic of leaving any unwanted letter unopened, and any plea that was connected with Medora seems to have gone straight into the Dead Letter Office that she had made of her mind. In a letter she wrote three years before her own death she confessed her failure to be of any help to those she had loved, and yet if that moment of almost Byronic insight is worth cherishing, a list of victims the length of her lifetime underlines the ruthlessness with which she visited her own inadequacies on those she knew that she had failed.

In 1849 the violent rupture with her son-in-law and daughter was still nearly two years away, but Byron, Augusta, Medora, Marie, Mrs. Jameson—the list could go almost indefinitely—were among those from whom she withdrew her love or affection. During the Brighton years that began around the time of Medora's death the friendship of Frederick Robertson briefly filled this void, but when in a characteristic gesture of self-dramatising humility, she found herself only four years later walking behind the coffin of her last "soul mate," all that remained was the preparation for posterity of her "history" that would become the final "duty" of these last years.

With her manic hoarding of letters and evidence since the time of the separation, her whole life had in a sense been a preparation for this, but it was Robertson's sympathy that gave her intentions coherent shape. From the earliest conversations with him she had found a willing listener, and as she unfolded the story of her marriage and Medora's life, a plan was born for Robertson to tell Annabella's history.

Given the ultimate integrity of Robertson, it is doubtful that this could ever have emerged in any shape that would have satisfied Annabella, but the alliance did produce one concrete outcome. When Annabella had parted with Medora in 1843 she had severed relations with all the Leighs, but as she rehearsed again for Robertson's benefit the miseries of her long infatuation with the Byrons, the lure of old affections and the chance of extorting one last confession out of Augusta proved too hard to resist.

Augusta had, in fact, written to Annabella in 1848, begging for financial help, but the letter had been returned unopened, with a note that any future communication should go to her lawyer. Over the next few months desperation had forced Augusta to try again, but with Medora's accusations still fresh in mind, there was no budging Annabella and a humiliated Augusta was forced to turn to the grandson of Byron's old guardian and satirical butt, Lord Carlisle.

Augusta's pathetic attempts to awaken Annabella's sympathy show the levels to which poverty had reduced her, but in the Leigh household there was worse to come. During the 1840s the disintegration of her family had continued along its old predictable lines, with her sons turning out everything they had always promised, Georgey estranged from her mother and only her youngest daughter, Emily, of any comfort to Augusta.

Punctuated by long bouts of torpor and depression, George Leigh, too, had continued his feckless path to the grave, his long career with the turf climaxing when he was arrested for debt on the racecourse at Newmarket. There is a poignant entry in Augusta's commonplace book that suggests how attritional the effects of life with him must have been, but whatever his failings, loyalty and affection were so deeply ingrained in her character that his death in May 1850 proved a decisive blow.

For over forty years she had been covering for him, begging for him, and pandering to his temper, and yet if George Leigh had done nothing else he had given the purpose and focus to life Augusta had always needed. With his death it was at last possible to make economies that had been out of the question during his lifetime, but with no one to look after there was no one to live for and Augusta's health suffered the collapse that would lead ultimately to her death.

By the end of 1850 she was beyond looking after family affairs, and in the February of the following year, with "ruin staring us in the face," her daughter Emily approached Lushington in one last attempt to enlist her godmother's support. "My Mother has been trying for some time to enable her to make an arrangement with creditors," she wrote with the mix of subservience and fear that had come to mark the Leighs' dealings with Annabella,

> There is no channel that she has not tried. But Alas! all to no purpose & I now turn to Lady Byron as our last & only

hope . . . Nothing would have induced me to make this application but my unhappiness at seeing My Mother in this wretched state & health . . . I should feel so grateful if you would have the kindness to communicate it to Lady Byron as I fear from her not having answered my letters she was displeased but the recollection of her kindness to me when a child at Brighton induces me to hope she would forgive my appealing to her.4

This plea arrived at a time when Annabella's dialogue with Robertson had stirred all her old, ambivalent feelings about Augusta, and, giving only the post-office at Brighton as her address, she set out the terms on which they might meet. Over the next weeks letters went backwards and forwards between Brighton and London refining the place and rules of engagement, with an exhausted and bewildered Augusta—the black-edged mourning paper of her letters as prophetic as it was commemorative—reluctant to have a witness to their meeting and Annabella adamant. "I can give no better proof of my wishing to see you," Augusta at last wrote, caving in as she had almost always done before the implacable will of her "sometime sister,"

than by the sacrifice of my own feelings in consenting to see any third person during any part of our interview which must be of a painful nature & may be the last we may ever have in this world—however such are your terms, & be it so.5

The letter has a faint but recognisable fatalism about it, and even if Augusta had guessed Annabella's full intentions, she would probably have made no attempt to escape. There was one further delay due to illness but on 8 April she left her daughter, Emily, and her maid, behind, and boarded the train at London Bridge for Reigate and the fly waiting to take her to the White Hart, a sick woman of sixty-seven held together by nothing more than a deluded confidence in a providence about to desert her.

Because if neither Augusta nor Annabella could have pulled back from that final meeting, its failure was just as certain. In the days before Reigate Annabella had worked herself up to a pitch of nervous excitement, and with her burning belief that Byron would have returned to her had he lived, nothing Augusta could say could ever make up for the life that had ended with the separation.

But if Annabella believed, when she left Reigate with Robertson in the train for Brighton on that Tuesday in 1851, that she could erase Augusta from her mind as easily as she had Medora, she was mistaken. It was characteristic that the last letter she ever received from Augusta should be returned unopened, but when two months after the meeting she received a letter from Augusta's daughter, Emily, she could no more resist its claim on her kindness than she had been able to nearly forty years before.

"I saw death in her face at once,"[6] Annabella had said after meeting Augusta at the White Hart, and she had been right. Augusta had returned from their meeting in a state of emotional and physical collapse, and by June the end was certain enough for her to make her will. "Fairly worn out with trouble & anxiety,"[7] her daughter reported, her illness had turned to dropsy. Down at Moore Place, Annabella gave instructions that she was to be kept informed, and at the beginning of October wrote to Emily with a last message for her mother. "About a week ago I felt so great a desire to send her a message," she told Robertson,

> that after fully considering what might be the effects I determined to disregard all but those which it might possibly have upon herself—I wrote to ask the daughter to whisper two words from me—words of affection long since disused."[8]

On 5 October Emily wrote back. "She desires me to say," she answered on her dying mother's behalf,

> that the tears which refused to flow from sorrow were produced by the joy of hearing "Dearest Augusta" from you— that they were her greatest consolation—her voice has grown so weak and thick that it is with difficulty that I can make out what she says—she said a great deal more to me that I could not hear distinctly—I dare say that she will mention the subject again.[9]

She never did—"A *second* message lost"[10] was Annabella's wry response, the first being from Missolonghi in April 1824—and a week after Emily wrote to her again from the apartment in St. James's that had been Augusta's only refuge. "My dear Aunt," she wrote a brief note early on Sunday, 12 October 1851,

> Poor Mamma died this morning after three having suffered most dreadfully since yesterday afternoon—it is indeed a most happy release but her loss can never be made up to me.[11]

"I feel it every moment & hour of the day," she wrote again, when she was more able to compose herself, sending her black-edged letter, in its black-edged envelope with its black sealing wax and penny red stamp to her aunt at Moore Place,

> & yet it is a merciful release [from] her sufferings that have been dreadful . . . It is a great consolation to me that I have always been with her & that she died with her dear hands in mine & that she said I had always been such a comfort to her.[12]

This death bed reconciliation was perhaps Annabella's first unalloyed gesture of generosity towards Augusta in almost forty years, but it was no more than tacit acknowledgement of what their friendship had meant. In the aftermath of Augusta's death she would inevitably retreat from any public admission of such a truth, but a letter to Emily the following year probably comes as close to the complex reality of her feelings as a lifetime's self-justification could allow. "I found that Mrs. Villiers had touched in conversation with you on my conduct towards your mother," she wrote on 2 July 1852,

> Before my marriage, when your mother was a stranger to me, I resolved to be to her as an own sister. Mine is not a nature in which affection *can* fade away. Nearly forty years have shown this in regard to *her*. She was throughout the object of my unvarying devotedness. It was her infatuation (pardon the word) not to recognise in me her truest friend . . .
>
> I failed in other attempts to serve her & her children, but there never was a time when her welfare was not my first object. I could not give up the *rights* of others or my own, & I was in consequence forced into an *apparently* unfriendly posi-

tion but the closing of her life & my previous wish for an
interview with her, must prove that my affection had with-
stood every trial;—all;—and your expression as the effect of
my last message upon her afforded me the consolation that
she was at last sensible how truly I had loved her.[13]

The death of Augusta in October 1851 could not have come at a
worse time for Annabella, because it coincided almost exactly with a
double-blow that rammed home the hollowness of all her "victo-
ries." For the best part of forty years she had done her best to redeem
the Byron bloodline from itself, and if she had failed with the Leighs
she had at least been able to console herself with the fiction that she
had saved Ada from her inheritance.

   She had felt sure enough of this to mark her daughter's first
Christmas as a married woman by trusting her with the portrait of
Byron in Albanian costume that had hung behind the curtain at
Kirkby, and Ada's support during the Medora saga had seemed to
endorse her judgement. In her son-in law, William King—now the
Earl of Lovelace—Annabella had also found a supporter ready to
cede her all the influence she could want. During the 1840s she had
virtually run his domestic and public life for him, overseeing his children and his children's tutors, his speeches in parliament and his phi-
lanthropies at home, his improvements to his country estates and his
place in town—in all things, as she announced with barely the slightest trace of irony, "*the Omnipotent.*"[14]

   With the swings of mood to which Ada had always been subject,
there were times when she savagely resented this interference, but
between her ambivalent attitude towards motherhood and ill health,
she, too, put up little resistance. Throughout her childhood she had
been subject to bouts of mysterious illness, and these had continued
into married life, with sporadic and grotesque attacks of swelling and
nervous paralysis—heightened by a regime of opium and laudanum—violently punctuating the chronic miseries of asthma and
anorexia.

   But illnesses apart, Ada was unfitted by temperament and intellect
for domestic life, and happy to leave its tedious details to her mother
and husband. From her earliest days she had shown an aptitude for
science, and if she was never the figure in the history of Babbage's

inventions legend has made of her, she had become a mathematician of real talent, with a passionate desire for intellectual fulfilment and a mystical belief in her own genius that makes her father's claim to be Napoleon's equal seem modest:

> I do not believe, that my father was (or ever could have been) such a *Poet* as I shall be an Analyst (& Metaphysician).[15]

"I believe no creature ever could will things like a Byron," she wrote again, striking that note of enthusiasm and excess her mother had spent her life trying to eradicate,

> And perhaps that is the bottom of the genius-like tendencies in my family. We can throw our *whole life* and *existence* for the time being into whatever we *will* to do and accomplish.[16]

As her sense of her powers had grown, even her illnesses seemed providential. "With all my wiry power and strength," she wrote,

> I am prone at times to bodily sufferings and peculiarities of my physical constitution. They have taught me, and continue to teach me, that which I think nothing else could have developed. It is a force and control put upon me by Providence, which I *must* obey. And the effects of this continual discipline are mighty. They *tame* in the best sense of that word, and they *fan* into existence a pure, bright holy, unselfish flame within that sheds cheerfulness and light on many.[17]

Increasingly bored with her husband, impatient of the constraints of rank, and only sporadically interested in her children, her life took on a frenetic urgency the constant threat of illness only intensified. During the early years of marriage there had been periods of acute depression in which she felt herself no more than a "walking intellect," but as Lovelace took his refuge in estate improvements and the approbation of Annabella, Ada found in the friendships of scientists and the risks of the turf the excitement and *life* her whole upbringing had tried to stifle.

With a devoted son-in-law, one of her old "spies' still reporting, and a controlling say in all the Lovelaces' affairs, only Annabella's faith in her own judgement could have blinded her to the danger. In the 1830s she had confidently prescribed mathematics as a "cure" for Ada's imagination, and although she might dislike men like Babbage and her other new friends on social grounds, she seemed utterly blind to the intoxicating possibilities of the world they had opened up for Ada.

Her disillusionment was abrupt, and came from an unexpected quarter, when on an extended tour of the northern counties, Ada wrote to her mother with the news that she had visited Newstead for the first time. Over thirty years earlier Annabella had made the same pilgrimage to the Byron family home, but while she had been happy enough to allow herself the luxury of a versifying melancholy she could not bear the place to have the same impact on Byron's daughter.

It might have been better and cleaner in the long run if Annabella had known that Ada had arranged with its new owner to be buried beside her father in the family vault at Hucknall, but even in her ignorance her anger had all the furious implacability of wounded feelings. In her own eyes she had always done her best to protect Byron's memory for his daughter, but when Ada wrote of her gradually thawing feelings for the "*Mausoleum*" of her race—of the way in which images of melancholy and death had changed to "resurrection"[18]—it seemed as though all the suffering and moral struggle of Annabella's life was being thrown in her face. "I was his best friend," she wrote back in a letter stiff with resentment and threat,

> It often occurs to me that my attempts to influence your Children favourably in their early years—will be frustrated & turned to mischief,—so that it would be better for them not to have known me,—if they are allowed to adopt the unfounded popular notion of my having abandoned my husband from want of devotedness & entire sympathy—or if they suppose me to have been under the influence, at any time, of cold, calculating, & unforgiving feelings,—such having been his published description of me, whilst he wrote to me privately (as will hereafter appear) "I did—do—and ever shall—love you."[19]

Although it was the reports of Newstead that upset Annabella at the time, Ada's news of the great Voltigeur's success at Doncaster in one the most famous of all horse races hid a more desperate threat to her mother's regime. It is not possible to say when Ada had begun to gamble heavily, but by the time that Voltigeur completed his extraordinary St. Leger/Doncaster Cup double in 1850 she was an addict, immersed in the clandestine world of the Victorian turf, deep in debt and—abetted it would seem by Babbage—as supremely confident as any self-respecting punter would be of mathematical systems that would get her out of gaol.

A fascination with gambling always seems to require some explanation—as if it were not the most natural, intellectually stimulating and satisfying of all human activities—but in Ada's case it probably does. Through the early years of the 1840s she had enjoyed the most fulfilling period of her life, and yet there seems to have been a restless dissatisfaction that craved some more lurid outlet than a life of intellectual bohemianism, a need for stimulus—her father's old battle cry—that must have seemed in the face of worsening health its own proof to her that she was *alive*.

Lovelace had known for some time that she was gambling, without ever having any idea of the stakes involved, but when the small syndicate to which she belonged sustained massive losses on the 1851 Derby, secrecy became impossible. Through her various contacts Ada managed to borrow her own share of the debt, but under the pressure of blackmail from another member of her consortium she had no choice but to turn for help to her husband.

After years of anxieties, she was also seriously—probably terminally—ill again, as an examination conducted by the family doctor, Laycock, in the month after the Derby confirmed. There had seemed a brief hope in 1850 that her health might recover, but even though she was not told the likely prognosis she was already consciously living her life with the sense that she might not have long. "I'd rather," she wrote, with a genuinely Byronic bravado, to a friend,

> have 10 or five what I call *real* years of life, than 20 or 30 such as I see people usually dwelling on, without any spirit.[20]

The last person Ada wanted to see in such circumstances was Annabella, but Lovelace's response to any domestic or public problem was to consult his mother-in-law, and on 19 June 1851 he went to Leamington Spa, where she was nursing her own ill-health. He took with him a diagnosis of cervical cancer from Ada's doctor, but if Annabella seemed bizarrely unmoved by Laycock's grim prognosis the revelations of Ada's gambling provoked an anger that eclipsed even her Newstead bitterness.

Coming only two months after the last abortive meeting with Augusta at Reigate, the news seems to have almost unhinged Annabella. It would have been bad enough for her to have been excluded from her daughter's confidence, but as with Medora almost a decade earlier she found herself confronting, in the spectre of Byronic "sin" triumphant, the failure of her whole life's work.

It was, though, oddly, Lovelace himself who bore the brunt of her bitterness, and with his revelations her affection and trust turned into an immediate and implacable hostility. In Annabella's eyes he had not only failed Ada but betrayed *her* too, and letter after bewildered letter from him did nothing more than give her the chance to crystallise her fury into a moral indignation from which there could be no retreat.

It was the first time that Lovelace had felt the full force of a personality that had been petrifying with age and the almost unopposed exercise of her own will. To the end of her life Annabella retained an extraordinary ability to inspire devotion in her friends, but when "the devil of the North Pole was upon her," as one Esher acquaintance put it, "she was stern, unyielding, and unforgiving in her hate." "The touch of her hand," at such times, William Howitt wrote in the *Daily News* in 1869, "was like that of death; in her manner was the silence of the grave." A "woman of the most honourable and conscientious intention," he remembered her,

> she was subject to a constitutional idiosyncrasy of a most peculiar kind, which rendered her, when under its influence, absolutely and persistently unjust ... Through this the changes in her mood were sudden, and most painful to all about her. I have seen her of an evening in the most amiable, cordial and sunny humour, full of interest and sympathy; and I have seen her the next morning come down as if she had lain all night not on a feather-bed, but on a glacier—frozen as it were to the very soul ... .[21]

"There was a strong vein of eccentricity in her character," Robertson's biographer, Frederick Arnold, recalled, pushing Howitt's observations a step further,

> She would take violent and unreasonable prejudices. She was capable of a very strong tinge of bitterness. She would show great and lavish kindness, and the kindness, without any reason would be capriciously withdrawn. Indeed one of her medical friends who had watched her very narrowly has declared that in his judgement her mental balance was impaired.[22]

To Lovelace's credit, after years of doing what he was told, he refused to allow Annabella to confront Ada personally, but with the cancer now clearly terminal some kind of rapprochement was inevitable. Through the second half of 1851 Ada managed with the help of laudanum to maintain some semblance of independence, but when at the beginning of 1852 her condition declined sharply neither she nor Lovelace any longer had the strength to hold out.

It was the opportunity Annabella had been waiting for, and by the end of May she was at her daughter's bedside, in control of her debts, her medication and her conscience. Over the previous weeks Ada had been brought to admit some of her losses to Annabella's lawyer, but it was the catharsis of personal confrontation, confession and remorse that her mother demanded and Ada found herself as powerless before her as she had been as child.

Within days the details of Ada's gambling began to emerge—the scale of the losses, the secret pawning of the Lovelace jewels, the paste replicas made to replace them—and with every confession Annabella's sense of divinely elected purpose increased. It had been typical of her disbelief in any but her own illness that the first news of Ada's should leave her unmoved, but as the cancer spread, and with a kind of horrific symmetry inexorably destroyed Ada's womb, her mother saw with all the blinkered certainty of Annabella Milbanke her own appointed role in an illness sanctioned by heaven.

There may perhaps have been deaths more lingering, more excruciatingly painful, more emotionally disturbing than that of Ada, but the presence there for week after week through the summer of 1852 of Annabella gives it a horror all its own. From the moment that

Ada's husband had revealed his wife's gambling he had been cut off as if he was almost not there, and in an atmosphere of unsuppressed hostility Annabella sat at her daughter's side, surrounded by a sea of mattresses on which the tortured Ada would throw herself, the "angel of mercy" of Annabella's acolytes revealed in all the retributive and unbending rigour of Victorian moral tyranny. The "greatest of all mercies," shown her, she wrote of what she called the "blessing" of Ada's cancer, in September,

> has been her disease—weaning her from temptation, & turning her thoughts to higher and better things.[23]

There are certain historical habits of thought and feeling that in spite of all effort remain beyond grasp, and no movement of imaginative sympathy can take one into the mind of Annabella as she sat at her daughter's deathbed. It was one thing for her fellow "souls" to see Ada's agonies as a redeeming mercy of God sent to break a rebellious spirit, but as her mother watched over her last interminable days, and one by one the broken confessions of excess and sexual infidelities came out, consuming teller and hearer in the same misery of blighted faith and memories, it beggars belief that she can have escaped her own part in Ada's tragedy.

Because it was not just the destructive work of cancer Annabella was witnessing, but the physical devastation of a lifetime's campaign of emotional suppression and control. As a child Ada had fantasies of flying, and was afraid to sleep within the prison of a fourposter, wrapping herself in blankets on the floor. Now she had nightmares of being buried alive. As the illness dragged on, and she lay there, compulsively fiddling with a handkerchief,—"spreading it, measuring it, & waving it about with her hands"[24]—it was her constant refrain that they should make no mistake over her death. Her husband was moved by her courage, but the simple truth was she was broken. As the bullfinch sang in its cage, Ada's groans filled the room, a repentant sinner brought back to her mother's faith. Her punishment at God's hands, the proud, materialist mathematician, told Annabella, would last a million years. It had been revealed to her in a dream.

If this was Annabella's victory, however, it was a pyrrhic one, as empty as every other in her struggle against Byronism. As her daughter rambled of her sins and God's punishment it might have seemed that she had won her back, but as she learned for the first time now that Ada would be buried with her father, her coffin next to his in the Byron crypt at Hucknall—the prophecy of *Childe Harold* fulfilled—Annabella must have recognised a gesture of rejection too complete and symbolic to escape.

As she sat there, sketching Ada's face as it lay sunk in a pillow, the hard, ugly lines of the drawing petering away into nothing, a thin, disembodied hand seeming all that is left of her daughter's tortured form, it is hard to believe that she could not also see there the mirror of her own life. For more than forty years she had tried to project her own emotional and sexual longings onto one external threat or another, but in the shattered body of a daughter she had so success-fully created in her own image it was as if she was at last brought face to face—Dorian Grey like—with the reality of her own inner world.

By the end, too, Ada's pain was such that not even Annabella could extract any emotional or spiritual comfort from it. On 26 November she confessed to a friend that some respite was needed if Ada was to *feel* as she should, but the only respite open to her daugh-ter now was drug-induced, and on the next evening she finally slipped insensibly away, after all her agonies dying at last with some-thing of the quiet of the young Paul Dombey, whose end—the figure of his father just beyond his fading gaze—Dickens himself had been asked to read to Ada at her death bed.*

And it is, in the end, in the literature of the nineteenth century and not in medical case notes so typical of an age buckling under the pressure of its divided identity that we can best feel the tragedy that reached its grim conclusion with Ada's death. In the text books of hysteria her symptoms and those both of Annabella and Medora can be found time and again, but in the generation before Freud it was left to the great novelists to recognise the full, destructive horror that lay at the heart of Annabella's story.

It is hard to pick up a nineteenth-century novel and not find a trace of Byron in some form, but in less obvious ways his wife's his-

---

*Dickens had first met Ada in 1843, when she had been wary that he only wanted to know her because of the Byron connection. Judging from dinner guest lists in Forster's biography, he often subsequently saw her—certainly often enough for her to ask him to come when she was dying and for him to hurry to comply.

tory made an equally profound impression. In her posthumous "Vindication" of Lady Byron, Mrs. Stowe claimed that anyone who wanted to understand Annabella's sufferings need only read *Romola*, but a striking coincidence of dates suggests that it is rather in *Middlemarch* and Dorothea Brooke's resurrection from the emotional and sexual trauma of marriage, that George Eliot gave her own answer to the moral death Annabella had brought on herself.*

It is a sobering thought, in fact, that to the nineteenth-century writer with the most profoundly *moral* sense of life and art, the story of Annabella's revenge seemed too shocking to be allowed into the light of day. "It remains a grievously pitiable thing to me," Eliot wrote to Sara Hennell, when Annabella's carefully controlled version of her story, with its insistent theme of self-justification and vengeance finally became public in 1869,

> that man or woman who has cared about a future life in the minds of coming generations should have deliberately, persistently mingled with that prospect the ignoble desire to perpetuate personal animosities, which can never be rightly judged by those immediately engaged in them. To write a cruel letter in a rage is very pardonable—even a letter full of gall and bitterness, meant as a sort of poisoned dagger. We poor mortals can hardly escape these sins of passion. But I have no pity to spare for the rancour that corrects its proofs . . . chuckling with the sense of its future publicity.[26]

It was probably always Annabella's fate to fall short of George Eliot's standards of humanity, and yet it is also possible that with her generosity of mind Eliot could simply not bear the human reality that faced her in Annabella's story. In Dorothea Brooke she created and then redeemed a heroine with the same priggish and evangelical nar-

---

*George Eliot began the restructuring of *Middlemarch*, for the first time sketching in the character of Dorothea, almost to the day that the controversy over the Byron marriage burst again on nineteenth-century England in 1869. It is quite possible that the process was an unconscious one, but as her letters show, Annabella and the separation story were at the front of her mind as she fleshed out her modern day St. Theresa. Another member of the Byron family also provided the inspiration for *Daniel Deronda*. In the autumn of 1872 George Eliot was in Hamburg, and was upset to see "Miss Leigh, Byron's grandniece," gambling, "her fresh face among all the hags and stupid men around her"[25]—the spark for the character of Gwendolen Harleth.

rowness as the young Annabella Milbanke, but the desolate truth is that outside the life-enhancing world of Eliot's imagination it is hard to think that anyone could have recovered the trust or suppleness of spirit that Annabella lost when she lost Byron.

While George Eliot in the end shied away from the full tragedy of Annabella's life, there is one novelist who did not, and in the character of Miss Havisham, Dickens has left a portrait that might stand as the obituary notice for Annabella Byron. There is no more question that Dickens knew of her story than that Eliot did, and with his profound sense of the relationship of the inner and outer life, and intuitive sense of the pathology of emotional disorders, the man who sat at Ada's deathbed need have looked no further for his inspiration.

It is difficult to believe, in fact, that with the evidence of what Annabella had done to her daughter and to herself, he did not have her in his mind when only weeks after Lady Byron's death he began *Great Expectations*. The genesis of any character in a novel is a complex and uncertain business of invention and borrowing of course, but if the external trappings of Miss Havisham's character come from any number of sources, the *emotional* truth is the truth of Annabella's life. The woman who sat "corpse like" among the decay of Satis House, her "withered bridal dress . . . grave clothes," her yellowing veil a shroud, the clock and watch stuck for ever at the same time, is the Annabella Byron who clung obsessively to the humiliations of her own wedding day. The woman who used and perverted her adopted child Estella to take her revenge on the world that had rejected her, is the same Annabella who turned Medora against her mother. "What have I done?" Miss Havisham demands of Pip (coincidentally the Byron nickname Medora revived for Annabella) when she at last sees the human destruction a lifetime of obsession and revenge has caused: "I knew not how to answer, or how to comfort her," Dickens's narrator recalls in one of the supreme passages of human understanding in English fiction,

> That she had done a grievous thing in taking an impressionable child to mould into the form that her wild resentment, spurned affection, and wounded pride, found vengeance in, I knew full well. But that, in shutting out the light of the day, she had shut out infinitely more; that, in seclusion, she had secluded herself from a thousand natural and healing

influences; that, her mind brooding solitary, had grown diseased, as all minds do and must and will that reverse the
appointed order of their Maker; I knew equally well. And
could I look upon her without compassion, seeing her punishment in the ruin she was, in her profound unfitness for this
earth on which she was placed, in the vanity of sorrow which
had become a master mania, like the vanity of penitence, the
vanity of remorse, the vanity of unworthiness, and other
monstrous vanities that have been curses in this world?[27]

If there had ever been a stage, however, when Annabella could have
asked herself Miss Havisham's question and answered it with any
honesty that had long since passed. At the time of Ada's death she
made the best public face she could of her daughter's choice of burial place, but as she moved back to Brighton and resumed the
rhythms of her old life again, prosecuting her feud with Lovelace
with an icy determination, that last, symbolic rejection became just
one more detail that had to be rewritten for the posthumous legend
she was determined to leave.

   It was one of the ironies of Annabella's history, in fact, that
through all her long "preparation for invisibility," as she phrased it,
no one could have been more concerned with the verdict of this
world. Throughout her life she had obsessively hoarded every scrap
of evidence that might bear on her reputation, making notes and
depositions in a hand that only ever wavered under the most intense
emotional strain, copying letters and minuting conversations, filling
notebook after notebook—little red, green, and marbled covered
monuments to mania—with observations, judgements, character
analyses, morality lessons, auto-descriptions, pen-portraits, religious
scruples, and fantasies of deluded self-justification.

   The death of Robertson in 1853, at the Byronic age of thirty-six,
robbed her of the collaborator she would most have wanted to put
this mass into order, but in the same year Annabella first met the
woman with whom her revelations will always be associated, the novelist and abolitionist, Harriet Beecher Stowe.

   Although in one sense Annabella could have found no more disas-
trous confidante than a woman as entirely innocent of the workings
of English social life as Mrs. Stowe, there was no one more prepared
to see her struggle in the terms she wanted it. In her childhood fan-

tasies Annabella had dreamed of herself at Thermopylae or "with Howard in the cheerless dungeon," and the author of *Uncle Tom's Cabin* was ready to champion her in the same terms, portraying her as the spiritual companion of Clarkson and Wilberforce, of Francis Xavier, Fenelon and the protestant martyrs, her life torn between a Christ-like love for the wayward souls who had wronged her and a final duty—"no matter at what expense to her own feelings"—to denounce corruption. "By nature and principle truthful," Mrs. Stowe wrote of her, when almost ten years after her death she went public with Annabella's version of her marriage, passed from one soul mate to another like some Olymypic flame of moral truth,

> she had the opportunity of silently watching the operation of a permitted lie upon a whole generation. She had been placed in a position in which it was necessary, by silence, to allow the spread and propagation through society of a radical falsehood. Lord Byron's life, fame, and genius had all struck their roots into this lie, been nourished by it, and had derived thence a poisonous power.
>
> Was this falsehood to go on corrupting literature as long as history lasted? Had the world no right to true history? Had she who possessed the truth no responsibility to the world? Was not a final silence a confirmation of a lie with all its consequences?
>
> Lady Byron has been falsely accused of having ruined *the* man of his generation, and caused all his vices and crimes, and all their evil effect on society. She submitted to the accusation for a certain number of years for reasons which commended themselves to her conscience; but when all the personal considerations were removed, and she was about passing from life, it was right, it was just, it was strictly in accordance with the philosophical and ethical character of her mind, and with her habit of considering things in their widest relations to the good of mankind, that she should give serious consideration to the last duty which she might owe to abstract truth and justice in her generation.[28]

It was not only her version of her marriage story she entrusted to Mrs. Stowe, but the image of herself in old age that she wanted perpetuated for posterity. Until the end of her life Annabella remained as alert as ever to the practical aspects of things, and yet the picture she left was of a woman who had already abandoned this earth, all inessentials distilled away to leave only that terrible creation of the Victorian mind—the all-seeing, all forgiving angel of compassion and death, hovering somewhere between the next world and this in sexless and untouchable serenity. "To talk to her seemed to the writer of this sketch," Mrs. Stowe wrote,

> the nearest possible approach to talking with one of the spir-
> its of the just made perfect . . . We have already spoken of
> that singular sense of the reality of the spiritual world which
> seemed to encompass Lady Byron during the last part of her
> life, and which made her words and actions seem more like
> those of a blessed being detached from earth than of an
> ordinary mortal. All her modes of looking at things, all her
> motives of action, all her involuntary actions of emotion,
> were so high above any common level, and so entirely regu-
> lated by the most worthy causes, that it would seem difficult
> to make the ordinary world understand exactly how the
> thing seemed to lie before her mind. What impressed the
> writer more strongly than ever was Lady Byron's perfect con-
> viction that her husband was now a redeemed spirit; that he
> looked back with pain and shame and regret on all that was
> unworthy in his past life; and that, if he could speak or could
> act in the case, he would desire to prevent the further circula-
> tion of base falsehoods, and of seductive poetry, which had
> been made the vehicle of morbid and unworthy passions.[29]

There is, in fact, something absolutely seamless in Annabella's descent to the grave, in the unchanging internal and external rhythms, the mental obsessions, the invalidism, the constant, restless wandering. For a time after Ada's death in 1852 she had taken apartments in Dover Street in London, but after that it was back to the old vagrant pattern, moving between Brighton and Hastings, London, Esher, Ham, Richmond, and finally London again, where at 11 St. George's Terrace, on 16 May 1860—one day short of her sixty-eighth birthday—the end finally came.

With her was her friend, Mrs. Barwell, and her devoted granddaughter, Lady Anne King. She had been suffering from bronchitis for weeks, complicated at the last by pleurisy, but death itself was quiet, Annabella slipping gently and calmly from sleep into the sleep of death, as her grandaughter wrote gratefully to Mrs. George Lamb. Shortly after, Annabella's grandson, Ralph, arrived, and the family sent for the Pre-Raphaelite sculptor, Thomas Woolner. The next day Woolner described the scene that met him. "I had to go and see a Cast taken of the left hand of Lady Byron, wife of the poet; he wrote to Tennyson's wife,

> The summons said it was essential an honourable man should do it, or I should not have been troubled. I do not much like taking casts of any one dead, but could not refuse in this case, as I know so many of their friends. But I was glad I did go, for a nobler sight I never saw—she looked as if she was living, and had just dropped to sleep, and as proud as a queen in her splendour . . . She seemed to have been almost adored by those around her.[30]

EPILOGUE

I t is fitting that Annabella's febrile wanderings should only end with death, because her kind of chronic restlessness—Tolstoy movingly portrayed it in old Prince Bolkonski—is a frequent symptom of terminal illness, and her whole widowhood had been little more than one long dying. In a perceptive obituary Harriet Martineau linked her bedouin life to the traumas of her marriage home with Byron, and if this outer life does offer any clue to her inner state then something in Annabella as surely died with her marriage as it did in Miss Havisham on her wedding day.

"Is her memory to be regarded with the deepest horror or the most profound compassion?"[1] John Paget demanded when Annabella's story was finally published in 1869, but Dickens had already answered that question ten years earlier. In her *Lady Byron Vindicated* Mrs. Stowe did her best to co-opt Annabella for the cause of women's freedom, but while there are certainly other economic and social patterns of nineteenth-century feminist history to which her life belongs it is the insights that Dickens offers that take us to the heart of her tragedy.

It is right that the decisive word on Annabella should be with him, too, because no novelist was better equipped to see not just the consequences of repression but also the relationship of the individual to the whole. There is such an outlandish quality to the sufferings of Miss Havisham that she seems to come from a planet of her own, but what Dickens saw was that the gothic horror of her bridal chamber and the physical and mental aberrations of a Jaggers or Wemmick are all of a piece in a society that has suppressed and warped its most generous instincts.

And that in the end is the fascination and importance of Annabella Byron, because her story is in miniature the story of the age; her descent from the passionate possibilities of her youth to the chillier virtues of justice and charity, the classic movement of the century. In a moment of savage disillusion Byron once labelled her "the moral Clytemnestra of her lord,"[2] and yet if this is a Greek tragedy it is a very English one, and Annabella a Clytemnestra of the sort Lord Leighton might paint, the embodiment of an England—the England of Lawrence's timeless battle of the community and the individual— that had come inexorably into its own with the Victorian era.

It is this, too, that gives such a monitory quality to her life, because the price she paid when she killed off in herself all those finer impulses, is just that which Europeans like Mazzini recognised England had paid when it drove Byron into exile. In her own warped and obsessive way, Annabella went on loving him until the end of her life, and yet it was a Byron of her own invention she always wanted, the outsider reabsorbed into the fold, the man who had lived with such vivid and dangerous intensity "purified and ennobled," "the shadows of earth for ever dissipated," "the angel in him," as she expressed it to Mrs. Stowe, "made perfect according to its divine ideal."[3]

It was only nine years after Annabella's death that Mrs. Stowe published *Lady Byron Vindicated,* and yet it is no exaggeration to say that the row she started is still not over. In the months after the separation the rumours of incest had been common currency in aristocratic London, but when Mrs. Stowe's revelations and Medora's *Autobiography* were published in the same year, the story broke on a mid-Victorian England that had buried those scandals beneath memories of Greek liberty and Missolonghi. "Who that has a spark of generous feeling," George Eliot had asked fourteen years earlier in her great essay on the Evangelical Dr. Cumming,

> that rejoices in the presence of good in a fellow-being, has not dwelt with pleasure on the thought that Lord Byron's unhappy career was ennobled and purified towards its close by a high and sympathetic purpose, by honest and energetic efforts for his fellow-men? Who has not read with deep emo-

tion those last pathetic lines, beautiful as the afterglow of sunset, in which love and resignation are mingled with something of a melancholy heroism? Who has not lingered with compassion over the dying scene at Missolonghi—the sufferer's inability to make his farewell messages of love intelligible, and the last long hours of silent pain?[4]

To George Eliot it seemed unbearable—in fact wicked—that Mrs. Stowe should shatter this image of Byron, and the public response was even more extreme. It is typical that in a fit of xenophobic snobbery it was Mrs. Stowe who bore the brunt of national anger, but when the dust had settled, all those who did not believe that she had simply misunderstood, or that Annabella was deranged, took out their disillusionment on Byron's widow in full measure. She was "an absolute moral monstrosity, an anomaly in the types of female hideousness." "It is said," declared *Blackwood's*—her champion back in 1819,

> that there are some poisons so subtle that they will destroy life, and may yet leave no trace of their action. The murderer who uses them may escape the vengeance of the law; but he is not the less guilty. So the slanderer who makes no charge; who deals in hints and insinuations: who knows melancholy facts he would not divulge;—things too painful to state; who forbears, expresses pity, sometimes even affection, for his victim . . . is far more guilty than he who tells the bold falsehood.
>
> Lady Byron has been called
>
> *"The moral Clytemnestra of her lord."*
>
> The "moral Brinvilliers" [the notorious 17th century French murderess who in one year killed her father, sister and two brothers and—famous for her charity—was said to try out her poisons on the sick in hospitals] would have been a truer designation.[5]

There can be few women who have received the posthumous mauling that Annabella Byron has suffered, but if England shot the messenger that does not mean that it did not listen to the message. In the century and a half since Mrs. Stowe's *Lady Byron Vindicated* there is scarcely a calumny that has not been piled on Annabella's head, but if nobody has ever thanked her for destroying Byron one only has to stand in the church at Hucknall where this book began to recognise the triumph of her bloodless vision over a tougher reality.

"And all men kill the thing they love,"[6]—the line has the same swelling insistence in this context as in Wilde's Ballad—and if there is anywhere to feel how England has traditionally done that best, the place is St. Mary's, Hucknall. This is not the only country that knows how to deal with its rebels of course, but there can be nowhere else that combines ruthlessness and re-assimilation with the same certainty of touch, demonising and then sanitising into posthumous harmlessness its aberrant genius—reabsorbing Shelley as the ineffectual angel of Victorian myth, the pariah Wilde as the author of *The Ideal Husband*, the blazing "Pilgrim of Eternity," that Shelley dubbed Byron, as the simple Christian "pilgrim" of Canon Barber's version.

The church—famous and visited for only one thing—is a hymn to this instinct for re-absorption. Near the porch, a small exhibition now preserves fragments of Byron's coffin and other memorabilia. At the west end, a Byron funeral hatchment hangs. On the south wall of the chancel, a tablet to Byron's memory records, all scandal hushed, that it was placed there by his sister. A medallion portrait—face in profile, hair curled, open neck—shows the ideal of what a poet *should* look like. In the floor is set a single slab of black marble, a gift of the King of Greece, with Byron's name and dates, surrounded by a hero's wreath.

What more perfect revenge could there be? Even Byron's corpse, hacked and battered by the doctors at Missolonghi, has shared in the same metamorphosis, brutal reality subsumed into the demands of Christian-classical mythology. What has happened to the disfigured and unrecognisable face that Hobhouse could scarcely bring himself to look at? Where in the idealising account of Canon Barber—the "custos of the body" as he called himself—are the crushed skull, the skeletalised limbs, the severed foot lying in the corner of his coffin? Where, for that matter, the "unusually pronounced sexual organ" privately noted by one of his churchwardens that June evening in 1938?

The cloven footed, priapic satyr of Byronic legend still has its place in popular demonology of course, but in its own way, that myth is no more threatening than the embalmed and ennobled corpse of Canon Barber's fiction. For the nineteenth century the gothic trappings of Byronism at least masked a real urgency of concern, but that anxiety has long since evaporated to leave the Byron of contemporary popular culture—the Byron routinely dragged up among the usual suspects at any identification parade of Don Juans or sexual deviants—with about as much historical solidity or danger about him as Bram Stoker's vampire.

"Byron, thou should be living at this hour!"[7] Auden invoked him on the eve of the Second World War—as Lawrence had done the aristocratic outsider on the eve of the First—but no generation has ever really wanted him as he *was*. In the same way that every age comes up with its own Shakespeare, so too it invents its own Byron, but it is always a Byron that is smaller and more manageable than the original, a writer of lyrics in one generation or letters in another, the author of the "Hebrew Melodies" or *Beppo*, the champion of political and sexual freedoms or a psychological case study.

Byron, though, is more serious than that. If he was right about England, England too was right about him, right that it could not afford to hold him. For a couple of years his contemporaries imagined, like Annabella, that they could enjoy the frisson of Byronic romanticism without any of its consequences, but as events rammed home that he had *meant* what he said they were left with nothing behind which to hide. They could take the libertine, Francis Jeffrey admitted. They could even take the atheist. What they could not take was the brilliant, unremitting stare that Byron turned on all their beliefs, illusions and self-deceptions. "The reveller may pursue his orgies," Jeffrey wrote in the *Edinburgh Review*, with all the desolation of a man who has heard the echo in the Marabar Caves,

> and the wanton display her enchantments with comparative safety to those around them . . . But if the priest pass from the altar, with exhortations to peace and purity still trembling on his tongue, to join familiarly in the grossest and most profane debauchery . . . our notions of right and wrong are at once confounded—our confidence in virtue shaken to the foundations—and our reliance on truth and fidelity at an end for ever.
>
> *This* is the charge which we bring against Lord Byron. We say that, under some misapprehension as to the truth, and the duty of proclaiming it, he has exerted all the powers of

his powerful mind to convince his readers, both directly and indirectly, that all ennobling pursuits, and disinterested virtues, are more deceits or illusions—hollow and despicable mockeries for the most part, and, at best, but laborious follies. Love, patriotism, valour, devotion, constancy, ambition—all are to be laughed at, disbelieved in, and despised! . . . Thus all good feelings are excited only to accustom us to their speedy and complete extinction, to the staple and substantial doctrine of the work—the non-existence of constancy in women or honour in men, and the folly of expecting to meet with any such virtues, or of cultivating them, for an undeserving world;—and all this mixed up with so much wit and cleverness, and knowledge of human nature, as to make it irresistibly pleasant and plausible—while there is not only no antidote supplied, but every thing that might have operated in that way has been anticipated, and presented already in as strong and engaging a form as possible—but under such associations as to rob it of all efficacy, or even turn it into an auxiliary of the poison.[8]

There is always so much sense in what Jeffrey writes of Byron—and such a palpable openness to his qualities—that it is hard to understand why he did not see that Byron was himself the "antidote." It would be hard to think of another satirist who fed so voraciously off himself as Byron did, but in an odd way it is that very egotism his critics railed against that is the guarantee of a shared humanity that ultimately roots even his most savage satire in a sense of common frailty.

In the end, though, it is not the quality of self-knowledge which distinguishes Byron—nor even the exuberance and fun with which he could go on looking at the world's follies—but something more profound. In the greatest of all English tragedies Shakespeare constructed a universe of faithlessness and cruelty and found within it the courage to *live*, and that essentially is what Byron did—saw humanity and his own character with all the clarity of *Lear*, saw life with its lies and deceptions, its cruelties, injustices, absurdities, abuses and hypocrisies, and discovered within *himself* the grace and bravery to live it with the intelligence and decency he showed in Greece.

It is easier, though, to fall back on other myths, and idealised hero or demonised caricature, Hucknall seems to have him both ways. On a cold, drizzling day in the early December of last year, the church was shut for lunch to pilgrims. At the far end of the High street, though, down from Byron Carpets, along the same route that his black-plumed funeral carriage was drawn in 1824, the Byron Cinema—Bingo twice a week—was showing *The Exorcist*.

It had a nice irony to it. It is not finally, though, at Hucknall but further south in west London's Kensal Green cemetery that one can fully count the cost of Annabella's crusade against the Byrons. It is where Augusta lies, and where no more than a hundred yards from her, Annabella was buried.

The way to approach that grave is from the main entrance of the cemetery, at the west end. As one goes through John Griffith's massive classical gateway, the path forks to left and right, the left hand path leading, as a contemporary noted with satisfaction,

> to the abodes of the Turks, Jews, Infidels, Heretics and "unbaptised folk" and the right hand after passing among the beautiful and consecrated graves of the faithful, leads to the Episcopal chapel. This chapel is a beautifully executed work, in the same style as the entrance buildings and is fitted up in excellent taste.9

It is down in the massive, barrel-vaulted catacomb beneath this chapel, that Augusta lies. With the encroaching pieties of old age she would probably have been pleased to find herself there, but there seems something very forlorn about her coffin, tucked away on the bottom shelf next to that "precious piece of helplessness" George Leigh, the wood beginning to disintegrate, a plain lead coffin plate the only identification, and above her head—as crushing a weight in death as in life—the great and uncompromising mass of religious and social orthodoxy enshrined in the grim doric of Griffith's chapel.

It is hard not to feel that Byron's Astarte—his Zuleika—would be happier among the Turks and infidels, but there are no such doubts as one stands by the grave of Lady Byron a minute's walk to the east. About twenty yards from where she is buried is the tomb of the hated Hobhouse, but there is a kind of inviolable self-sufficiency about Annabella's plain grave that no contagion can disturb. It is a single, flat stone. On it—the Anne of Anne Isabella Byron misspelled—is her name and dates. That misspelling, though, is the only liberty.

Next to her, like the slaves of some despot slaughtered on her death, lie the family of her lawyer Lushington. All around, too, monuments are collapsing in the heavy clay, marble columns and Egyptian obelisks falling, Ozymandias-like, into yawning graves. But not hers. Even its iron railings, fencing her off from the world around, have survived. "Let the English take care," Chateaubriand warned, "if they break the mould of the man—Byron—who had made them revive, what will remain?" What remains—and standing there on the white cliffs of Dover, child in her arms, Albion's daughter on perpetual guard, what always remains—is Lady Byron.

Notes,
Select Bibliography,
Acknowledgements,
Index

Notes

Abbreviations in Notes:

Ada — Moore, D. L., *Ada, Countess of Lovelace, Byron's Legitimate Daughter*, London, 1977

Astarte — Lovelace, R. M., *Astarte: A Fragment of Truth Concerning George Gordon Byron*, New York, 1921

Blessington — Lovell, J. (ed.), *Lady Blessington's Conversations of Lord Byron*, Princeton, 1969

Byron (McGann) — Byron, (ed. McGann, J. J.), *Lord Byron: The Complete Poetical Works*, Oxford, 1980

BLJ — Marchand, L. (ed.), *Byron's Letters and Journals*, London, Vols. 1–12, 1973–82

Byron, Lady, *Auto-Description*, 1831 — Byron Lovelace Papers, Bodleian Library, Byron, Lady, *Auto-Description*, 1831

Elwin (LBF) — Elwin, M., *Lord Byron's Family, Annabella, Ada and Augusta, 1816–1824*, London, 1975

Elwin (LBW) — Elwin, M., *Lord Byron's Wife*, London, 1962

Gunn — Gunn, P., *My Dearest Augusta*, London, 1968

Mayne — Mayne, E. C., *The Life and Letters of Anne Isabella, Lady Noel Byron*, London, 1929

Medora (Mackay) — Mackay, C. (ed.), *Medora Leigh; A History and an Autobiography*, London, 1869

Stowe — Stowe, H. B., *Lady Byron Vindicated*, London, 1870

Prologue

1 Lawrence, D. H., *Pheonix: The Posthumous Papers of D. H. Lawrence*, ed. Edward McDonald, London, 1936. *Study of Thomas Hardy*, pp. 398–516

2 Nicholson, Andrew (ed), *Lord Byron, the Complete Miscellaneous Prose*, Oxford, 1991, p. 97

3 Barber, T. G., *Byron and Where He Is Buried*, Hucknall, 1939, pp. 136–7

4 *Blackwood's*, 1825, quoted in Stowe, p. 315

5 BM Add Ms 31038

6 Byron (McGann) Vol. II, p. 180

7 Carlyle, T., *The Love Letters of Thomas Carlyle and Jane Welsh*, London, 1909, p. 366

8 Quoted in Elwin (LBW), p. 63

9 Trelawny, E. J., *Recollections of the Last Days of Shelley and Byron*, London, 1858, pp. 222–4

10 *Byroniana*, London, 1834, p. 111

11 *The Quarterly Review*, XXVII, quoted in Redpath, T., *The Young Romantics & Critical Opinion 1807–1824*, London, 1975, p. 191

12 Stowe, p. 80

13 *Blackwood's*, 1819, quoted in Stowe, p. 314

14 Wilde, O. (ed. Fong, B. & Beckson, K.), *The Complete Works of Oscar Wilde*, Oxford, 2000, Vol. I, p. 196

15 Lawrence, D. H., op. cit., pp. 398–516

16 Lawrence, D. H., *ibid*.

17 Byron (McGann), Vol. I, p. 107

18 Trelawny, E. J., *Records of Shelley, Byron and the Author*, London, 1878, Vol. I, pp. 30–1

19 Stowe, p. 128

A Meeting of Opposites

1 Stowe, p. 290

2 Stowe, p. 300

3 Ibid.

4 Byron, Lady, *Auto-Description*, 1831

5 Quoted in Mayne, p. 9

6 Byron, Lady, *Auto-Description*, 1831

7 Byron, Lady, *Auto-Description*, 1831, quoted in Mayne, pp. 4–5

8 Lamb, C., *Glenarvon*, London, 1995, pp. 29–30

9 Byron, Lady, *Auto-Description*, 1831, quoted in Mayne, p. 15

10 Quoted in Goldring, D., *Regency Portrait Painter, the life of Sir Thomas Lawrence, PRA*, London, 1951, p. 262

11 Byron, Lady, quoted in Mayne, pp. 36–7

12 Byron, Lady, quoted in Mayne, p. 38

13 Byron, Lady, *Auto-Description*, 1831, quoted in Mayne, p. 39

14 Marchand, L. (ed.), *Byron's Letters and Journals*, London, 1973–82, Vol. 4, pp. 182–3

15 Morgan, Lady, *Lady Morgan's Memoirs*, London, 1882, Vol. II, p. 200

16 Lovell, J. (ed.), *Lady Blessington's Conversations of Lord Byron*, Princeton, 1969, pp. 132–3

17 Lamb, C., op. cit., pp. 10–11

18 BLJ, Vol. 2, pp. 175–6

19 BLJ, Vol. 2, p. 218

20 BLJ, Vol. 2, p. 199

21 Byron, Lady, quoted in Mayne, pp. 48–9

22 BLJ, Vol. 2, pp. 226–7

23 Gronow, Captain, *Reminiscence of Captain Gronow*, Frome, 1984, Vol. 1, p. 150

24 Medwin, T., *Conversations of Lord Byron; noted during a residence with his lordship at Pisa*, London, 1824, p. 88

25 Cecil, D., *Melbourne*, London, 1955, p. 80

26 Blessington, p. 149

27 BLJ, Vol. 2, p. 238

28 BLJ, Vol. 2, p. 233

29 BLJ, Vol. 2, p. 242

30 BLJ, Vol. 3, p. 32

31 Hayman, R., *Nietzsche: A Critical Life*, London 1980, p. 35

32 Lawrence, D. H., op. cit., pp. 398–516

33 BLJ, Vol. 3, p. 225

34 BLJ, Vol. 3, p. 204

35 Lawrence, D. H., op. cit., pp. 398–516

36 BLJ, Vol. 3, p. 69

37 Lawrence, D. H., op. cit., pp. 398–516

38 BLJ, Vol. 3, p. 69

39 Lawrence, D. H., op. cit., pp. 398–516

40 Medwin, T., op. cit., p. 69

41 *The Town and Country Magazine*, January 1779, quoted in Gunn, p. 11

42 Osborne, Lady M., quoted in Gunn, P., op.cit, p. 38

43 BLJ, Vol. 3, p. 32

44 Byron (McGann), Vol. IV, p. 40

45 BLJ, Vol. 5, pp. 273–4

46 BLJ, Vol. 3, p. 68

47 Byron (McGann), Vol. III, p. 120

48 quoted in Astarte, p. 263

49 Byron (McGann), Vol. III, p. 120

50 BLJ, Vol. 3, p. 205

51 Byron (McGann), Vol. III, p. 159

52 Byron, Lady, quoted in Mayne, p. 48

53 BLJ, Vol. 4, p. 36

54 BLJ, Vol. 4, p. 39

55 Byron (McGann), Vol. III, pp. 359–60

56 BLJ, Vol. 3, p. 179

57 BLJ, Vol. 4, p. 45

58 BLJ, Vol. 4, pp. 110–11
59 BLJ, Vol. 4, p. 104
60 Stowe, p. 121
61 Byron, Lady, quoted in Mayne, pp. 57–8
62 Byron, Lady, quoted in Mayne, pp. 57–8
63 Byron, Lady, quoted in Mayne, p. 73
64 Byron, Lady, quoted in Mayne, p. 58
65 BLJ, Vol. 3, p. 99
66 BLJ, Vol. 3, p. 174
67 Moore, T., *The Letters and Journals of Lord Byron, with notices of his life*, Paris, 1829, Vol. 1, p. 581
68 Byron, Lady, quoted in Mayne, p. 111
69 Quoted in Eisler, B., *Byron*, New York, 1999, p. 447
70 Byron, Lady, quoted in Mayne, p. 408
71 Quoted in Gunn, p. 265
72 Byron, Lady, quoted in Mayne, p. 406

A Sense of Failure

1 Keynes, G. (ed.), *The Complete Writings of William Blake*, London, 1957, p. 75–6
2 Byron, Lady, quoted in Mayne, p. 409
3 Byron, Lady, quoted in Mayne, p. 408
4 Byron, Lady, *Memorandum of my interview with Mrs. Leigh at Reigate*, Lovelace Byron papers
5 Byron, Lady, quoted in Mayne, p. 409
6 Byron, Lady, quoted in Mayne, p. 410
7 Byron, Lady, quoted in Mayne, p. 403
8 Leigh, A., quoted in Gunn, p. 262
9 Robertson, F., quoted in Arnold, F., *Robertson of Brighton, with Some Notices of His Times and Contemporaries*, London, 1886, pp. 184–6
10 Byron, Lady, quoted in Mayne, p. 399

11 Arnold, F., op.cit., p. 155
12 Byron, Lady, quoted in Ada, p. 297

Marriage

1 Quoted in Stowe, p. 287
2 Byron, Lady, quoted in Elwin (LBW), p. 250
3 Martineau, H., quoted in Mayne, p. 287
4 Elwin (LBW), p. 254
5 Byron, Lady, quoted in Elwin (LBW), p. 254
6 Leigh, A., quoted in Gunn, p. 123
7 Byron, Lady, quoted in Elwin (LBW), p. 257
8 BLJ, Vol. 4, p. 249
9 BLJ, Vol. 4, pp. 252–2
10 BLJ, Vol. 4, pp. 263–4
11 Bence-Jones, Dr., quoted in Elwin (LBW), p. 285
12 BLJ, Vol. 4, p. 262
13 Byron, Lady, quoted in Elwin (LBW), p. 192
14 Byron, Lady, quoted in Elwin (LBW), pp. 294–5
15 BLJ, Vol. 4, p. 285
16 Ibid.
17 Leigh, Augusta, quoted in Elwin (LBW), p. 300
18 Byron, Lady, quoted in Mayne, p. 183
19 Byron, Lady, quoted in Mayne, p. 181
20 Ticknor, G., *Life, Letters and Journals of George Ticknor*, 1876, Vol. 1, pp. 50–56
21 Ibid.
22 Byron, Lady, quoted in Mayne, p. 181
23 Byron, Lady, quoted in Mayne, p. 194
24 Lawrence, D. H., op. cit., pp. 398–516
25 Byron, Lady, quoted in Mayne, p. 195
26 Barnard, Lady A., quoted in Stowe, p. 306
27 BLJ, Vol. 5, p. 14–15

28 Byron, Lady, quoted in Elwin
    (LBW), p. 346
29 Byron, Lady, quoted in Mayne,
    pp. 200–1

Sleeping with the Vampire

1 Byron, Lady, quoted in Gunn, p. 154
2 Byron, Lady, quoted in Mayne,
    p. 203
3 BM Add MS 31037
4 Ibid.
5 BLJ, Vol. 5, p. 20
6 Ibid.
7 Leigh, A., quoted in Elwin (LBW),
    p. 384
8 Leigh, A., quoted in Elwin (LBW),
    p. 428
9 Byron, Lady, quoted in Elwin
    (LBW), p. 426
10 Byron, Lady, quoted in Elwin
    (LBW), p. 456
11 Ibid.
12 Byron, Lady, quoted in Elwin
    (LBW), p. 457
13 Ibid.
14 Byron, Lady, quoted in Elwin
    (LBW), p. 459
15 Byron (McGann), pp. 386–8
16 Byron, Lady, quoted in Elwin
    (LBW), p. 463
17 Nicholson, Andrew (ed.), *Lord Byron,*
    The Complete Miscellaneous Prose, Ox-
    ford, 1991, p. 95
18 Robinson, H. C., quoted in Stowe,
    p. 186
19 Wordsworth, W., quoted in Red-
    path, T., *The Young Romantics & Criti-*
    cal Opinion 1807–1824, London, 1975,
    p. 199
20 Barnard, Lady A., quoted in Stowe,
    p. 306
21 quoted in Stowe, p. 80
22 Byron, Lady, *Auto-Description,* 1831
23 Elwin (LSW) p. 115
24 BLJ, Vol. 2, p. 175
25 BLJ, Vol. 4, pp. 229–231
26 Leigh, Augusta, quoted in Elwin
    (LBW), p. 275
27 BLJ, Vol. 5, p. 24
28 Byron, Lady, quoted in Ada, p. 141
29 Byron (McGann), Vol. 2, p. 119
30 Polidori, J., *The Vampyre and Other*
    Tales of the Macabre, Oxford, 1997,
    p. 3
31 Byron (McGann), Vol. III,
    pp. 380–2
32 Byron (McGann), Vol. III, p. 383
33 Byron (McGann), Vol. IV, pp. 1–2
34 BLJ, Vol. 5, p. 66
35 Byron (McGann), Vol. III, p. 64
36 Tennyson, A., in Ricks C. (ed.) *The*
    Poems of Tennyson, Avon, 1969, p. 321

The Kindness of Sisters

1 Lamb, Mrs G., quoted in
    Grosskurth, P., *Byron, the Flawed*
    Angel, London, 1997, p. 272
2 Byron, Lady, quoted in Elwin
    (LBF), p. 45
3 Ibid.
4 Byron, Lady, quoted in Elwin
    (LBF), p. 54
5 Byron, Lady, quoted in Mayne,
    p. 181
6 Clermont, Mrs., quoted in Fox, Sir
    J., *The Byron Mystery,* London, 1924,
    p. 147
7 Byron, Lady, quoted in Medora
    (Mackay), p. 55
8 Byron, Lady, quoted in Medora
    (Mackay), pp. 54–5
9 BLJ, Vol. 5, p. 66
10 Byron, Lady, quoted in Elwin (LBF),
    p. 30
11 Villiers, The Hon. Mrs. G., quoted
    in Elwin (LBF), p. 30
12 Byron, Lady, quoted in Elwin (LBF),
    p. 30
13 Villiers, The Hon Mrs. G., quoted
    in Elwin (LBF), pp. 33–4
14 Byron, Lady, quoted in Elwin (LBF),
    p. 42
15 Byron, Lady, quoted in Elwin (LBF),
    p. 35
16 Leigh, A., quoted in Elwin (LBF),
    p. 42

17 Byron, Lady, quoted in Elwin (LBF), p. 33

18 Leigh, A., quoted in Astarte, p. 224

19 Byron, Lady, quoted in Astarte, pp. 247–8

20 Leigh, A., quoted in Astarte, pp. 249–50

21 Hobhouse, J. C., quoted in Grosskurth, P., *Byron, the Flawed Angel*, London, 1997, p. 27

22 BLJ, Vol. 6, p. 232

23 Byron (McGann), Vol. IV, p. 74

24 Villiers, The Hon. Mrs. G., quoted in Astarte, p. 69

25 BLJ, Vol. 5, p. 91

26 BLJ, Vol. 5, p. 115

27 BLJ, Vol. 5, p. 190

28 BLJ, Vol. 5, pp. 231–2

29 BLJ, Vol. 6, pp. 129–130

30 BLJ, Vol. 6, p. 129

31 BLJ, Vol. 8, p. 139

32 Astarte, pp. 61–2

33 Quoted in Edel, L., *Henry James, the Middle Years 1884–94*, London, 1963, p. 243

34 quoted in Edel, op.cit, p. 244

35 Austen, J., *Persuasion*, London, 1965, p. 238

An Instrument of Destruction

1 Byron, Lady, quoted in Mayne, p. 267

2 Byron, Lady, quoted in Elwin (LBF), p. 161

3 Lockhart, J. G., *Life of Scott*, Edinburgh, 1839, Vol. 5, p. 253

4 Byron, Lady, quoted in Mayne, pp. 277–8

5 Byron, Lady, quoted in Mayne, p. 272

6 Johnson, S., *The Works of Samuel Johnson*, London, 1825, Vol. 7, p. 119

7 Byron, Lady, quoted in Ada, pp. 8–9

8 Byron, Lady, quoted in Mayne, p. 292

9 Byron, Lady, quoted in Ada, p. 373

10 Leigh, A., quoted in Gunn, pp. 225–6

11 Leigh, A., quoted in Gunn, pp. 226–7

12 Trevanion, H., *The Influence of Apathy*, London, 1829, pp. 122–3

13 Medora (Mackay), pp. 122–4

14 Leigh, Medora, Byron Lovelace Papers, Bodleian Library, Box 86, f.18

15 Medora (Mackay), p. 124

16 Medora (Mackay), pp. 125–6

17 Leigh, A., quoted in Mayne, p. 342

18 Leigh, A., quoted in Mayne, pp. 342–4

19 Leigh, A., quoted in Mayne, pp. 344–5

20 Medora (Mackay), pp. 126–7

21 Medora (Mackay), p. 128

22 Medora (Mackay), p. 129

23 Medora (Mackay), p. 119

24 Medora (Mackay), p. 131–2

25 Villiers, The Hon. Mrs. G., quoted in Mayne, p. 351

26 Medora (Mackay), p. 132

27 Leigh, Medora quoted in Mayne, p. 352

28 Medora (Mackay), pp. 133–4

The End of the Affair

1 Byron, Lady, quoted in Gunn, p. 233

2 Leigh, A., quoted in Gunn, p. 234

3 Leigh, A., quoted in Gunn, p. 235

4 Campbell, T., *New Monthly Magazine*, 1830, quoted in Stowe, p. 85

5 *Blackwood's* quoted in Arnold, F., Arnold, F., *Robertson of Brighton, with Some Notices of His Times and Contemporaries*, London, 1886, p. 163

6 Gallinge, Mr., quoted in Arnold F., *op.cit.*, p.169

7 Byron, Lady, quoted in Elwin (LBF), pp. 236–7

8 Byron, Lady, quoted in Ada, p. 31

9 de Morgan, S., quoted in Ada, p. 34

10 Woolley, B., *The Bride of Science: Romance, Reason, and Byron's Daughter*, London, 1999, p. 90

11 Briggs, Miss, quoted in Ada, pp. 47–8

12 Woolley, B, op.cit., p. 120

13 Trench, F., quoted in Arnold, F., op.cit., p. 170
14 King, Lord, quoted in Ada, p. 65
15 Byron, Ada, quoted in Ada, p. 66
16 Byron, Lady, quoted in Ada, p. 72
17 Medora (Mackay), pp. 135–7
18 Byron, Ada, quoted in Ada, p. 124
19 Byron, Ada, quoted in Ada, p. 125
20 Ibid.
21 Byron, Lady, quoted in Mayne, p. 350
22 Byron, Lady, quoted in Mayne, p. 353
23 Byron, Lady, quoted in Mayne, p. 358
24 Ibid.
25 Leigh, Medora, Byron Lovelace Papers, Bodleian Library, Box 86, ff.151–171
26 Jameson, A., quoted in Ada, p. 138
27 Medora (Mackay), pp. 137–8
28 Byron, Lady, quoted in Ada, p. 140
29 Medora (Mackay), p. 141
30 Leigh, M., quoted in Mayne, pp. 360–2
31 Medora (Mackay), pp. 91–3
32 Byron, Ada, quoted in Ada, p. 172

A Preparation for Invisibility

1 Stowe, p. 135
2 Arnold, F., op.cit., p. 193
3 Stowe, pp. 140–1
4 Leigh, Emily, quoted in Gunn, pp. 255–6
5 Leigh, A., quoted in Gunn, p. 259
6 Byron, Lady, quoted in Mayne, p. 408
7 Leigh, Emily, Byron Lovelace Papers, Bodleian Library, Box 85, f.3
8 Byron, Lady, quoted in Gunn, pp. 264–5
9 Leigh, Emily, quoted in Gunn, p. 265
10 Byron, Lady, quoted in Mayne, p. 414
11 Leigh, Emily, Byron Lovelace Papers, Bodleian Library, Box 85, f.18
12 Leigh, Emily, Byron Lovelace Papers, Bodleian Library, Box 85, f.22
13 Byron, Lady, Byron Lovelace Papers, Bodleian Library, Box 85, f.73
14 Byron, Lady, quoted in Ada, p. 152
15 Byron, Ada, quoted in Ada, p. 76
16 Byron, Ada, quoted in Arnold, F., op.cit., p. 171
17 Byron, Ada, quoted in Arnold, F., op.cit., p. 173
18 Byron, Ada, quoted in Ada, p. 268
19 Byron, Lady, quoted in Ada, p. 271
20 Byron, Ada, quoted in Woolley, B., op.cit., pp. 344–5
21 Howitt, W., *Daily News*, 2 September 1869
22 Arnold, F., op.cit., p. 193
23 Byron, Lady, quoted in Ada, p. 312
24 Lovelace Journal quoted in Ada, p. 325
25 Eliot, G. (ed. Haight G.), *The George Eliot Letters*, London, 1956, Vol. 5, p. 314
26 Eliot, G. (ed. Haight G.), *The George Eliot Letters*, London, 1956, Vol. 6, pp. 371–2
27 Dickens, C., *Great Expectations*, London, 1965, p. 411
28 Stowe, pp. 245–6
29 Stowe, pp. 301–2
30 Amy Woolner, Thomas Woolner, R. A., *Sculptor and Poet, His Life in Letters*, London, 1917

Epilogue

1 Paget, J., quoted in Stowe, p. 122
2 Byron, (McGann), Vol. IV, p. 44
3 Stowe, p. 299
4 Eliot, G., *Selected Critical Writings*, Oxford, 1992, p. 148
5 *Blackwood's*, 1825, quoted in Stowe, p. 122
6 Wilde, O., op.cit., p. 216
7 Auden, W. H., "Letter to Lord Byron" in *Collected Poems*, ed. E. Mendekon, London, 1976, p. 86
8 Jeffrey, F., quoted in Redpath, op.cit., p. 289
9 Collison, G., *Cemetery Interment*, London, 1840, p. 157

Select Bibliography

Arnold, Rev. Frederick. *Robertson of Brighton with Some Notices of His Times and Contemporaries*, London 1886

Barber, Rev., Canon T. G. *Byron and Where He Is Buried*, Hucknall 1939

Broughton, Lord [J. C. Hobhouse]. *Recollections of a Long Life*, 6 vols., ed. Lady Dorchester, London 1911

Eisler, Benita. *Byron: Child of Passion, Fool of Fame*, New York 1999

Elwin, Malcolm. *The Noels and the Milbankes*, London 1967

Elwin, Malcolm. *Lord Byron's Wife*, London 1962

Elwin, Malcolm. *Lord Byron's Family*, London 1975

Fox, Sir John. *The Byron Mystery*, London 1924

Grosskurth, Phyllis. *Byron, The Flawed Angel*, London 1997

Gunn, Peter. *My Dearest Augusta*, London 1968

Knight, G. Wilson. *Lord Byron's Marriage: The Evidence of Asterisks*, London 1957

Lovelace, Ralph Milbanke. *Lady Noel Byron and the Leighs: Some Authentic Records of Certain Circumstances, etc.*, privately printed, 1887

Lovelace, Ralph Milbanke. *Astarte: A Fragment of Truth Concerning George Gordon Byron, Sixth Lord Byron. Recorded by His Grandson, Ralph Milbanke, Earl of Lovelace*, New York 1921

Marchand, Leslie. *Byron, A Biography*, 3 vols., New York 1957

Marchand, Leslie. (ed.) *Byron's Letters and Journals*, 12 vols., London 1982

Maurois, Andre. *Byron*, New York 1930

Mayne, Ethel Colburn. *The Life and Letters of Anne Isabella, Lady Noel Byron*, London 1929

Mackay, Charles. *Medora Leigh; A History and an Autobiography*, London 1869

McGann, Jerome J. (ed.) *Byron: The Complete Poetical Works*, 7 vols., Oxford 1993

Moore, Doris Langley. *Ada Countess of Lovelace, Byron's Legitimate Daughter*, London 1977

Moore, Doris Langley. *The Late Lord Byron*, London 1962

Nicholson, Andrew. (ed.) *Lord Byron, The Complete Miscellaneous Prose*, Oxford 1991

Pierson, Joan. *The Real Lady Byron*, London 1992

Stowe, Harriet Beecher. *Lady Byron Vindicated, A History of the Byron Controversy*, London 1870

Woolley, Benjamin. *The Bride of Science: Romance, Reason, and Byron's Daughter*, London 1999

Acknowledgements

No one can write about Byron without first acknowledging a debt to the vast mass of literature on the subject that has gone on before. From the moment that Byron died in 1824 the biographers and memoirists went to work on him, and if two major biographies in the last five years—and a third on the way—are anything to go by, the search is by no means over.

With so much written on Byron's life and posthumous reputation, it would be impossible to acknowledge every influence, but certain debts incurred here will be obvious. Like everyone else who writes on Byron the scholarship of Professor Leslie Marchand provides an indispensable framework, but given the particular emphasis of this book the work of Malcolm Elwin and Doris Langley Moore in disentangling the massive archive in the Bodleian Library known as the Lovelace Byron Papers has been of equal importance. I have often disagreed with their conclusions, but could not have begun without their scholarship, and am very grateful. Quotations from the Lovelace Byron Papers are included with the permission of the Earl of Lytton and Laurence Pollinger Ltd.

On a more personal note, it is a pleasure to thank all those who have helped with the writing of this book: Haidee Jackson, for her time and kindness on more than one visit to Newstead; Ryan Davis for the photographs of the catacombs at Kensal Green Cemetery; Perran Wood for hours of conversation on the Byrons and the photographs of Medora Leigh's last home in the south of France; Derek Johns for his encouragement and suggestions; Catherine Eldridge for her attempts to provide a scientific answer to the issue of Medora's paternity. I am also especially grateful to Alan Petty, Stella Tillyard and Elisabeth Green who read all or parts of this in manuscript, and to Min Stacpoole who waded through it more than once to help make it a better book than it would otherwise have been.

I would also like to thank everyone at Harper Collins who has worked on this, but especially Arabella Pike, whose enthusiasm and commitment has survived some fairly radical changes of direction since the first draft was stolen by some very disappointed burglars. Finally, this book is for Honor, who has helped at every stage, and whose unfailing support has made it possible.

Index

A Note About the Author

David Crane teaches English literature in London. His first book, *Lord Byron's Jackal*, a biography of Edward Trelawny, was published in 1998. He lives in northwest Scotland.

A Note on the Type

This book was set in a type called Baskerville.
The face itself is a facsimile reproduction of types
cast from the molds made for John Baskerville
(1706–1775) from his designs. Baskerville's original
face was one of the forerunners of the type style
known to printers as "modern face"—a
"modern" of the period A.D. 1800.

Composed by North Market Street Graphics,
Lancaster, Pennsylvania
Printed and bound by R. R. Donnelley & Sons,
Harrisonburg, Virginia
Designed by Anthea Lingeman